CHRISTOPHER HADLEY is a writer and historian writing at the murky, wonderful intersection of history and folklore. His pieces have appeared in the *Independent*, the *Guardian*, *The Times*, *London Review of Books* and *Esquire*, among many other publications. His previous book, *Hollow Places: An unusual history of land and legend*, was a *Sunday Times* book of the year.

Praise for

THE ROAD

Shortlisted for the 2023 East Anglian Book Awards

'Magnificent ... This is no dry and prosaic history, but a work of imagination and a deeply literary book ... wonderful prose ... striking images and lapidary sentences ... enthralling. It's an absolute joy to read and an early contender for every list of History Books of the Year' *Sunday Telegraph*

'The breadth of his knowledge ... the beauty of his prose ... This book deserves to be read at least twice, first to appreciate what it reveals and then to luxuriate in its effervescent voice. On nearly every page a random passage takes one's breath away' *The Times*

'A set of musical variations ... ingeniously written to create a narrative that draws the reader through the book ... scholarly ... wears its learning lightly ... engagingly written ... always a pleasure to read' *Country Life*

'The book offers a wealth of historical knowledge in a fashion which is entertaining and readable ... combines scholarly depth with wonderfully lyrical depictions of the English landscape. This exhilarating mixture of travel writing and history reminds us that ... the wild banks and stony lanes of rural England may speak as eloquently of the deep Roman past as the marble-clad ruins in the Forum' *Literary Review*

'Richly written ... we pick up some wonderful things along the way' *The Oldie*

'Inspired by this rolling landscapes of pasts, histories and possibilities ... in this magnificent book ... Hadley takes us down a different way, looking through a gentler window on that road's long lost days. He reveals The Road's own intimate knowledge of the land it knew and the folk it's known, turning the tables on what we think we're reading; because *The Road* is not really about it, it's about us' *Mythical Britain*

'An eclectic mix of history, archaeology, geography, and observation ... *The Road* is about journeying into our past ... successfully transfers [his] enthusiasm to the reader ... well-researched and engaging' *Current Archaeology*

'Scholarly insights are wrapped in gorgeous prose. It's a profoundly lyrical book ... one can imagine any reader enjoying it, whether they were interested in Roman road research or not ... For its insights and enthusiastic cadence, I'd say the book is an essential purchase for any with an interest or curiosity about Roman roads' *Itinera*

'Hadley's lyrical descriptions ... take him on fascinating tangents ... Hadley's style and use of poetry, prose and myths indicate a new path for historical explanation'
New Zealand Listener

'Hadley travels through time as well as space, so that he finds himself walking in step not just with Roman legionaries but also with medieval drovers, speculative antiquarians, and officials from the Ordnance Survey. Highly recommended'
Historic Houses Magazine

ALSO BY CHRISTOPHER HADLEY

Hollow Places

THE ROAD

A STORY OF ROMANS AND WAYS TO THE PAST

CHRISTOPHER HADLEY

WILLIAM
COLLINS

William Collins
An imprint of HarperCollins*Publishers*
1 London Bridge Street
London SE1 9GF

WilliamCollinsBooks.com

HarperCollins*Publishers*
Macken House, 39/40 Mayor Street Upper
Dublin 1, D01 C9W8, Ireland

First published in Great Britain in 2023 by William Collins
This William Collins paperback edition published in 2024

1

A catalogue record for this book is
available from the British Library

ISBN 978-0-00-835672-9

Maps drawn by Martin Brown

Set in Sabon LT Pro
Printed and bound in the UK using 100%
renewable electricity at CPI Group (UK) Ltd

This book contains FSC™ certified paper and other controlled
sources to ensure responsible forest management.

For more information visit: www.harpercollins.co.uk/green

For Rebecca

Alder was a mender. He could rejoin. He could make whole. A broken tool, a knife blade or an axle snapped, a pottery bowl shattered: he could bring the fragments back together without joint or seam or weakness … 'It was a joy to me … Working out the spells and finding sometimes how to use one of the True Words in the work … to put back together a barrel that's dried, the staves all fallen in from the hoops – that's a real pleasure, seeing it build up again, and swell out in the right curve, and stand there on its bottom ready for the wine.'

Ursula K. Le Guin, *The Other Wind*

CONTENTS

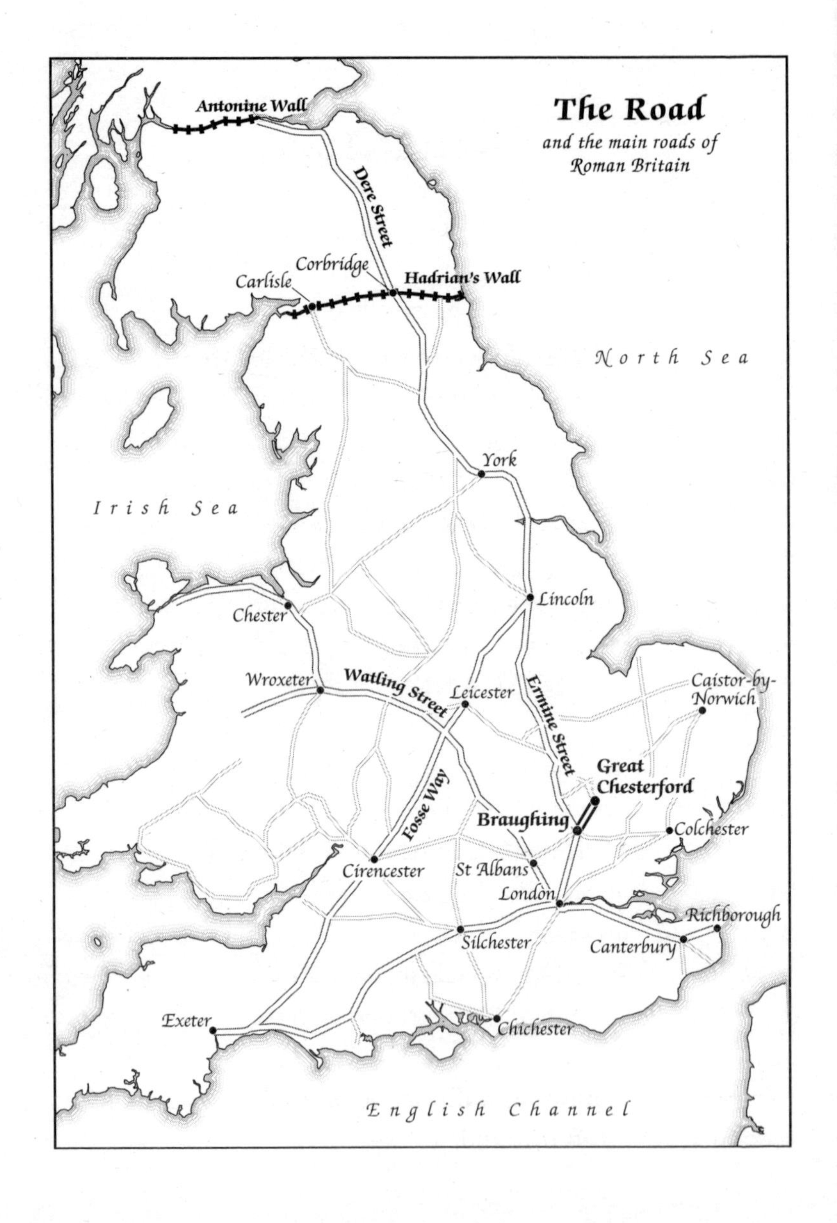

The Road
and the main roads of Roman Britain
Antonine Wall
Dere Street
Corbridge
Carlisle
Hadrian's Wall
North Sea
York
Irish Sea
Lincoln
Chester
Wroxeter
Watling Street
Leicester
Ermine Street
Caistor-by-Norwich
Great Chesterford
Fosse Way
Braughing
Colchester
Cirencester
St Albans
London
Richborough
Silchester
Canterbury
Exeter
Chichester
English Channel

PREFACE

There has never been a better time for lovers of Roman roads – those seeking, and seeking to understand, the indelible but elusive lines tattooed onto the face of Britain by the Roman occupiers long ago. Thanks to new technologies and the recent labours of archaeologists and the Roman Roads Research Association, we can track and map thousands of miles of road more accurately than ever before and explain the extraordinary role that they played in the military, social and economic life of Roman Britain, as well as during the centuries that followed. As I write, our understanding of the roads is changing constantly, with the map being redrawn weekly, not only because previously lost roads are being rediscovered, but also because we are learning that even those well known and long known didn't go where we thought they did. Such knowledge changes our ideas about trade and industry and communications, about where forts were built, and about why and how the Roman invasion and occupation progressed. It changes the maps we have in our minds when we think about the past.

Roman road hunting is a well-established if not always venerable tradition in the historiography of Roman Britain.

Confirming a route is called 'proving the line'. It is the province of antiquaries, poets and local enthusiasts, as well as academic historians and archaeologists. I am interested in all these perspectives. This book, like my last, *Hollow Places*, is about a personal hunt across time. I go in search of one road in particular and in doing so hope to tell the wider story of Britain's Roman roads. I could have trekked one of the great ways or iconic roads – Ermine Street, say, between Lincoln and the Humber, the Ackling Dyke from Old Sarum to Badbury Rings, or the Stanegate in the shadow of Hadrian's Wall – instead I follow one of the lesser ways. Not an insignificant way. Oliver Rackham, the great historian of the English countryside, wrote about those Roman roads that survive only in bits and pieces between places that stopped being important long ago, calling them 'more eloquent' than any that became modern roads. He singled out one in particular. 'But what of the road between Braughing and Great Chesterford?' he wrote. 'There were still people in these Essex-Hertfordshire backwoods for whom bits of it were of use as local roads. Every few years, through the darkest of the Dark Ages, there has been somebody ... to take a billhook to the blackthorn on two short stretches of Roman road, which stand out by their straightness amid the maze of lanes.'

This is the road we shall follow. An 'eloquent road', so it will speak to us if we are prepared to listen. Eloquent suggests fluent, forcible, powerfully expressive, lyrical. It can be all these things. Let's have a conversation with this road. It will tell us stories.

While this book celebrates the new precision, the latest findings and the determination to set Roman road research on sound academic footings, I am determined not to turn my back on the amateurs, the romantics and even the dilettantes, nor to shun those qualities of a Roman road that give them their greatest allure. We mustn't reduce these magical relics to three-letter acronyms, to GIS and to CAM, or to GPS. Here you'll find that the imagination is just as essential a tool for getting at the roads as are aerial photography and LiDAR. The hunt for a road's essence and why it fascinates us is as important as the hunt for its physical remains, which is why I widen the customary evidence base for a road to poems, church walls and hag stones; oxlips, killing places and Rebecca West; hauntings and immortals and things buried too deep for archaeology. After two thousand years, the road I am hunting is now made of these things as much as it is of gravel and sand. It is important to remember at the outset that many of us who love Roman roads love them not because they are roads, but for what they have become over centuries of use and misuse.

There have already been many excellent histories and technical treatises on the roads the Romans built during their occupation of Britain. I haven't set out to write another, although you will find some road history and a bit of technical stuff here. Nor is this book a general history of the Roman province of Britannia, but inevitably there are quite a few stories from those times in these pages. They are irresistible.

This book is not one of those poetic encounters with nature: a walk to exalt in the countryside and the act of walking, while exorcising demons or mulling over some personal tragedy, and yet it bears a passing resemblance to such writing from time to time.

It is a hunt through time and space – for a physical road but mostly for its quiddity and for its charms too – though even that often seems like a proxy for searching for something else. I think that *something else* might be the power to time travel. I have discovered various ways to accomplish that. I began by pretending to walk in the footsteps of the legions but I want to get beyond that cliché; to get at what it is to encounter something concealed in the landscape that transports us into the past, or transports the past to us in the present. A Roman road is uncanny, singular in its capacity to reflect both continuity and change over such a long period of time; it can manipulate time and space and open up no end of ways to the past: historical, archaeological, anthropological, technological and poetic. It makes a fine time machine.

Many accounts of walking in someone's footsteps are about the famous – writers or artists, soldiers, explorers, the great and the (not always) good. Their journey is reconstructed from written accounts, histories and letters and diaries and such like. There is nothing so grand or definitive here to guide my steps, only the merest trace of the road written in the landscape in a strange alphabet that can be read only with a remarkable array of tools and strategies. Many of them are technical, some are literary and artistic, but chief among them is a restless curiosity and a romanticism. A Roman road is surprisingly good at feeding that.

Which is all a long-winded way to say that this book is, in part, of course, all the things I've insisted it isn't. It is also a paean, an ekphrasis, a love letter, an attempt to describe the remains of one of these extraordinary feats of human endeavour that are hidden all around us, not as we might usually describe a layer of stones laid across the land, but with much the same reverence and attention that we might give to a great painting, a cathedral or a poem.

Let's begin at the real beginning (which is also an ending). How would a road disappear, what actually happened to it, and, most importantly, how should I describe this process? These were the questions I was struggling with when I began to write the opening sentences of this book. I was at a loss how to start, but I then came across Richard Jefferies' strange novel of 1885, *After London*, and there on the opening pages was my cadence and with that everything else fell into place. And so I began ... I begin, with that brilliant writer's voice in my head and with the encroaching grass ...

PART I

ENDINGS AND BEGINNINGS

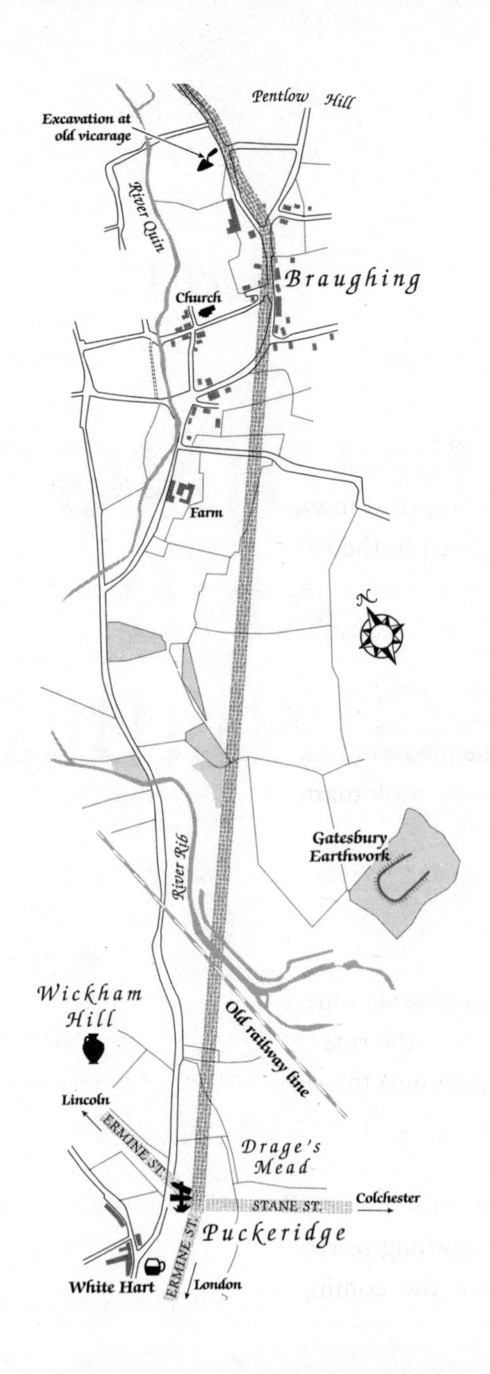

Pentlow Hill
Excavation at old vicarage
River Quin
Braughing
Church
Farm
N
Gatesbury Earthwork
River Rib
Old railway line
Wickham Hill
Lincoln
ERMINE ST.
Drage's Mead
STANE ST.
Colchester
Puckeridge
ERMINE ST.
White Hart
London

The grass spread inwards from the margins and turned the road green in the years after the legions left. Willowherb, groundsel and bindweed tunnelled through the gravel and chalk and few did anything to tame them. Those who knew where the road had gone and where it came from said it only brought trouble and sickness now, and so did nothing to discourage the brambles where they caught at passing feet. In places people took mattocks to it, violently, as sure as raising a drawbridge.

When spring arrived, the bluebells painted the surface brighter each year. Dog's mercury poisoned the berm. Most used the lesser ways now, local ways, older ways and newer ways. Cloudbursts mired the once great road, loosening the pebbles where the ruts cut deepest so that some washed from the metalling into the side ditches. This achievement of man, a link in a great web at the edge of empire, now weighed heavy on a land the Romans had spent nearly four hundred years inscribing with roads. Ten thousand miles of them. There would be nothing to rival the endeavour for over a thousand years, until the coming of the railways in the nineteenth century; no one would build and repair roads on the same scale until the first motorways in the twentieth.

Time and weather erased these Roman labours.

They rotted the bridges and brought down trees across the route so that travellers went a different way round. The clay itself began to swallow lengths of the road, drawing its hoggin back into the land. When the crossing places slipped and drifted, the road lost its purposefulness, its directness. Carters found an easier ford downstream, a kinder gradient out of the valley, and they robbed out the old ways and broke up its milestones to mend the new ones.

Abandoned Roman farmsteads on the heavy lands disassembled themselves and their contents into fragments of tile and sherd to temper the black earth and give testimony that people travelled this way once and stayed a while. When the population shrank again – after plague and calamity – few farmed the clay anymore so the hilltops over which the road ran tumbled down to woodland. In parts now, it was a blackthorn hedge, in others a thicket where founderous ash and oak took root, until entire woods hid what was left. Within them, swine rooted among the stones. Only flights of rooks remembered the road's long cambered trail and followed the shadow path that still showed at first light.

In later years, the men who returned to cultivate the clay stocked up the smooth ginks and the flints and with their ploughshares and mouldboards ate at the foundations ever more ruinously. They severed the ways with glebe and quarry, founding estates across it that forbade trespass. An entombing till and silt slid off the valley sides, a slow deceitful fluxion of the earth, an eroding, concealing, smoring, gnawing thing.

The *wanton outrage* of improvement quickened: the road thinned and denuded by the great plough, the steam plough, the mole plough, the bulldozer.

And then it was gone. Wasn't it?

Some knew the roads were there. Some had never stopped using them. Some turned them to other ends. In time, the curious began their search for them. The Romans built roads that endured; triumphs of humanity's struggle against distance. They circumscribe the journeys we take and how we negotiate hills and valleys and rivers – even when they are no longer roads. They are things of permanence and also of immanence. Lengths of them call to travellers: incomers – guttural and wild, say the old stories – came up the valley and, on finding a firm footing, followed its ridge north-east, intent on clearing the land again and staking a claim to a homestead and a new life. Their children nursed its fragments where it served their purpose. Riders paused to let their horses drink from ponds that had once been gravel pits, quarried to make the road, and drovers favoured the hollows alongside it.

Folk who know it is here, that it has always been here, stop late on a winter's day and look back along their route, listening. The sky and the dusk conspire to burden the land so that there is no telling one from the other. They add a grey mass to everything, erasing the horizontals, the dips and the rises, accentuating the verticals so that all the trees are sinister silhouettes looming out of the mist. A flat wind climbs keenly towards the chalk scarp, the land ever paler, ever colder. Britannia, that place cut off at the world's end. Ahead on the road, a lone traveller emerges from this grey light, one who set off long ago. He pulls up the hood of his *birrus*, clasps its woollen folds about him, trying not to think again of warmer lands where he would return if the roads still went there. He is oblivious to the drayman in his Leyland hauling empty casks homeward, avoiding potholes in another day's dusk, in another time, past the manor house where one of Sir John's men leads the mortuary cow ahead of the bier, startled when he hears ... what? The tramp of feet? Wellies, cavalry boots, the *caligae* of a soldier, his sharp-edged *dolabra* hanging from his belt, forever retracing his steps searching for the lost *fibula* that pinned his cloak, unaware that Mr Sworder's men found it when they carted away the last stones in the year Prince Albert died.

A patch of burdock now, a drainage ditch cut deep through Crooks Crout and Further Jefferies field, *dark-toned anomalies* in the soil. After a thousand years and more they came to this corner of Hertfordshire and Essex looking for the road, first on foot and horseback, later from the skies. Callous in their curiosity, they prayed that the parched earth would give up its secrets. But the harder they looked, the more they seemed to doubt it was there.

Two thousand years after the road opened to the traffic of Roman Britain, sections of it remain, not as the motorway it was in ancient times – there to speed an army to its fort or bring pots from the kilns – but as a bridleway, as the footings of a windmill, a green baulk, a country road, or the line of a parish boundary. It is some fourteen miles from end to end – a day's march. A little over a mile and a half is still road, in three short sections. Another two and a half miles are public rights of way now – green-dashed footpaths and bridleways on the map. For the rest of its course, the road is lost, severed by cornfield, woodland, lake and pond, driveway, paddock, riverbed, garden and building, across fourteen parishes, five of the old hundreds, three counties, five rivers, countless tributaries and one watershed.

It was still there if you knew where to look. Erased and indelible. Mutable and constant.

Look. There. Running straight towards that boundary oak. Running back in time. Was that a thickening, a deepening, a terracing, a bounding and bordering, a resistance to a fence post, a ringing of the pick handle on the ground? *No trace … Faint trace … Possible line … Little trace … No surface indication … Suggestion of course … no trace … course uncertain … no trace.*

♦ ♦ ♦

In the beginning was the road.

Joseph Bédier, *Les légendes épiques* (1908)

♦ ♦ ♦

The roads begin at a beachhead on the Kent coast, in the forty-third year of the first millennium. They begin with the Roman general Aulus Plautius, the man leading the invasion of Britain. It is he who is charged with capturing glory for Emperor Claudius, with plundering the island's rumoured precious metals and pearls, with helping the 'traitor' Verica put down the too-powerful Catuvellauni tribe. By some counts, Plautius lands on the Kent coast with an expeditionary force ten times the size of the Norman army that will invade in 1066: four legions totalling twenty thousand men and a similar number of auxiliary forces – slingers, archers and cavalry, supplied by client states. Once they win the initial skirmishes, the invaders begin their march inland along the line of what will, centuries later, be called Watling Street, the first and most important of Britannia's Roman roads.

Temporary campaign roads roll out westwards, establishing routes that will be highways for two millennia and more; no small testament to the courage and expertise of scouts and surveyors taking the measure of a hostile land. The legions arrive at Rochester and their first major battle, traditionally at the Medway – the first of the two river battles attested a century and a half later by the Roman historian Cassius Dio. The Britons fall back to the far bank of the Thames and the line of Watling Street pursues them to the river's edge, bringing troops and supplies and military despatches. Togodumnus, one of the sons of the late king Cunobelin – the hound of Belos, the War Dog, Shakespeare's Cymbeline – loses his life, after Batavian auxiliaries swim the river and take the Britons by surprise. In the months and years of the fighting that follow, Watling Street will reach the River Severn and the great legionary fortress that will be built at Wroxeter over 270 miles from the Kent coast.

Perhaps the next major road to be planned is that from London to Colchester in Essex, by then the capital of the Catuvellauni. 'Perhaps' because modern historians are careful not to speak with certainty about the course of the invasion, nor to tie every archaeological find to an event described in the few questionable sources that have come down to us. But a historian of an earlier generation did not hesitate to describe the Colchester road colourfully as wide at its incept, 'an unprecedented width', because he thought it must be intended to carry a large army and baggage train on the march, as well as the elephants and camels that will come with the emperor when he arrives in Britain just in time to see Colchester fall. In time, roads will radiate out from Colchester like great spokes from a hub, north to the Wash, north-west to Cambridge, west into Hertfordshire to intersect Ermine Street, and thrusting north to link the Thames to the Humber.

And the Romans keep marching, surveying, laying out and engineering roads, establishing supply lines from the harbours to the marching camps and forts. A network gradually taking shape from individual roads built for a specific military purpose – both a symbol and a concrete expression of Roman imperial might. Another road from London reaches Exeter and branching from it at Axmouth, the Fosse Way sets out towards Lincoln, in a line of linked roads that look both outward and inwards, there to supply the advance and from where the legions might police the province. Roads built to carry an army into the interior become transport routes to carry minerals to the continent; within six years of the invasion, lead from the Mendips is finding its way to Gaul, no doubt silver too.

The conquest lasted forty years under eleven governors and eight emperors (albeit four of those emperors squabbled for supremacy in a single year – 69 CE). Penetration roads would be built north to York on the east coast and to Chester on the west, often thought to represent the advance of two legions: IX Hispana and XX Valeria Victrix. The first volume in the story of Roman Britain doesn't end until Governor Julius Agricola's subjugation of the north after the decisive defeat of the chieftain Calgacus at Mons Graupius near Inverness in 83 or 84 CE. It is a story picked out in roads, one that archaeologists can still read in the soil today. The invasion of Britain cost tens if not hundreds of thousands of lives – 250,000 is a modern estimate – as the legions pushed west into Wales and north into Scotland in search of booty, mineral wealth, land and tribute, leaving behind a vast web of military roads, changing the landscape permanently, etching the story of the Roman advance into the face of the land.

The key moments of those first forty years were once found – vividly illustrated – in every history primer: the fall of Colchester to the emperor Claudius and his famous elephants, the surrender of eleven British kings to the emperor before he headed back to Rome after just sixteen days in Britain; the long resistance of Cunobelin's other son Caratacus before his final betrayal by Cartimandua, the queen of the Brigantes in the north; the destruction of the druids and their sacred groves on Anglesey. There was the role Britain played in the rise of the Flavian dynasty: the emperor who came out on top in 69 CE was its patriarch, Vespasian, Titus Flavius Vespasianus, who had been there when Watling Street was just a line in a surveyor's sandpit. He made his name commanding the II Augusta Legion in the first four years after the invasion. Advancing towards the Solent along Stane Street from London to Chichester, he fought thirty battles, accepted the submission of two tribes, captured twenty hillforts and seized the Isle of Wight. That's what the coming of the *Pax Romana*, the Roman peace, really meant to the Britons and if we were to draw a picture of it, it would be one framed and criss-crossed by roads and the troops marching along them. No march was more famous than that of the troops racing back from campaigning in Wales to confront the dreadful rage of Queen Boudicca and the uprising of her Iceni near Norwich. In the immediate aftermath of that disaster yet another road was built, branching north-east from Ermine Street at Braughing, in Hertfordshire, driven directly over the low hills towards East Anglia – our eloquent road.

♦ ♦ ♦

Thy Roman fame o'er England still
Swells many a lingering scar,
Where Caesars led, with conquering skill,
Their legions on to war:
And camps and stations still abide
On many a sloping hill;
Though Time had done its all to hide,
Thy presence guards them still.

John Clare, 'Antiquity! Thou Dark Sublime!' (1821–22)

♦ ♦ ♦

In a field somewhere you've never heard of, behind a pub on the goblin ridge, is one of the busiest road hubs in Roman Britain. An octopus of routes stretches to the points of the compass from this eight dials in Hertfordshire: all the way to Kent, to the sea and beyond to the continent along ancient roads. An *unbroken channel of communication* far beyond Hertfordshire and Essex, to the potteries on the banks of the River Guadalquivir in southern Spain, to the imperial mint at Arles on Gaul's Mediterranean coast. As far away as the vineyards of Campania on the Tyrrhenian Sea and beyond into Asia Minor and North Africa, from the Nile to the Atlantic at Rabat along a coast road nearly three thousand miles long. Closer to home, roads once led east to Camulodunum and west to Verulamium, south to Londinium and north to Lindum and Eburacum. Direct roads from a tiny Hertfordshire village to five of the six most important towns in all of Britannia: today's Colchester, St Albans, London, Lincoln and York.

We know the road hub is there thanks to Eric Stacey. I imagine young Eric in an oversized woolly jumper, short trousers and gumboots, looking like an extra from *The Railway Children* or *Goodnight Mister Tom*, no doubt thinking about which ditch he is going to scour for treasure next, although Eric wouldn't have called it treasure: at twelve years old he was already taking his archaeology very seriously. On Monday 14 July 1941, as the German Panzer divisions pushed east towards Kiev and Allied troops continued to hold out in the Libyan fortress of Tobruk, Eric started keeping a diary.

MAPPED PART OF THE LARKS HILL CAMP WITH A FRIEND, he printed in careful capitals, beginning his endeavours by exploring a non-existent Roman encampment imagined years earlier by the English antiquary Nathaniel Salmon. The earthworks there are really field lynchets, but Eric wasn't to know. Salmon's eighteenth-century description had caught his imagination.

There was nothing else until 1 August:

> TODAY I WAS WITH SOME OF MY EVACUEE PALS AT GATESBURY MILL AND WE WERE ABOUT TO CROSS THE RIVER RIB VIA A FALLEN TREE TRUNK, WHEN, ONE OF THE BOYS PICKED UP A LARGE PIECE OF TERRA COTTA POTTERY.

Eric writes in pencil, in capital letters on blue-lined notepaper that will yellow over the years, its corners dog-eared and rusted by old paperclips. He has formed an archaeological society and appointed himself secretary. Soon he is writing letters to museums asking for information and advice. He visits the Hertfordshire Museum, whose curator Herbert Andrews encourages him in his fossicking, and Eric starts to present his finds to the museum, initially from a 'burial site' on Ford Street in Braughing where he has been picking up bits of pot and oyster shells with his friend Evans and developing a rivalry with another gang of schoolboys – more evacuees from London. One Saturday during October 1941, Eric complains that they are digging without permission at Weirs Farm.

> TODAY I WENT TO SEARCH FOR POTTERY AT WIERS [*sic*]. I GOT THERE AND DISCOVERED SOME BOYS SEARCHING FOR POTTERY WITHOUT PERMISSION. I TOLD THEM TO GO IN CASE THEY GOT IN A ROW, THEY DID BUT CAME BACK AGAIN. THEY HAD ALREADY DUG OUT A COMPLETE OR NEARLY COMPLETE POT. IT WAS A FLAGON WITH ITS NECK & HANDLE BROKEN OFF ... I THEN INSPECTED THE EXCAVATIONS THEY HAD MADE. POTTERY FRAGMENTS WERE ALL OVER THE PLACE; AND BROKEN.

We can hear his youthful, earnest indignation across the years, while delighting in the fact that these teenagers' idea of mischief is a morning of illicit archaeology. But all is not lost. A short while later his friend Jimmy Cox appears wading through the River Quin.

> HE WALKED ALONG IN THE WATER INSPECTING THE BANK. PRESENTLY HE DISCOVERED A LARGE PIECE OF SAMIAM [*sic*] AND LIFTING IT UP, HE UNCOVERED A CINERARY URN; FULL OF BONES. OUT OF THE BANK TUMBLED A SMALL FLAGON, ANOTHER POT AND A SMALL FUNNEL SHAPED SAMIAM [*sic*] DRINKING CUP.

Eric would later lament that the interlopers carried away several complete pots, which eventually went back to London with them. And even worse, the landowner wouldn't allow him to search the land again, because the boys had damaged the fences and gates. Or perhaps Farmer Weir had realised what was being pulled from his field. Roman urns were tumbling from the riverbank and while these would have been cremation burials, the ancient methods left an unnerving quantity of charred bone.

Where there is a Roman cemetery there is often a road since Roman law forbade burial within settlements, and on Sunday 30 November, Eric spots his first one.

> TODAY I WAS PROCEEDING ACROSS THE 'MEADS' TO THE BUNTINGFORD ROAD WITH MY FRIEND EVANS. THE FIRST THING WE OBSERVED WAS A PERFECTLY STRAIGHT RIDGE

RUNNING TOWARDS THE RIVER WHERE IT ENDED IN A MASS OF MUD NEAR THE MODERN FOOT-BRIDGE.

ON THE OTHER BANK IT WAS PRECISELY THE SAME; THE END OF THE RIDGE THIS SIDE ENDING IN SWAMPY GROUND HALF WAY BETWEEN THE RAILWAY LINE AND THE RIVER.

His thoughts turn back to this probable road nearly a month later on Christmas Eve when he first considers where it might be going. Although his initial ideas are wrong, they still lead Eric in the right direction. I HAVE COME TO THE CONCLUSION THAT IF THE RIDGE AT THE MEADS SIDE OF LARK HILL IS A ROAD, he begins and continues with various speculations as to where the road is going, concluding: IT IS LIKELY THAT IT CONTINUES THE WHOLE LENGTH OF THE BRAUGHING VALLEY ...

In the entries that follow we find Eric mulling over and exploring possible routes. He has caught the road-hunting bug and spends his time marking Roman roads on an Ordnance Survey map, but the weather keeps him indoors. It's some six weeks before he ventures out again in the footsteps of the legions towards a hamlet called Bozen Green.

THE WEATHER IS STILL RATHER UNSETTLED AND HAS MADE MOST FIELDS AND TRACKWAYS INTO BOGS THUS PREVENTING PROPER SEARCH.

DESPITE THIS I WENT ALONG NUMEROUS CART TRACKS TO SOMEWHERE NEAR BOZEN GREEN WHERE ONE OF THE ROADS (ROMAN) ENDS OR RATHER DISAPPEARS. THE PART SURROUNDING THE TRACKS IS WOOD & GRASS

FIELD WHICH ARE EXCELLENT FOR SEARCHING IN. IF I AM STILL HERE THIS SUMMER I INTEND TO SEARCH FOR THE LOST ROUTES.

He ponders its course through grassland and woodland, looking forward to searching for it 'undisturbed'. IS IT 'LOST' OR JUST NOT RECORDED AS BEING FOUND? he wonders. It's an excellent question. Come spring, Eric turns his attention to tiles and clues to the location of buildings, but he hasn't completely forgotten the roads. Over the coming months, he will continue to explore possible routes, marking them on maps, inventing names for them. He is developing the skills necessary to follow the roads. Tracking them across fields, trying to understand the topography like a Roman surveyor. Earlier that year, he'd made a discovery that would teach him a valuable lesson about how to find roads and other remains too.

SINCE THE BIG FIELD BY BRAUGHING RAILWAY STATION HAS BEEN PLOUGHED A NUMBER OF LIGHT PATCHES HAVE APPEARED ACROSS THE TOP OF THE HILL. THIS LOOKS PRETTY OBVIOUS, PROBABLY MORTAR DUST FROM BURIED FRAGMENTS OF WALLS.

'Mortar dust' is ingenious and charming. These are the soil marks of the Roman buildings that one day Eric and a local schoolmaster, John Holmes, will find and record, but in January 1942 he doesn't understand what he is looking at. In time, he will develop an excellent eye for this sort of work.

People had been spotting strange shapes and trails in soil and crops for centuries. Both were caused by features hidden under the ground. Soil marks were simply darker or lighter lines created by buried structures that made the ground wetter or drier. Once the fields were put to crop, the traces became even more obvious. A ditch that had been filled in would hold more moisture and the crop above it would grow stronger, whereas a wall or foundation stunted growth. The result? Magically distinctive marks that might show the outlines of a building or road long hidden in the earth. Cereal crops growing on chalky, well-draining soil gave up their secrets best of all, especially in dry summers when the difference in crop colour or height would be most marked. Clay soils were more concealing and it required a drought to grow the shadow of a road, or etch the playing card shape of a lost fort into the wheat.

One of the earliest accounts of a cropmark comes to us from the antiquary John Leland, who in the early 1500s travelled through Britain describing its ruins. Of the Roman site at Silchester, in about 1540, he wrote: 'There is one straung thing seen ther that in certen Partes of the Ground withyn the Waules, the Corne is mervelus faire to the Yee, and ready to show Perfecture, it decayith.' *Marvellous fair to the eye.*

Leland's successor, William Camden, would also record cropmarks in his sixteenth-century description of Britain, *Britannia*. Writing of the settlement that once stood outside the Roman fort at Richborough, in Kent, he observed:

> But now age has eras'd the very tracks of it; and to teach us that Cities dye as well as men, it is at this day a corn-field, wherein when the corn is grown up, one may observe the draughts of streets crossing one another (for where they have gone the corn is thinner).

The locals named these crossings St Augustine's Cross, after the monk from Rome who had landed there at the end of the sixth century and gone on to become the first Archbishop of Canterbury. By the second half of the nineteenth century, archaeologists had a better understanding of what they were looking at. In 1857, Stephen Stone wrote a detailed account of his excavations at Standlake, in Oxfordshire. After observing that the soil in the neighbourhood didn't retain much moisture, he explained:

> The crops of corn, or clover, or whatever else may chance to have been planted, are so quickly affected by drought, that a few successive days of dry sunny weather in summer are sufficient to show the situation and extent of every excavation underneath the soil as clearly as though a plan had been prepared and drawn upon paper.

Braughing's fields were a blotter for similar diagrams, as Eric Stacey eventually discovered. His boyhood interest never dwindled, and his knowledge and experience grew, as did the debt future students of ancient Braughing would owe him. By the 1950s, Eric and John Holmes were exploring the land by the railway station on nearby Wickham Hill, basing many of their conclusions on the patterns in the soil and its crops, finding in them a plan of the narrow corridors of the supposed temple there. Holmes would later write: 'The crop marks were produced by the stunted growth and earlier ripening of the wheat wherever the roots encountered walls or other solid structures. They began to appear in June and were at their best about mid-July, when the stunted wheat had turned brown but most of the field was still yellow.' The marks became clearer as the summer of 1954 advanced and eventually 'a photograph was taken on 14 July from the roof of the station building and shows the streets and the walls for the temple at their clearest'.

Eric was an old hand when, five years later, he spotted a rather special cropmark that would come to define Roman Braughing, emphasising the startling contrast between the place's modern-day obscurity and its importance in antiquity. In 1959, a field known as Drage's Mead, behind the White Hart Inn in Puckeridge, a village bordering Braughing, was ploughed and sown with wheat for the first time in living memory. The following summer, in June 1960, the soil sprouted something more impressive than cereal: a diagram in corn of the meeting of ways, a rune or cuneiform wedge of Roman roads imprinted in the crop by the stones beneath the soil. One line came in from the south, thickened, changed angle and headed off north-west. This was the great Ermine Street. Another was but a hint of something, a faint mark continuing the line of a hedge running east to west. Here was the Essex Stane Street, the Colchester Road, on its heading from Horse Cross just over a mile and a half away, along which ghostly monks were said to walk every five years. But it is the third, nameless trace that should interest us the most: from the junction it travelled a few yards north to the field boundary, where it disappeared into a hedge. It is our road at its origin.

♦ ♦ ♦

I stand one spring day at a Bermuda triangle of roads, in Eric Stacey's footsteps, on ghost roads that will sometimes reveal themselves when the sun is low enough in the sky. Half a century ago, Eric sank a trial trench here and found a road surface sixteen inches below ground on the edge of Pumps Mead. This finally confirmed the course of the mighty Ermine Street just before it met our road.

Ermine Street was the second great road of Britannia. Running north from Bishopsgate in London, it heads to Ware in Hertfordshire where it changes alignment, seemingly diverting to this very spot, before turning north-west to continue its march up to Lincoln and beyond to York, the most important town in the north of the Roman province. Much of Ermine Street is still followed today by modern roads, by the A10 and A1. It has been suggested that the apparent diversion means our road was the original planned course of Ermine Street at the beginning of the occupation. Whatever the truth of the matter, here in this field near

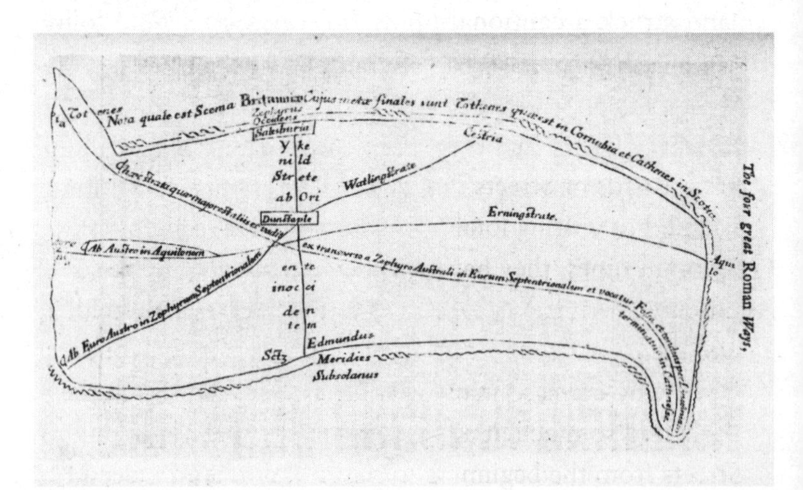

Braughing lie the remains of one of the Four Great Ways of the realm; the others were the Fosse Way, Watling Street and the Icknield Way.

Legend says that the Great Ways were established not by the Romans, but by Belinus, a king of the Britons. According to the fourteenth-century Cornish writer John Trevisa, Belinus's father had declared that the people should have free use of all highways leading to towns or cities:

> But afterward, for that wayes were uncertayne and stryf was had, therefore Belinus, the kyng ... for to put away all doubt and stryfe, made four hyghe kynges wayes, pryveleged with all pryveleges and fredom. And the wayes stretch thorugh the Ilonde.

No two of the early authors who wrote about the Great Ways seem able to agree on where they started and ended, let alone the course they took. Nearly five hundred years ago, John Leland struck a cautionary note for any who would follow them:

> It is the general voice of all our Historians that four great Roads or Streets ran from several points cross this Island; but writing long after they were made, and in ignorant times, they have left their accounts of them so obscure and uncertain, both as to the courses they held, and the names they were known by, that it is no wonder if we, who come so many ages after them, are still in the dark, and so much at a loss to trace any one of these Streets from the beginning to the end of it. And indeed I

> now conclude it is impossible to do it without great interruptions, time and other accidents destroying every day more and more of their mouldering remains.

And that's the Four Great Ways. What hope have all the little ones got?

Eric's discoveries drew the archaeologists the following year. They excavated and tracked the course of the shadow of Stane Street, to its meeting with our road. And they measured the newly uncovered section of Ermine Street: it was forty feet wide and three feet thick and had been resurfaced at least three times, sealing the ephemeral into its substance: a cook's mortar that must have come up the road one day in the late first century. When, nearly two thousand years later, the mortar was found it still bore the stamp of Matugenus, a potter known to have worked at kilns near present-day Stanmore in north London. Best of all, archaeologists picked up a brooch, lost or discarded in the first years after the invasion and tamped down hard beneath a four-inch layer of gravel: a simple bronze brooch with a flat, fluted bow, a type fashionable on the continent before the conquest. A Briton or a traveller from Gaul came this way – it was not a brooch worn by a Roman – with their clothes gathered and pinned at the shoulder. Did they catch their cloak on something? Did the spring give out or did a hand yank the cloth and snap the pin against the catch plate? We will never know who they were or how far they had come or why their brooch was tumbled into gravel used to surface a road. They passed this way before it was built, unaware that their little misfortune would give a date to it nearly two thousand years later.

If the road is part of an unbroken line of communication across space, it is one across time as well. It is a spur to the historical imagination, conjuring carts laden with earthenware made by Matugenus that give way to slabs of venison heading the other way to the table of Edward II, to the lord of the manor on horseback visiting his vineyard, or to carts on market day in the fourteenth century. Ermine Street was a coaching road, a turnpike road and until the bypass was built in the 1970s, the trucks of the Old North Road still thundered down Puckeridge's pretty high street, rattling the glass out of the casements and threatening to shake the pargeting from the timber-framed inns.

The author Herbert Tompkins caught the mood in 1903 while contemplating the highways and byways:

> What is to be gained from tramping on the King's highway in such frosty weather unless it be the memory that old Pepys went this way before me and that Turpin galloped up the hill towards High Cross, rattled merrily through Collier's End, clattered along the narrow street of Puckeridge, rounded the dangerous twist near the Old George inn and raced for dear life towards Royston.

After running through the respective fates of a list of notables who trod these ways, Tompkins adds:

> They are all gone; almost forgotten; for they are ne'er thought of save by some collegiate fellow with his nose in a folio, or some vagabond rambler who, as he

> wanders from village to village, has sometimes little enough to think about unless he remembers those worthies who once owned the land upon which he treads.

And so, with a proper place to start, I imagine this vagabond on my road and set out to follow him. Trusting that the land lying before me will prove the way as clearly as the corn in Drage's Mead and is prepared to give up its secrets.

♦ ♦ ♦

> We are coldly drawn unto discourses of antiquities, who have scarce time before us to comprehend new things, or make out learned novelties. But seeing they arose as they lay, almost in silence among us, at least in short account suddenly passed over; we were very unwilling they should die again, and be buried twice among us.
>
> Thomas Browne, *Hydriotaphia, Urne-Buriall* (1658)

♦ ♦ ♦

Buried twice among us. If only so few times. I soon came to realise that this old road was always being rediscovered, lost, forgotten and found again, and despite this, or because of it, few could agree where precisely it was. Its general course, its alignment, had been guessed at since the mid-nineteenth century when the Cambridge botanist and antiquary Cardale Babington published a description of a road he thought the

Romans had built between the villages of Great Chesterford in Essex and Braughing in Hertfordshire. In an afterthought of a section headed 'Other supposed roads in Cambridge', he had then dismissed the great William Stukeley's idea that a lost road had linked Cambridge with Braughing. The polymathic Babington postulated the course of the road through Essex as far as a village called Elmdon, but he was then unsure where it went next as it passed 'through a country with which I am totally unacquainted'.

And he was none the wiser when he brought out a revised edition of his *Ancient Cambridgeshire* in 1883. A short section of the road heading south-west from Great Chesterford was marked in contingent dotted lines on the map at the back of the book as only 'probably' a Roman road. Twenty years later, the engineer Thomas Codrington wrote the first comprehensive account of the known Roman roads in Britain, remarking briefly on a road which 'seems to have continued on from Braughing to the north-east, in the direction of Great Chesterford'. He was more forthright when he came to draw his map, adding a bolder, straighter line than Babington's, scored confidently into the two-dimensional landscape that exaggerates the straightness of roads. At one end, he found it arrived at Great Chesterford and at the other it met the road into Braughing a little under two miles north of the road hub.

Codrington's conviction would be undermined on later maps and the doubts persist – nearly 80 per cent of the lost road's course remains unmarked on modern Ordnance Survey maps – but his line will be our default. A hypothesis. An alignment, an imagined road, a route, a survey line, the straight road as an ideal of Roman roadness in the popular imagination, and as something else as well, *a fixed materialisation of human longing, and of the human notion that it is better to be in one place than in another.*

♦ ♦ ♦

In short, the only means to recover the tract of these Ways, besides what we may pick out of our Historians, is diligently to trace what is left of them where any footsteps or names of them are yet apparent; and where no such are to be found, by observing where they show themselves again after any discontinuance, and filling up the intermediate loss upon the best conjectures we can make.

Roger Gale, 'Essay Towards the Recovery of the Courses of the Four Great Roman Ways' (1711)

♦ ♦ ♦

Nodules of flint litter the field edges like newborn lambs encased in their cauls. Hard-going underfoot, walking on the chines of the long dead, rinsed and boned by a land that has rejected them. I am stalking the missing miles to the alignment. Trying to fill up the *intermediate loss*.

Nature is washed out to lime greens by sunshine and rainfall. There is a clear trail here, but it is the memory of an old railway line. The road must have crossed it heading for the banks of the Rib, the river that winds its way from the chalk hills to the north towards the River Lea. The railway line might answer some important questions. What was this place to the Romans, this meeting of great ways, this little village of no obvious significance? What was Braughing in 43 CE or even in 55 BCE when Julius Caesar first visited? After all, the first test a true Roman road must pass is to start and finish at a recognised Roman settlement. As we know, no civil engineering achievement would rival the Roman road network in Britain until the building of the railways, so it is pleasing to learn that the cutting of the line in 1861 gave the first real indication that Braughing might have been something to the Romans. The navvies unearthed 'thousands' of Roman and Iron Age coins spanning over four hundred years, from the rule of the late first-century BCE British chieftain Tasciovanus to that of the first Christian Roman emperor Constantine the Great. 'A field called Wickhams, on a portion of which the Railway station is erected, is so rich in Roman coins that one is almost inclined to believe the legend of Tom Tiddler's ground to be no fable,' wrote one antiquary:

> After heavy rain coins are frequently to be found on the surface, and at nearly every furrow the plough is almost certain to disclose one or more pieces of Roman money. In the summer of 1869, when the beans growing in the field were being hoed, one man succeeded in obtaining thirty-three of these coins; in fact the productiveness of this veritable mine of curiosities far exceeds the expectations of the most sanguine antiquarian.

While the fields proved rich in coins, the riverbank has shed a greater prize in recent years. Where invasive Himalayan balsam has blocked the flow, water erodes the bank and from it fall ancient coin moulds, grey clay trays with holes for casting pellets of metal. The many kilos of moulds that have been found in the area – more than anywhere else in Europe – could mean that Braughing was an Iron Age mint, a place where gold, silver and bronze coins were hammered out, and so possibly a royal centre.

But the episodes of minting appear to have happened in the late summer and early autumn, according to archaeologist Mark Landon. 'We know because bits of chaff are caught in the coin mould, so the coins were being made at the time when there was a lot of reaping debris floating around,' he says. 'And just about all of the major assemblages here produced evidence of harvest time.' This fits a theory that Braughing was not a central place, but where people came to meet at the end of summer, a place of ceremony and ritual where ancient trackways met. Those husks of corn are one of my favourite pieces of evidence – so ephemeral and yet fixed there for ever. And I cannot help thinking of the ears of corn on the ancient gold coins of Cunobelin, king of the Britons.

The archaeology of minting is hard to unravel. We don't know if the moulds were made where the pellets were cast or the coins hammered. That would make sense to us, but the evidence suggests otherwise – it is extremely rare to find moulds in the same place as dies and punches used to mint coins. So this area may not have been a mint at all, but somewhere the coin moulds were ceremonially gathered. The moulds have been deposited together, but the clays come from different places. And oddly, two out of every three finds appear to have been dug up and re-deposited in early Roman times. Stranger still, bits of the mould are always missing. There are never enough corners. Eighty per cent not enough. And no one knows why.

Was Braughing a lost *oppidum*? An Iron Age tribal capital? It has been suggested that some nearby earthworks could be associated with one of the great events of early Romano-British history. In the summer of 55 BCE, Julius Caesar, then the Roman governor of Gaul, an area covering most of Western Europe between the Rhine and the Pyrenees, narrowly avoided disaster on the Kent coast. The weather and tides wreaked havoc on the future dictator's transports and prevented his cavalry landing. Although he stayed in Britain for only twenty days and returned empty-handed, having pushed the limits of his luck both at the landing and in the

skirmishes that followed, he had still pulled off a huge propaganda coup in Rome: Caesar was feted for travelling to the ends of the earth. In his own account of that first expedition, he claimed it to be in retaliation for the British tribes sending warriors to aid the Gauls who had resisted the Roman occupation.

The following summer he returned with a far more ambitious and far-reaching invasion, intent on winning booty and perhaps even adding a new province to Rome's dominions. He had used the winter well, building ships that could better cope with the shallow coastal waters, and amassing a huge expeditionary force of 800 vessels packed with six legions of 30,000 soldiers, 2,000 cavalry and a large number of auxiliaries. This time Caesar quickly established a beachhead and marched inland with four of his legions. After two battles, and having successfully repelled numerous skirmishes involving the formidable British chariots, the *essedarii*, the invaders crossed the Thames probably somewhere near Tilbury and pushed on north, seeking to engage the British war leader Cassivellaunus in battle. Chief of the Catuvellauni tribe, centred on modern-day Hertfordshire, and the most powerful king in Britain, Cassivellaunus had made enemies by extending his powerbase, most notably into territory to the east belonging to the Trinovantes, who controlled much of what is now Essex. They surrendered and revealed the location of their rival's stronghold. Caesar gives us few clues as to where this was, describing it as 'protected by forests and marshes, and filled with a large number of men and cattle'.

It's a vague description that could fit any number of locations in Hertfordshire, but archaeologists have pointed to earthworks in Braughing when trying to identify the *oppidum* of Cassivellaunus, writing, 'The fortification stormed by Caesar could feasibly be represented by no more than the Gatesbury enclosure and its surrounding steep-sided natural ravines. Certainly, the Iron Age topography around Braughing ... featured the "forests and marshes" ... noted by Caesar.' It is stirring stuff. Did Braughing play a bit part in one of few stories that has come down to us from that time?

It's now thought that Cassivellaunus sited his main capital at Wheathampstead, some twenty miles west of Braughing, centred on the Devil's Dyke earthworks, but would envoys from other tribes have ventured that far into enemy territory? Braughing, on the other hand, lay on the boundary between territories. A war camp in the tribal capital would hardly have been a secret location. Is it not more likely that the British king had amassed his forces elsewhere? Surely the great chieftain had more than one stronghold? Whatever the truth of the matter, the Romans quickly overran the earthworks and the defenders were forced to sue for peace. Laden with hostages and an agreement from the Britons to pay tribute to Rome, Caesar returned to Gaul, this time to put down an uprising there. The might of Rome wouldn't return to Britain for nearly a century.

After Caesar's departure, it appears that at least a few Roman merchants stuck around. It's almost certain that Romans or Romanised traders of local or continental origin were living in the area well before it became part of the empire, servicing a population with Mediterranean tastes. Archaeologists have surmised that in the period between

Caesar's excursion and the Claudian conquest, the British settlement that would eventually become Roman Braughing was one of the most important Iron Age settlements.

Mortaria – cookware used in the preparation of Roman food – has been found from the right period along with the remains of enough luxury imported goods to suggest that Braughing was the most important Iron Age settlement in south-east England. Someone was shipping in amphorae of Spanish and Italian wine and oil, and fine tableware from Gaul and Italy bearing some of the earliest continental potters' stamps to be found in Britain. They were eating fish, which was, surprisingly, exceptionally rare in Iron Age Britain. We imagine merchants and their heavily laden mules arriving here along Iron Age trackways or in flat-bottomed coracles drawn upstream: Samian ware from Gaul in 40 CE; from Italy, fancy Arretine ware and Falernian wine. Braughing was at the centre of a skein of trade, travel and ceremony. We are at the beginning of the road and we are at the very beginning of the history of the Romans in Britain.

♦ ♦ ♦

The walls of St Mary's, Braughing, are fashioned mostly of flint and fragments of boulder from the glacial till, but here and there they are adulterated by Roman history – lumps of masonry, chunks of portico. The fragments are big and, says Mark Landon, they are not very abraded so they've not been knocking around in a field: 'They probably came from standing masonry.' In other words, from Roman buildings that were still there nearby when the church was built.

Look closely and you'll spot the chamfering on an arched block of stone that gives away its former life as part of a medieval window, probably from the church's original nave. Here is an unfilled putlog hole that held the medieval scaffolding, and there are stones that must have once nested elsewhere since their outward faces are pecked and keyed for mortar. Mark points this out to me before observing that the footings of the tower have a less solid provenance. They are 'fart and biscuit,' he says, chuckling. 'And they carry the whole weight of the thing.'

On the south side, we travel further back in time: 'Just there. It's a bit of Saxon archway upside down and along from it, a bit of carved stone with some interlace,' says Mark, pointing out more bewitching coils of Anglo-Saxon carving.

'That inscribed stone, can you see it?' He is pointing high up on the wall and I use my camera to zoom in and examine it. 'It needs rotating. You can make out the letters "CIV … PER …". Mark thinks it could be a bit of Roman milestone or a boundary stone. Something granting civic rights or responsibilities.

The render has come away to reveal the words and I suggest that someone has helped it along. 'Differential expansion and contraction, I assure you,' he says. Not him up a ladder in the dead of night with a hammer and chisel? 'What expanding and contracting? Just expanding these days.' And he can't stop laughing.

Low down in one wall is a healthy serving of Hertfordshire puddingstone. It was part of a beehive quern-stone for grinding corn. How can you tell? 'By the profile. It's shaped like an old-fashioned bee skep.' Two more lumps flank a window.

'Did that signify something? Another possible piece of milestone there.'

We are staring at the outer walls of the south aisle. There are layers of brick, thicker than Roman but thinner than modern frogged bricks. Probably Tudor: 'As thick as they could make a slab of clay without it exploding in the kiln.' Then there are much slighter biscuits of brick, older, and unmistakably Roman. Most telling of all, the higher your eyes follow the wall, the smaller the stones get until the topmost course is almost all gravel. It's as if they ran out of big stones.

And where might they have harvested the little ones? How about from a Roman road, robbed out and reduced to a ridgeline on the edge of the church estate?

Others have suggested that our road made its way past the nearby cemetery at Ford Street, where Eric Stacey and his pals vied for cinerary urns in the riverbank, roughly following the modern road, before turning up towards St Mary's. It's even been said the church was built on the road. It is not unknown for buildings to use roads as their foundations. The church at Welwyn, twelve miles to the south-west as the crow files, is built on a Roman road. Could St Mary's be blamed for severing the route? Were those scant footings – the 'fart and biscuit' – originally laid by Romans to bear the weight of sandalled feet and cart wheels?

One summer a few years ago, Landon decided that a visual assessment wasn't enough. It was time for ground-truthing, 'an antidote to baroque fancies', as he puts it. That meant it was time to dig a hole. He and a group of local volunteers sank a trench along the supposed line north of the church – and found nothing.

He came up with another theory, one that meant the road took a completely different route out of Braughing. Not under the church but some 150 metres east of it. His team of volunteers started to excavate a bank in the grounds of the Old Vicarage. They found lots of Tudor brick. Late medieval pottery. Some fill. More medieval pottery. Some Roman pottery. And there it was, not the running surface, but one of the outlying road ditches.

It took some eight weeks of Saturdays and Sundays, but eventually they found cobbles too. 'The "best fit" explanation for these features,' Mark would later write, 'is that together they are the remains of a cobbled road, with a top surface of smaller rammed gravel set on a base of hoggin made with clay and larger pebbles, which had shallow "scoop" ditches on either side.' There was an extraction pit too, where materials for the road had been dug out, and a large sherd of amphora had lain hidden since the days when the grapes on Mount Falernus were still thought to produce the best wine in the world.

Mark estimated that the road had been about twelve metres wide from ditch to ditch and it appeared to have been adopted as the easternmost boundary of the church estate, which tells us that it must have still been a significant feature when the church was gifted the land in the tenth century. The ditch looked to have been re-cut many times over the centuries and in the fill they found sherds of medieval grey ware pottery. What looked like repairs had been made at a date late enough for Tudor brick to be sealed into the surface. The road was still being used and maintained over a thousand years after the Romans left.

Roman Braughing's glory had been short-lived. Its heyday had already passed when Claudius arrived. And yet it was not nothing to the occupiers. There were a large porticoed stone building, which may or may not have been a temple, a bath house or two and various other stone buildings, possibly even a street layout that would indicate a Roman town. If it had been an *oppidum* it may have become a *pagus* – a tribal centre under the Romans.

The traditional model for the early growth of settlements and road networks assumes they had military origins and grew around forts that were built in the aftermath of the invasion to garrison the roads. 'You have built a strategic road and you desire to hold it,' writes one historian. 'So you place garrisons along it, normally at a day's march apart – say 15–20 miles. You often combine the strategic plan with local tactical advantage by placing your fort at a river-crossing, to protect the bridge and to keep your men and horses watered.' Braughing fits the bill, but no fort has ever been found there, although archaeologists think that only about a quarter of all Romano-British forts have been discovered to date. And none in Hertfordshire.

The Romans side-lined Braughing. Before the end of the first century, it had become 'no more than a small undefended roadside town'. Even *town* might be too grand a description. All well and good. It's now understood that roadside settlements were vital to the economy and society of the countryside in Roman Britain. They were witness to a constant flow of people trading and exchanging news, practising their religions and socialising at hostelries and bath houses. They came along roads built for speed and wheeled transport in all weathers,

whether it be for an army on the march or a family in a covered carriage. Picture Braughing teeming with traffic: porters and pack animals, four-wheeled wagons and carts on two wheels of all weights and speeds, slow creaking farm wagons drawn by horses, mules, oxen or men. Most comfortable of all, the rich in litters on the shoulders of slaves, spared from feeling every stone on the road in an age without suspension. Swiftest of all, the couriers of the *cursus publicus*, the imperial postal service, carrying urgent dispatches on horseback or by light carriage. These messengers could regularly cover as much as fifty miles a day and twice as many in extremis.

One of the stone buildings, usually described as a double-winged villa, was possibly a *mansio* – an official overnight stopping place for imperial couriers and travellers on state business. Our rider stops for a while, visits the bath house, takes a meal, exchanges news and perhaps horses too, and then canters away north or south, or maybe climbs steeply north-east in the same direction we are headed, leaving Roman Braughing far behind.

♦ ♦ ♦

If only the Romans had left a map behind to guide us on this journey. The best we have is a kind of roadmap, just without the map. The *Antonine Itinerary* is an ancient roadbook, a series of 225 iters or journeys across the Roman Empire. Surviving today in numerous manuscripts, it was traditionally thought to have taken its name from the emperor Antoninus Pius, one of the 'Five Good Emperors' who ruled in the first and second century between the tyrants Domitian and Commodus. (Antoninus, the adopted heir of Hadrian, also gave his name to a dynasty and to the Antonine Wall, that short-lived northern extremity of the empire that runs between the Firths of Forth and Clyde.) Clues in the text tell modern scholars that the *Itinerary* was probably compiled after his reign, which ended in 161 CE. Since some *iters* take the long way round and certain key roads and road junctions are missing, it's now considered to be less of a list of recommended routes and more a plan or description of specific journeys, say by tax officials collecting food and supplies for the army. The longest tour describes a journey from Rome to Egypt and might represent one taken in the early third century by Antoninus Caracalla, who became emperor in Britain when his father Septimius Severus died at York and so lends his name to the compilation, even though the other journeys may date from different periods. Recent interpretations have pointed out that many of the *iters* seem to start from ports, which might mean we need to think of Roman officials first travelling along the coast by boat before beginning their pre-arranged journeys. All these theories come with a health warning.

The British section of the *Antonine Itinerary* survives in only five manuscripts; the oldest of which is in Vienna and dates to the eighth century. It comes at the end of all the other journeys – Britannia, after all, lay at the furthest extremity of the empire, at the ends of the earth. Fifteen journeys are listed, with their start and end points, the total Roman mileage, the names of places en route and the distances between them. When an edition was first printed in 1512, it immediately attracted the attention of scholars who wanted to match the names of the Roman military 'stations' (as they thought of them) to modern locations. And over the last few centuries, an immense quantity of mental energy and frustration has been expended by students of Roman Britain trying to identify all the places and reconcile the mileages along known Roman roads, or to discover new roads that ought to have existed if the names on the list are correctly identified and in the right order.

Despite their efforts, the *Itinerary* still holds many mysteries and is riddled with apparent errors that cannot be explained away by the mistakes of scribes over the years or mis-measurements by the original authors in Roman times. And yet for all its difficulties it is easy to forget how important and remarkable is its survival. Many of its conundrums have now been solved and thanks to its existence we know the names in the first and second centuries of a large number of places with some degree of certainty. As many as 99 of the 153 stages given agree within one mile with the measurements on the ground.

Antiquaries intent on fitting names in the *Itinerary* to modern towns and villages were not always disinterested in the results of their workings out. 'The study of Roman antiquities,' observed the historian of antiquarianism Rosemary Sweet, 'was something akin to a perpetual guessing game in which each antiquary attempted to join the dots of the Antonine Itinerary in such a way as would demonstrate the importance of his own locality within the Roman imperium.' She cited one wit who wrote caustically that while we might think it unfortunate that the scribes made so many errors, in fact it is a 'happiness. Had it not been for this delicious puzzle, many a dull learned man would not have been able to have employed his time, in a tedious peregrination thro' a muzzy life.' The eighteenth-century Hertfordshire historian Nathaniel Salmon played this game, deciding that Braughing was 'anciently the most considerable place of the County, except Verulamium [St Albans]'. He had found its name on the *Itinerary*. It was the '*Caesaromagus* of the Romans,' wrote Salmon, guessing that the name meant 'Caesar's Town', which must indicate that the emperor Claudius 'in his sixteen days campaign here ... fixed a mansion after his victory at Camulodunum [Colchester]'.

Caesaromagus appears in both the fifth and the ninth British itineraries. Salmon noticed that in the former it was twenty-eight miles from London and thirty-one miles in the latter, and he somehow measured both as being right using slightly different routes. The fifth records a journey of 443 miles from London to Carlisle and Caesaromagus is the first stop, for which Braughing would be a reasonable identification along Ermine Street.

'The grandeur of the name is equal to any,' wrote Salmon, although a more accurate rendering would give a less grand but actually more interesting 'Marketplace of Caesar'. More interesting because it combines Latin and Celtic elements – *magus* being a Celtic term for a marketplace. (It is one of the few Roman place names that can be translated.) What's more, Salmon had it all wrong, because modern scholars have decided that this market was held twenty-six miles to the east: Caesaromagus was at Chelmsford, in Essex. We will have to look elsewhere.

We might try the British Museum. In 2007, the trustees acquired tweezers and hair pins, a finger ring, an ear scoop, a buckle and something simply catalogued as 'of uncertain use' – a box of artefacts that had been collected by a William Allen in the nineteenth century and passed down in his family. Here are various *fibulae* – Roman brooches – both of the annular (ring-shaped) and penannular (shaped like a broken ring) varieties, a rosette brooch, a plate brooch, a bow brooch – all once used to pin the folds of a cloak. Turquoise and green with age, some are plain, others patterned; one of them is shaped like a crude bird. There is a cube of Egyptian blue tesserae from a mosaic pavement, and fragments of a yellow glass bowl too. All are clipped to old index cards, labelled in faded brown ink capitals with the place where they were found. I'm fond of a simple copper brooch, with the pin that once closed it missing. It has a note handwritten in the centre of its unclosed circle: 'Fibula from AD. FINES'.

Ad Fines. Meaning: 'At the Frontier'. The start of our road was the 'AD FINES of the Romans,' wrote Professor Babington confidently, taking his cue from the greatest of the early Roman road hunters, the Reverend Thomas Leman. In 1809, Leman described 'Broughing' – as he called it – as 'a post at the confluence of the Rib and the Quin, where was probably the station Ad Fines'. The frontier in question, imagined Leman, was that between three Iron Age tribes, 'the boundary between the countries of the Iceni, the Cassii and the Trinobantes'. He knew this thanks to the genius of a twenty-three-year-old Englishman, Charles Bertram.

In 1747, Bertram had written to the eminent antiquary William Stukeley from his home in Copenhagen, revealing that he had a copy of part of a manuscript written by a fourteenth-century monk. This remarkable document was called *De Situ Britanniae*, 'Of the situation of Britain', and it would be greeted as one of the most exciting antiquarian discoveries of the age. It completely changed our view of the topography of Roman Britain and made good many of the deficiencies of the *Antonine Itinerary*. The author, who came to be identified as Richard of Cirencester, clearly had had access to now lost sources. He clarified the boundaries of the provinces Britannia had been divided into, as well as identifying a new province no one had heard of before, and gave names to locations that nobody had ever thought of associating with Roman remains. Stukeley wrote effusively about this well-informed monk: 'He gives us more than a hundred names of cities, roads, people and the like: which till now were absolutely unknown to us. The whole is wrote with great judgment, perspicuity, and conciseness, as by one that was altogether master of his subject.'

Unfortunately, the whole thing was made up. Richard of Cirencester's description of Roman Britain was a phenomenally successful and long-lived forgery. Not everyone was taken in as easily as poor Stukeley. The historian Edward Gibbon – he of the *Decline and Fall of the Roman Empire* – noted shrewdly that the author's knowledge of antiquity was 'very extraordinary for a monk of the fourteenth century'. Gibbon assumed that the monk was the forger, who had made a fool of poor Bertram and his followers. The penny eventually dropped for some when they began to question the poor Latin, which belonged more to the eighteenth-century schoolroom than the fourteenth-century scriptorium. Others started to notice even more troubling discrepancies: how could it be that this classical text supposedly copied in the 1300s contained a passage written by an eighteenth-century editor of the Roman author Tacitus? This was just one of the more blatant errors Bertram had made as he invented his itinerary.

No manuscript, no new place names, no Ad Fines. It was extraordinary that it had fooled anybody, but Stukeley and his ilk desperately wanted it to be true: they wanted to know the names of places in Roman Britain, the nodes on the great web of roads and settlements. It was a new and exciting edition of their favourite game.

Bertram's adventure was not harmless. A number of his fabrications stuck. Throughout the nineteenth century, long after most classicists had seen through the charade, names from this fake itinerary continued to be added to Ordnance Survey maps. The 1878 large-scale survey has 'AD FINES' printed on it as the Roman name for the settlement at Braughing, and even today you see the error perpetuated by the unwary. Bertram was 'a nuisance whose influence on opinion dogged the Survey's work until 1920,' wrote one archaeologist. In fact, the last of his fabrications wasn't removed until the 1970s. By then our road's starting point had another name.

Ravenna in northern Italy was where the Western Roman emperors clung to the ruins of empire, and where, over two hundred years after the last of them was deposed, somebody compiled a unique geography of late antiquity. It has the best name of all the sources: the *Ravenna Cosmography*. Its British section has more topographical names than any other source; it is the most complete but also the most baffling of the lists left to us.

Probably written in the seventh century (or maybe the eighth) by an anonymous clerk, three manuscripts have survived. It was first published in the 1700s based on a copy unearthed in the Vatican, but it remained misunderstood until the mid-twentieth century when someone realised that its seemingly random list of five thousand place names had been arranged along Roman roads – a fact which appears to have evaded its own author, since he was copying originals that he didn't understand. While its entries overlap with those of other sources, many of its place names are preserved nowhere else. It is a cosmography because it attempts to describe the earth, parcelling out the continents to the sons of Noah (a fairly standard schemata for Christian geographers), but also dividing the world into twenty-four regions based on the hours of the day – the daytime regions of the south and the night-time regions of the north. From the Italian point of view, Britain was in perpetual night.

It would have stayed in darkness if not for the work of numerous scholars who have wrestled with the impenetrable manuscript in which towns are confused with rivers, rivers with islands and most letters of the alphabet with every other letter. Untangling it meant trying to reconstruct how this poor, careless scribe wrote down the names from one or more maps and itineraries he had in front of him, how he tried to amalgamate poor copies of poor sources, while patently unaware what his sources had originally been created for.

By his own admission, the scribe was selective in his choice of places in Britain, writing, 'In that Britain we read that there were many civitates and forts, of which we wish to name a few.' To make matters worse, the surviving manuscripts have in turn been copied by scribes who introduced their own errors. Of the 315 British place names, the three extant versions disagree on over a hundred spellings. All these barriers to comprehension did not deter the great twentieth century archaeologists O.G.S. Crawford and Sir Ian Richmond from using the *Cosmography* in the 1940s in an attempt to reconstruct a map of Roman Britain. While doing so they discovered a sequence of names that seemed to describe places along roads between Leicester and London, and north again via Chelmsford and Cambridge to Horncastle, north of Lincoln. They found a name that appeared in no other source, Durcinate, and decided that this was what the Romans called Braughing

There was an added twist of course. Durcinate was one of the words that had been 'corrupted' by the author and should surely have read 'Curcinate', which could mean the property of Curcinus. Giving us not only a name but a man from Roman Britain.

The name stuck for the next twenty years, until it finally came unstuck. There had been no such place as Curcinate, or even Durcinate. This time it hadn't been invented by a forger, just mangled by its copyists and optimistically interpreted. While Crawford and Richmond had been pioneers in proving that the *Cosmography* was immensely useful to Roman scholars, some of their conclusions were soon overturned. Since the 1970s scholars have agreed that Durcinate – bafflingly to the non-specialist in Latin philology – is a corruption of Duroliponte. That was a place name already well known from the *Antonine Itinerary* and firmly established as the Roman forerunner of somewhere called Cambridge.

I enjoy tracking this constant revision of short-lived certainties. The shift in key from 'there can be little doubt' to 'it seems most likely' to 'can only be guessed at'. Like those antiquaries who scoured the fragments of literature, milestones, coins and itineraries to fit their favourite place to a personal version of Roman Britain, I had hoped for a name, a Roman name, a definite Roman 'station' to start the road from, another to head towards, but I had something better: three names – Caesaromagus, Ad Fines, Curcinate – creative misreadings, errors, inventions and wild guesses. All spoke more eloquently to my endeavour as I set out across the clay plateau.

♦ ♦ ♦

... that Blind Road, by which I mean the track so slightly marked by the passengers' footsteps that it can but be traced by a slight shade of verdure from the darker heath around it, and, being only visible to the eye when at some distance, ceases to be distinguished while the foot is actually treading it.

Walter Scott, *Guy Mannering* (1815)

♦ ♦ ♦

Penned now by thick hedgerows and barely seven feet wide, a steep track climbs Pentlow Hill out of Braughing. In the nineteenth century it was *a private carriage and Drift Road or Way and public Bridle Way of the breadth of twenty feet.*

No carriage or cart would get through today. Although there is a slight dog-leg zigzag to break the climb, it would have taxed mule or oxen to reach the summit with any substantial load. Was this really the way? Some argue that Roman engineers tolerated steeper slopes than modern road builders would. John Holmes, the local archaeologist and schoolmaster, walked here in the 1950s, noting that parts of the track were 'hard and metalled with flint'; it is only where it 'deviates from the straight that it becomes worn and muddy'. This morning, someone has helpfully spray-painted bright circles around dog turds, a chicane for our times.

We must sport the appropriate footwear to follow in the footsteps of the Romans. The ubiquitous sandals – the *calligae* – of the Roman soldier perhaps, or better still the boots that later replaced them, with soles thickened by layers of cowhide hobnailed together – so hard-wearing they might last for two thousand years. At Vindolanda, beneath Hadrian's Wall, several thousand of them have been pulled from the dark anaerobic silt of the fort's ditches, wrinkled brown, dried out and, to the casual glance, curled up like corpses plucked from bogs or the sands of Egypt. They are deeply moving, since each was once shaped to an individual's foot. There are many more soles than uppers. Thousands of soles, a homophonically appropriate word, for they must stand in for those souls who once walked in them, carried their footfall through life. More than any other item of clothing, they are testament to someone passing this way, the weight of their bodies pressing down on the leather, on the soil, on a road's grassy verge, as they walked the roads of Britain so long ago.

Preserved in leather are the tastes and fashions of the years, for closed boots fretted with elaborate decorated open work, for designs with cross-lacing and intricate eyelets, for the single piece *carbatinae*, with toe-shapes pressed into the leather, sometimes shaped by their maker to emphasise the long second toe – an ancient ideal of beauty seen in classical statuary. Shoes come into fashion, multiply in the archaeological strata across the Roman world from the Tyne–Solway isthmus to the Netherlands and the Mediterranean coast, then disappear again. There are slippers for the home and clogs for the Roman baths, marching boots hobnailed and heeled. One sole is stamped with an eagle and is identical to a shoe found hundreds of miles away in London. Others are marked with urns, circles or florets. A sandal worn by Sulpicia Lepidina, wife of the fort's prefect, is here, stamped with her name and the name of its maker. (She is famous as the author of a birthday invitation found among the Vindolanda writing tablets.)

We can even guess how they walked in these shoes: the ever-widening soles of men's footwear must have made them strut, with a military stride, their shoulders thrown back.

Let us march after them, following in these strange footsteps uphill, past the wild clematis, old man's beard, in the hedgerow. Is this the tinder that set the hilltop ablaze in dry summers or do the field names Spark Hill and Kindle Croft commemorate where generations lit the bonfires in the high places at midsummer? At the top, to my right, a haystack towers monolithic and sentinel at the edge of the plateau. Westward, the chalky fields at the margin between slope and plateau crumble towards Quinbury Farm in the valley below. The English writer Rebecca West might have described this hilltop, the clouds above it, this path. She spent a year holed up in the farmhouse, the rent paid by the father of her newly born child, her lover, the novelist H.G. Wells. In her lifetime, West was called the greatest-living English writer. Her reputation today rests chiefly on *Black Lamb and Grey Falcon*, her extraordinary travelogue of the Balkans in the 1930s, one of the great non-fiction books of the twentieth century. At Heraclea, on a Roman road in Macedonia, the great Via Egnatia, nearly seven hundred miles long linking the Adriatic to Constantinople, she 'realized Macedonia to be the bridge between our age and the past' when she saw two peasant women meet for the first time and share food, reminding her of a similar incident in the life of St Monica some 1,500 years before. Places along a Roman road might be such a bridge anywhere in the world. West was probably just too late to see the past lived out near Quinbury. Certainly as late as 1900 – as had happened for centuries – old widows still went Thomasing there or goodening, carrying apples and hedgenuts around the houses on St Thomas's day, 21 December, when it had been customary to give alms to the poor.

West must have walked the hill and valley here. If only she had written something about the countryside hereabout. I scour an experimental short story of hers from the time, in the hope of clues. After an argument a man follows his wife out into a night 'flooded with the yellow moonshine of midsummer'. She slips through a hedge 'to tread a field path' and he pursues her through a muddy puddle over a stile beyond a mass of hawthorn bloom. I want it to be based on a night-time walk with Wells along the line of our road. He would publish his *Short History of the World* a few years later.

Writing in the adumbrated style that fitted so many centuries and certainties into so few pages, he outlined what he called the first stage of the expansion of Rome; he knew the secret of the early success of the Roman Republic as she gradually assimilated her neighbours. It was her roads: 'Great roads were made. The rapid Latinization of all Italy was the inevitable consequence of such a policy.'

◆ ◆ ◆

I am tracing a terraced bridleway above the valley in the wake of Roman engineers, who followed the slope of the valley's side, not wanting their soldiers to be silhouetted against the sky, certain that an attack could not come from below. I am also in the footsteps of the apex predator of road hunters, Ivan Margary. Reading his terse directions. Following him onto *higher ground beyond*. Upslope a badger has dug out a bumblebee nest to feast on the larvae, and bees lie dead around the hole.

Margary dedicated much of his life to recording and making sense of Roman roads in Britain. Where some devotees restrict themselves to searching out one road in great detail or all the roads in one part of the country, Margary was a completist, with the right kind of mind for the job and the good fortune to have inherited a vast sum of money with which to finance his passion. From the 1920s, his interest in Roman roads in Sussex led him to take on the seemingly impossible task of investigating every rumour of one in Britain, walking thousands of miles and eventually driving thousands more in his much-loved vintage Austin. He would have motored up the Great North

Road, today's A1, which then still followed much of Ermine Street, and remained in the hands of seventy-two separate local authorities between London and Carlisle. The first stretch of motorway was still over twenty years away. To Margary and other enthusiasts navigating Britain's early twentieth-century highways and byways, Roman roads must have been viewed with some degree of awe; an improbable lesson in what had once been possible and what may become possible again.

Margary has been everywhere before us and documented his passing. The greatest monument to his footfall was the publication in the mid-1950s of *Roman Roads in Britain*, which would go through two further editions as he and his disciples accumulated ever more miles and the evidence for them. Reading the book, it is hard to tell that roads were Margary's great passion, although they must have been. By repute, a quiet, self-effacing man, he gives no account of his enthusiasm or any clue as to what drove him or why he loved exploring the roads. He wrote a very knowledgeable introduction and informative descriptions of all the known routes, but no panegyric to them. No love letter. Perhaps he thought it was self-evident. Who doesn't love Roman roads?

His book is a phenomenal work of scholarship, on both roads and how they relate to the archaeology of Roman Britain that was known when Margary was writing. It is a reference book and of its time. Where he has something more to say than a dry account of place-names and waymarks, the route descriptions begin with a brief comment on the context, what it was for and why it was there. So Watling Street 'was of course the most important thoroughfare in Roman Britain, and nearly all those who came to the island province must have travelled along it to the capital', but the majority of Margary's entries simply describe the routes as he found them, his evidence carefully itemised. We wish he would let his personality come through; perhaps it is his personality. He was old school, said his obituary in *The Times*, 'in manner, dress and civility ... All he did was a combination of quiet dignity and assurance.'

Margary was no romantic. Here he is describing a section of the road closest to his heart, that from London to Lewes, in East Sussex: 'Its course is through Cobhambury; just west of Waystrode Farm, Cowden and Kitford Bridge, through Peter's Wood, Holtye (traces of the *agger* ...); west of Bassett's Farm, just east of Butcher's cross ...' And so on in this vein. This *agger*, the raised and cambered platform that once carried the road surface, is a forty-yard section, a few miles out of Holtye in East Sussex, that Margary excavated, fenced and preserved for posterity. He had discovered the road by chance in 1929 while photographing Ashdown Forest from the air. No Roman roads were known in the area, but some of the photographs revealed lines, absolutely straight and parallel, which on the ground proved to be shallow ditches wide apart, with a raised causeway and unmetalled side strips between them that Margary quickly recognised for what they are.

To keep track of his inventory, Margary devised a numbering system. London to Lewes is RR14. Roman Road 14. Which is not to say it is the fourteenth road he found or the fourteenth road built back in the first century, nor is it the fourteenth most important road. (Pay attention.) Think of it as one-four, rather than fourteen. The 'one', because the road branches off RR1, Watling Street. The 'four', because (pay extra special attention) it is the fifth road branching off RR1

– the fifth being numbered 'four' because the first road was numbered zero. (More accurately, it is the fifth road that Margary adjudged to be branching off Watling Street in a particular direction at the time he was assigning numbers.) The first three are RR10, 11 and 12, all leaving Watling Street at Canterbury in Kent. The next is RR13 from Rochester, Kent, to Hastings in East Sussex. Then Margary's London to Lewes road. In his numbering system, no road has more than three numbers. RR140, for instance, from Barcombe Mills in East Sussex to Hardham in West Sussex, is the first branch off RR14. By his accounting, there are 9 principal routes, 78 secondary ones and nearly 180 tertiary routes. Routes rather than roads, because they may be made up of what some would consider to be separate roads.

Margary's many colleagues and acolytes have continued to pursue the ultimate accolade: finding a previously unknown stretch of road and providing enough evidence for its course to convince the master and subsequent authorities and so bag a Margary number. Without one, it isn't a Roman road. The system is still used today by Historic England, local authorities and anyone else with an interest in the roads. It is not without fault, and experts debate the underlying philosophy of it. As we might expect, some roads are missing and plenty are now contested. Are they really Roman? Do they follow the route Margary describes?

Our road is RR21b. Reaching for greater precision and to break up his journeys, Margary sometimes split the routes into more than one section. So RR21a and RR21b are two branches off RR2, Ermine Street. That he considered them sections of the same road, begins to reveal the relative arbitrariness of his system. RR21a sets off from Ermine Street towards St Albans a little south of the main road hub and on a completely different alignment to RR21b.

That 'b' is so woolly and unexceptional, an adjunct of a road. An afterthought. Squeezed in somewhere between 21 and 22. A road you don't see coming.

♦ ♦ ♦

Everything we see hides another thing, we always want to see what is hidden by what we see ... The interest can take the form of a quite intense feeling, a sort of conflict, one might say, between the visible that is hidden and the visible that is apparent.

René Magritte, radio interview (1965)

♦ ♦ ♦

The line has evolved. It is now marked in red pen on copies of old Ordnance Survey maps, sometimes bold and certain, mostly tentative and exploratory, broken and dashed like a running stitch, here straying from the centre line, here returning to suggest possibilities across the plough, linking footpaths and hedge lines. It unfurls to two and a half metres long from origin to terminus on seven map sheets glued in a continuous sequence to a roll of thick lining paper, and I like to keep it open with stones picked up on walks so as to study the many handwritten annotations: parsimonious ontologies, dated and initialled, enclosed in rectangles tethered to the road's alignment with thin arrows that sometimes get lost among the contour and grid lines. NO TRACE IN CLOSE SCRUB OF COPPICE J.R.L. 2-75 and NO PHYSICAL SURFACE REMAINS FOUND F.I. F.D.C. 12/77, which in their reticence and caution typify the other comments, so that it seems like a record of something that doesn't exist or at best is permanently contingent. The route as far as the dog turds is shown as a broken red line following modern roads and glossed in blue pen with a paragraph initialled 'IDM' – for Ivan Margary – and followed with the anonymous '(No authority cited for this claim)'. It sets the mood: don't believe everything you read, question everything, even if the great Margary says something is so.

The original of this wonder is kept today at the Historic England archive in Swindon. It is the map at the heart of the old Ordnance Survey file for RR21b: buff tangrams cut from six-inch-to-the-mile map sheets from the early 1960s and fitted together, uncannily, because they don't unroll but unfold, deviously, like a magic trick, to reveal the condensed wisdom of the Ordnance Survey field investigators and local archaeologists who walked the road before me. These maps were a conversation between surveyors and archaeologists from across the years. I like to walk it with them before I set out.

I like to think that I am also walking in the footsteps of giants, or at least one in particular. At the funeral of Charles Phillips in October 1985, Professor Glyn Daniel concluded his address by saying: 'Future historians of British archaeology looking back at what was achieved in the twentieth century and remembering, as we do today, Charles Phillips, might well say in the words of Genesis IV: "There were giants in the earth in those days."'

It is mostly Phillips we must thank for the wonderful annotated maps. As an amateur, he supervised the excavation at England's most significant archaeological dig, at Sutton Hoo, the Anglo-Saxon royal burial site, and in the Second World War he worked on photo interpretation of enemy territory. In 1947 he was appointed archaeology officer of the Ordnance Survey's special Archaeology Division.

Phillips was a giant of twentieth-century archaeology and a giant of a man – too large to get through doorways, it was said – and famous for his 'Phillipics', his Saturday-night monologues on the state of the world when he worked as the librarian at Selwyn College, Cambridge. His years at the Ordnance Survey would prove revolutionary for archaeology at a time when it was growing in popularity, partly thanks to the proselytising of household names such as Sir Mortimer Wheeler and Glyn Daniel on the 1950s BBC TV programme *Animal, Vegetable, Mineral*?

Phillips made sure that work to save hidden archaeological sites from destruction was seen as urgent. Deep ploughing, the ploughing up of margins, the damage wreaked by large earth-moving machines, the Forestry Commission's breaking up of moorland to plant conifers, the building of new towns, the expansion of old ones, open-cast mining, quarrying – these destructive forces seemed never-ending to him. Ancient roads were being erased by the building of new ones. Technology was the enemy too. 'In earlier days the hummocky areas marking the sites of deserted villages were often left as pasture by farmers because the levelling of them was too difficult,' he wrote. 'But by the mid-20th century an earth moving machine would solve most of this problem in the course of a day.'

I don't know for certain if Phillips ever walked our road, although he had family nearby and he grew up over the border in Essex; from his office in Cambridge University he liked to explore the countryside in all directions on his bicycle. While his initials don't appear on the maps, Phillips is the authority cited on them for the suggested line of the road and his signature verifies this on one of the index cards, known to insiders as the 495s, from their Stationery Office reference number.

These were the eight-inch by five-inch record cards at the heart of Phillips' filing system, one card for every antiquity in the country. By 1951, his small team had created 15,000 index cards, and two years later there were 35,000 and growing rapidly. In his years at the Ordnance Survey, the Archaeology Division grew from a staff of four to fifty-five, with over twenty field investigators.

A decade after Phillips' retirement in 1965, one of those investigators came to follow the red line.

♦ ♦ ♦

Darwin, like Freud, always regards what he can see – in this case, the literally superficial layer of earth – as the result of a hidden process. And this process needs to be reconstructed from further evidence. The ground is as it is because something is happening underground; what is visible is, as it were, the end of the story.

Adam Phillips, *Darwin's Worms* (1999)

♦ ♦ ♦

The field investigator took the track up Pentlow Hill and walked the first stretch of terrace way, largely underwhelmed. Then he stopped and made a note that would eventually find its way on to the map, his very first recorded observation – TRACK & HIGH BANK ON LINE – and he signed and dated it J.R.L. 2-75.

I imagine J.R.L. in February 1975, boots claggy, clutching a mud-streaked map with cold fingers and over his shoulder his Survey drawing board – made of Formica with metal braces and a waterproof cover. In his haversack, his pencils and various coloured inks for his fountain pen, tape measures, a camera, compasses, a pocket sextant and a surveyor's optical square known as a 'popeye'. Hopefully some sandwiches too, and a flask of tea from the landlady of the B&B where he would be staying.

The Ordnance Survey field investigators had no real offices to work out of. In small teams of three, they based themselves at guesthouses, B&Bs and in rooms above pubs, racing against the clock to survey all the antiquities in an area ahead of the surveyors, who in the 1970s were revising the Ordnance Survey's maps. The investigators would work from a 6-inch sheet and batches of 495 index cards that had been generated over the years from local correspondents and the observations of nineteenth-century antiquaries. While investigators usually worked on a single map, moving systematically across the grid squares so as to visit sites in the most efficient order, most would work on linear features – canals, railways, viaducts, earthworks, roads – as a single entity from end to end. They often set off in pairs, so they could leave a car at the end of the day's planned walk, then drive back to the beginning.

Our investigator, J.R.L., has studied the maps and must be expecting this length of bridleway up ahead, knowing it is on the line of our road. In total, he adds eighteen comments to the map, all short and matter of fact. Most are negations of the road – NO TRACE – an observation of nothing, evidence of absence, nothing to see here. Such remarks say more than meets the eye. DEEP DRAINAGE CUT NO TRACE. It tells us that he looked for one. It boasts of his professional eye trained to see nothing where there is nothing – which is sometimes beyond my powers.

'You must remember,' says Stewart Ainsworth, 'that we carried around a lot more in our heads than made it onto the maps.' Ainsworth is best known as the landscape archaeologist from the Channel 4 television show *Time Team*. He joined the Ordnance Survey in 1969 and three years later moved to the Archaeology Division. While he and his colleagues might fill their personal notebooks with sketches, observations about changes of land use and theories as to why a road was abandoned or what things might have influenced its survival, these would not make it onto the working map. The notes written up in the evening on a large table in a pub would be brief and to the point, as J.R.L.'s comments attest. There might be a longer narrative behind them, but it had to be distilled to a synthesis. 'You took care to draught what was going on the record,' explains Ainsworth. 'You had one shot at it. And you have to remember that what was written down did not represent the understanding of the investigator or even the state of knowledge about the road at the time. It was what the system demanded.' Indeed, one of the ADIs, the Archaeology Division Instructions, read menacingly and depressingly: 'All written work ... must be set out to meet, but not to exceed, the purpose of the records requirements.'

While the entire point of the exercise was to capture any visual evidence for where the road was, so that it could be drawn on a map, many field investigators also wanted to get into its 'mentality', to gain a feel for the geography of it, how it related to the landscape, how that landscape had altered over time and what part the road played in that change or continuity. They worked end to end on a road, even if those ends led out of the area under survey, in order to get to know what Ainsworth calls 'the personality of the road'.

They also looked at comments made by other investigators to see if they were still valid, and updated or deleted them if necessary. Any new sections they found they surveyed onto their right position on the map. If anything had been destroyed, they would make annotations. Investigators were not supposed to look for 'invisibles' and certainly not to makes notes on them. Yet J.R.L. would have been trying to get into the heads of the Roman engineers. What problems had they met on the ground and what solutions had they used? At the front of their minds was always water, because drainage was everything. Ainsworth again: 'If you look at how a single Roman road adapts itself to the geography of a place – its topography – then the water, its drainage and run-off patterns, were always a major influence, especially in upland areas.' Roman roads would have had to contend with many different problems, such as flooding, streams to cross and surface run-off. Roads survived because the engineers had successfully solved the difficulties of boggy areas and how to cross the boulder clay where the drainage was easily and quickly blocked. 'There were multiple minor engineering feats for a Roman road to function,' says Ainsworth.

For all their precision and rigour, the Ordnance Survey investigators felt the weight and poetry of history too. Their interests often grew beyond those of the surveyor. They became sensitive to the special atmosphere that you feel when you travel along a Roman road – the thrill of walking in the footsteps of the legions. And of all those who came afterwards. With experience, many came to understand that few of the Roman roads they walked were in any sense still Roman. A lot had been patched up and reused or taken away. They were dealing with a route, rather than a physical entity, and the actual road became less interesting than the relationship that it had with the landscape, and its other infrastructure, what it was part of, what it revealed about the conquest and the occupation in military and economic terms. A good field

investigator couldn't divorce the road from two to three thousand years of other activity.

J.R.L. would be thinking about how the landscape had changed over those centuries. Tracing the repair, diversion and abandonment of a road is a key to the landscape it crosses: what happened there and the relationships between other things in it, its pastures, farms, woods, chapels, groves, kilns and rivers. He would look for sections that had been repaired and rebuilt by Romans or Saxons or Victorians as they reacted to landslips and alterations in land use when fields were enclosed in the eighteenth and nineteenth centuries. 'Seeing its changes over time helps you to understand the bits where it hasn't changed,' explains Ainsworth.

And where it hadn't changed can be seen in J.R.L.'s opening volley: TRACK & HIGH BANK ON LINE. This short comment is framed by a rectangle with two arrows connecting it to the beginning and end points on a stretch of bridleway less than 250 metres long, but pointing north-east on a bearing of thirty-five degrees and sitting precisely on Thomas Codrington's straight line, the theoretical line, Charles Phillips' central line, on the line of a Roman road built two thousand years ago, on an alignment that appears, at least for now, to continue at that same thirty-five degrees, unbroken, undaunted, until Bixett Wood in Littlebury, Essex, eight parishes and 9.4 miles hence. This blessed length of bridleway pointing north-east and to the past. We are finally on the line.

PART II

THE LINE

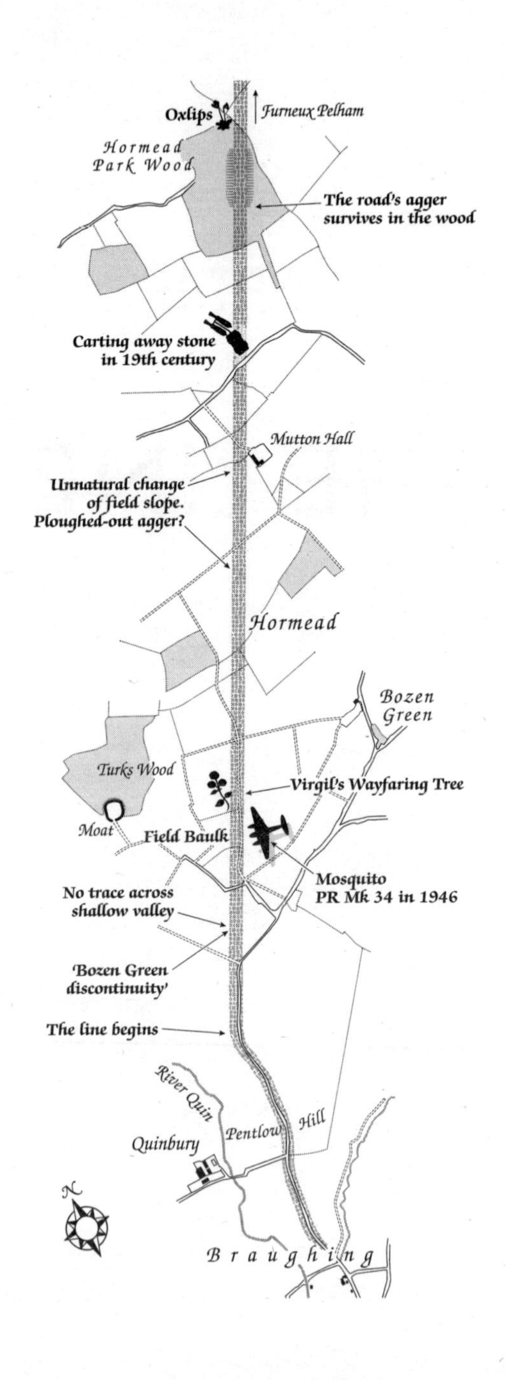
Oxlips
Furneux Pelham
Hormead
Park Wood
The road's agger
survives in the wood
Carting away stone
in 19th century
Mutton Hall
Unnatural change
of field slope.
Ploughed-out agger?
Hormead
Bozen
Green
Turks Wood
Virgil's Wayfaring Tree
Moat
Field Baulk
Mosquito
PR Mk 34 in 1946
No trace across
shallow valley
'Bozen Green
discontinuity'
The line begins
River Quin
Pentlow
Hill
Quinbury
N
Braughing

Intimate almost secretive. That's what someone called the clayland countryside here, and I know what they mean now. It is hiding the road in its embrace. After less than 250 metres, the bridleway on the line, pointing into the far distance, has gone astray. Abruptly, at a farm track heading east, it leaves the alignment and there is no sign of the road where it should be. I ignore the paths and trudge slowly across the adhering plough, where feet turn leprous with clay. Surely this is the way it must have come. Looking back from the field edge: is there a white patch in the middle of the plough? Gravel? Chalk? Is this field stonier than you'd expect? Clutching at straws. Cold going. Wind biting now and nothing to show for it. I turn to J.R.L.'s comments on this passage we share, hoping for solutions and solace in their found poetry.

NO TRACE ACROSS SHALLOW VALLEY, notes J.R.L. on the map, but Ivan Margary disagrees; he could see it. His observation, condensed for the OS's strip map, reads FAINT TRACES OF RIDGE. Yes, that's what I could see, that white patch. In reality, I can will no ridge into being and the satisfaction of walking directly towards some far goal along a dead straight pencil line vanishes in the soil. The first length of path has too quickly become the first break point. A discontinuity. J.R.L.'s NO TRACE takes issue with Margary's TRACES, but doesn't erase it. Elsewhere on the map, some of Margary's comments have been rubbed out or written over, but here J.R.L. has let it stand, as if acknowledging that the hint of a ridge might have been visible years before. Acknowledging that the road must have held its line. Where else could it be?

Another walker thought otherwise: the local archaeologist John Holmes wrote that the original road diverted from the alignment deliberately, zigzagging to NEGOTIATE STEEP VALLEY. The Ordnance Survey file on RR21b shows both of these possible routes as dashed red lines, one following the bridleway as it right angles around the field on the track to the clutch of houses at Bozen Green – once a medieval village, located just off the road – the other straight across the plough, where we want it to be. I give it a name, this disappointment, this challenge: it is the *Bozen Green Discontinuity*.

Hang on though, that's why J.R.L. calls it a *shallow* valley. He is conversing with Holmes, correcting his *steep valley*. J.R.L. could find no trace of the road on the alignment, but he must have thought it went straight ahead two thousand years ago because there was no *steep* valley and so no need to zigzag to reduce the gradient. We are eking out all we can from J.R.L.'s brevity. He must have stood here like me and tried to gauge the lie of the land. The *lie* of the land. Homonyms sending seekers awry. Yes, in the Middle Ages the track east became more important, but the road didn't originally go that way.

For surveyors turned archaeologists, there is always a tension between the continuous line for which the evidence has to be found and the distinct points on that line where the evidence resides. The enforced concision of his comments on the map of our road didn't allow J.R.L. to express this. They portray the road as distinct points in space – a pond bay, a field baulk, a ridge and mostly distinct negations, lacunae itemised. This is because he takes as his starting point the line that has already been established and expects little new evidence, only its gradual disappearance (or chance reappearance), or to judge an earlier interpretation as mistaken. His job was not to make the sections join up, to force the line, but to assess the evidence for them. He never strays from that in search of other possible routes when he finds no trace. Is there a conceivable reason why the Roman surveyors would have moved from the straight line in this landscape? On our road, the line made sense topographically. There was enough evidence to prove it perhaps, so why look anywhere else?

And so I don't. The road must go straight on along the pencil line, dipping across Rylands field to join up with another longer stretch of bridleway on the right alignment. It must have done. I squat on my haunches and look hard for it. The rain is pounding the ground again and I remember how Roman coins were said to float to the surface on Wickham Hill in heavy rain. Would the road rise revenant-like at any moment, some vestige of a lost civilisation resurfacing? I read J.R.L.'s words again: NO TRACE ACROSS SHALLOW VALLEY. Now I am annoyed with him. Is there a road here or isn't there? Why can't you tell? You're the expert. A short distance ahead, he will do better, observing that ploughing has formed an unnatural change in the field's slope. Presumably where farmers have ploughed out the *agger*. This is what we expect from an expert, a forensic certainty. Someone who can identify not only the course of the Roman road but the name of the particular soldier who turned that sod of earth and packed down that chalk two thousand years ago, from the angle of his spade cut. AN UNNATURAL CHANGE OF FIELD SLOPE. Now we're talking. This is *CSI*. This is the 'patient examination of the ground on foot' that Charles Phillips and his assistant A.L.F. Rivet call for in the Ordnance Survey archaeology field guide for beginners. There is still no substitute for it, they say. That may be so, but this intimate countryside won't give up all its secrets from the ground.

◆ ◆ ◆

The twin props of a Mosquito Mk 34 corral the skies above the Hertfordshire countryside into perfect whirlpools of blue. The ninth of July, 1946 is fair to fine, visibility moderate, wind calm to light-variable. It won't become cloudy until midday. The light wooden bomber works its way south-west over fields that have recently been filled with rusted machinery to prevent the enemy landing; others are seeded with the accidental wreckage of training flights. A little to the south of their current position lies a decoy airfield built to lure the destructive payloads of air-raids. The pilot and navigator are over friendly territory now and don't have to worry about contrails giving them away, or the shock of anti-aircraft fire. This Mk 34 has been customised by de Havilland for military photo reconnaissance, her bomb bays adapted and fitted with large fuel tanks to extend the range to over three and a half thousand miles. As many as six large cameras are now arrayed about the fuselage ready to capture frame after frame of the tessellated world below – to probe its secrets, vertically and obliquely. With the uncanny ability of aeroplanes to slow time, even at 300 mph, the Mosquito unrolls the land field by field, framing black and white photographs that in their ghostly details reverse time, so that features lost for centuries might be exposed on the film like a presence caught by spirit photography.

Less than two years earlier, these same planes of 540 Squadron had hunted the coastline around Tromsø in Norway, above the Arctic Circle, eventually capturing images in the water of what everyone was looking for – the wounded *Tirpitz*; a few weeks later the RAF returned and sank the great German battleship. And it was a 540 Squadron crew that shot arguably the most important photograph of the entire Second World War in November 1943, when a flight returning from an aborted mission over Berlin took a photograph at Peenemünde on Germany's Baltic coast. This seemingly unreadable image of a scarred and confused landform revealed a tiny winged tube on a launchpad – it was a V1 rocket. Nearby, the even more malign V2s sat on their transporters. Thanks to the skill and bravery of the pilots and photographers and the penetrating eyes of the photo interpreters on the ground, the RAF knew where to strike and thus save thousands of British lives from the flying bombs.

The men of 540 Squadron stationed at RAF Benson, in Oxfordshire, were honing their skills that summer, undertaking a photographic survey of the UK and further afield as well, preparing for the coming Cold War in which their aerial reconnaissance role would remain essential. To avoid shadows and haze they couldn't shoot before 'first photographic light', so they took off about three hours after sunrise. One of five survey flights that day, they released the shutter of the F52 camera with its thirty-six-inch lens every six hundred yards over an area covering some one and a half square miles – just shy of nine hundred acres of England frozen on film.

Before the flight moved off westwards that July day, they took twenty-three photos above the fields harbouring our road. The amount of information in just one of these frames is formidable. Simply processing the easily visible, the immediately readable, is hard, impressionistic to most of us: you can see blocks of woodland, hedgerows, roads like seams of a rare mineral or veins of fat in a side of beef. The eye tries to

amass odd polygons into ever-larger agglomerations of meaning. It is a deliberately analytical act in the face of what the artist John Piper called 'the most beautiful photographs ever taken'.

Another frame, numbered 5240, taken as the plane continued south-west, interrogates a field in Hormead known as Second Park Ley. Time and the ground darken in reply, leaching a widening black trail on the alignment across the hedgerow. Here is the road, where it should be. Here where J.R.L. would find NO TRACE ACROSS RIDGE EDGE. The Mosquito flight, nearly three-quarters of a century earlier, solved the mystery, found the missing trace, but nobody took heed. Frames 5240–5241. Two more lost pieces of a lost road.

♦ ♦ ♦

While military reconnaissance might have favoured first photographic light, those setting out deliberately to capture the elusive traces of past worlds preferred the early morning or dusk. They came to call it 'lynchet time'. With the sun low in the sky, the shadows of ridges of old field systems were thrown into relief, 'like the bony skeletons of an old horse'. *Aggers* of roads too. These were 'shadow sites'.

It was Osbert Crawford – O.G.S., Ogs or Uncle Ogs – appointed as the very first archaeology officer of the Ordnance Survey in 1920, who pioneered the use of aerial photography as a way to the past. While excavating in the Sudan at the outbreak of war in 1914, he had noticed box cameras suspended from kites being used to photograph excavations. By 1917 he had joined the Royal Flying Corps as an observer, flying reconnaissance missions over the trenches on the Western Front. The experience – photographing the topography of warfare and later interpreting those photos – would prove an extraordinary boon to twentieth-century archaeology. At the Ordnance Survey Crawford was tasked with ensuring that archaeological details – the course of a Roman road, for example – were accurate, yet it came as a surprise to his superiors when he started leaving the office for days on end on his bicycle. Within months of taking up the position, he had personally visited over two hundred sites in the Cotswolds. Personally, because he was on his own, no division, no branch, just Crawford. Something of an experiment. Resented in many parts of the Survey that, true to its military origins, demanded strict discipline and conformity from its officers.

His fieldwork was brilliant and revelatory – he knew that 'a furrow, grown over with weeds, might be the lasting register of the wheels of chariots on a Roman road' – and when in 1922 he saw aerial photographs of Hampshire taken by the RAF he realised that you could see the shadows of lynchets, the ancient field strips scored into the earth and now revealing their ghosts to the heavens. It was as though a long-sighted reader had just held a book at arm's length and watched the characters come into focus, revealing stories that had hitherto been unreadable.

O.G.S. read the history of the landscape in those photos. While people had long known that ancient structures could be recorded in fields of corn, Crawford expanded the potential of the science, noticing ever more subtle impressions, not just buildings but Iron Age field systems and other long-ago disturbances of the earth.

He reported excitedly to the Royal Geographical Society: 'It is difficult to express in suitable words my sense of the importance of air-photographs for archaeological study. They provide a new instrument of research comparable only to that provided by excavation. They are second only to excavation ... Their invention will prove as valuable to archaeology as that of the telescope has proved to astronomy.' He added his hope that Roman roads would be discovered too. A few years later the president of the Society of Antiquaries said, quite beautifully, that aerial photography had 'emphasized one thing, not quite appreciated hitherto, namely, how sensitive the soil is, how slowly nature heals the wound made by man'.

O.G.S. later improved on his own analogy, famously saying that a person on the ground was like a cat on a carpet: the cat was too close and couldn't make out the pattern, but the human eye was far enough away to make sense of it. Crawford even took a photograph of a carpet at cat's eye level, where the pattern was just a blur, and another from above, where it was revealed in all its intricacy. This way of seeing into the past was futuristic to many. In his 1933 vision of the future *The Shape of Things to Come*, H.G. Wells imagined a survey plane finding the submerged wreck of an ancient Greek glider that Daedalus had built for his son Icarus (instead of the more customary wings found in classical legend). The plane was called Crawford.

Crawford made a deal with the RAF and began a collection that is now kept at the Historic England Archive, in which our photographs of the road in the village of Hormead and elsewhere are filed. On his retirement in 1951, it was said that: 'No single scholar has done more than O.G.S. Crawford to place the study of the remoter past, and of the past of Britain in particular, on the secure and sound basis upon which it now rests.'

♦ ♦ ♦

The burial and subsequent re-emergence of an archaeological site directly mimics the effect of the uncanny as explained by Freud in his 1919 essay. 'The uncanny,' he writes, 'is something which is secretly familiar which had undergone repression and then returned from it' ... An aerial photograph of archaeological remains is almost a textbook case of the uncanny, for here is the apparent return of the dead, the return of that which was thought to have been unburied.

Kitty Hauser, *Shadow Sites* (2007)

♦ ♦ ♦

It is with a god's eye view that I sit at the kitchen table and navigate the road. Six months after the 540 Squadron photo was taken, a flight from 82 Squadron passed overhead and its camera recorded two frames of a January day above Hormead. There is no sign of life in these grey photographs. No movement. Only a stillness after some great event. It is as if the photo has been developed in the silvered emulsion of a photographic plate that someone has dropped, each field a sharp fragment of glass. Our road is a tiny shock of white with dark ditches on either side, no more than ten millimetres wide on my photocopy, but there is no doubting it, and so it gives substance to the fainter blurred white line pointing to the north-east. In the Ordnance Survey file for RR21b, someone has ringed the road with a yellow chinagraph pencil, a clumsy elongated oval, not swiftly circled, but drawn slowly by someone who must be saying, 'There you are.'

In the summer of 1976, Parliament passed an emergency powers bill followed quickly by the Drought Act in August. Reservoirs lay empty, bore holes had run dry, and the earth cracked, its top soil blowing away. Crops everywhere were failing, grasslands were browning and dying. On the afternoon of the last day of June, a plane flew low over the Hertfordshire countryside and took an oblique close-up of fields that look fossilised or as if someone has spilled bleach on them. It shows the *Bozen Green Discontinuity*, that first length of bridleway on the alignment, the 250-metre stretch that stops abruptly where it should run straight ahead. The withered earth can no longer contain its mysteries; drawn out by the heat, there it is, linking the first length of bridleway with the second across the shallow valley of Rylands field – a clear white ghost road. It is as if Roman roads were always meant to be seen from the air, as if they had been waiting for two thousand years to be seen as their makers intended.

The magic is not in the camera, in those vast grey cylinders, half the size of a man, loaded into bomb bays in the 1940s like a more sinister payload. The magic lies in the earth itself that draws the path of the road for us in whatever is to hand – wheat, barley, rapeseed, grass, soil. It is a latent magic, instilled by Roman engineers who gave much thought to making sure their roads would drain and be useful in all weathers, who built the hard, wide, raised running surface with evenly spaced drainage ditches. They wouldn't have known the roads would survive long enough to be seen by people who had learned how to fly and plot alignments through the clouds. That even images of the past, things lost to time, could be exposed on the photographic plate of the earth.

◆ ◆ ◆

Back on the ground now, on a grassy track where J.R.L. noted the slightest of clues, a DEEP DRAINAGE CUT. It is on the left as the road follows a second length of bridleway north-east. Looking back, the track I have climbed appears arrow straight, though it didn't seem so as I walked it. A hedgerow has been planted in recent years and I follow it up the gentle incline. I know that J.R.L.'s next comment was FIELD BAULK ON LINE, and it is still there, an innocuous firm length of grass, something of age and purpose written in the soil between the crops. Or is that just the impression of that solid, archaic word *baulk* – a ridge of unploughed land dividing field strips. This is the straightest stretch now, an open field on my left and a tall young hedgerow flanking the path on my right: field maple, hawthorn, blackthorn and appropriately there is viburnum here too – the Roman poet Virgil's tough wayfaring tree. I follow the path through the golden rapeseed, looking to my right for bumps in the field. Crossing a hedge line and a small wooden bridge, marked on the map by a watercourse. NO TRACE. What else would we expect?

There are settlements everywhere from across time. Not just the medieval site known as Turks, once home to an adulterine castle, but Iron Age and Roman too. Identified by their pottery scatter. The road must have played a part in their existence, their growth. We must remind ourselves that roads make sense only when we join the dots of evidence to make a whole. For a specialist like J.R.L. this is the only way they make sense, otherwise it's just stamp collecting.

The bridleway has become a lowly footpath leading to a road and beyond arable fields laid out before a block of woodland. Hormead Park Wood. I pause, thinking of words I can use to describe this ghost of the road. I have been making a list: trace, relict, stain, weal, ribbon, tread, footprint, furrow, scuffmark, impression, welt, wale, cicatrix. I like the last of these best: a scar or seam left after a wound has healed.

A short distance from here, the eighteenth-century antiquary Nathaniel Salmon was very taken with a large lump of stone by the roadside. He would go on to anoint it in his *History of Hertfordshire* as an important antiquity, calling it grandly a *Roman Lapis Milliaris*. He described it as lying in a *bottom*, on the road: a great stone, 'which antiently may have been set up for the Purpose [of marking the miles].' Early Ordnance Survey maps mark it as a boundary stone and it survives in sketches made in the early nineteenth century by the local rector and amateur artist, the Reverend Robert Newell. They show a large, jagged pyramid of granite emerging from an overgrown verge. It must have been impressive since Newell not only drew it but penned an ode to it too, six four-line stanzas beginning:

Rude relic of a by-gone age,
What changes hast thou seen!
What mark'd events in memory's page
Of nations that have been!

By 1914, it had moved opposite the nearby church, says the venerable *Victoria County History*, which dismisses it as nothing, but in mentioning it at all cannot resist its charms: 'There seems no reason for assigning a Roman date to the granite stone mentioned by Salmon as standing near the junction of Stonecross Lane and Ware Road, near Hare Street, and in 1900 among some nettles inside a field by a broken-down gateway at the top of the hill exactly opposite Little Hormead Church.' If it was a milestone, it has gone the way of most of its kind. It has vanished.

In Britain, fewer than a hundred Roman milestones are known to exist, and only four still stand in their original location. We must stray a few hundred miles to see the best of them, to a Northumbrian glade, a ridding, deep green after rainfall, where stands an ancient monolith. It has weathered for nearly two thousand years, pitted and lichen-covered with a depression in the top that you can probe with your fingertips, a stoup or font, a vessel for some sorcery, moss-filled and damp. I think it has been a rubbing stone for cattle, who over the centuries have pushed it to its precipitous angle, but like most such stones its roots are deep in the ground and it will never fall now. It stands on the first-century Stanegate, the stone road, just south of Hadrian's Wall where it passes the Roman fort of Vindolanda, marking the fifteenth Roman mile from Corbridge. If it has been a rubbing stone that would explain its inscrutability, because any inscription that might speak to us has been worn away (although it is just as likely that over the years the locals chipped bits off to put in their potions and cure their toothaches).

Many milestones carried inscriptions; some just painted on and easily lost. As Vindolanda is one of the most literate sites in all of Roman Britain, thanks to the discovery in the early 1970s of hundreds of thin wooden writing tablets from the first and second centuries, there is a certain irony in the stone's silence. Nearly two metres tall, with the girth of an old pillar box, the great pillar might be mute, but it is not ineloquent and speaks to an imagination intent on summoning the legions and the traffic of the Roman frontier lands and the passing of the seasons since.

The Corbridge milestone is one of over four thousand such stones to have been found throughout the former Roman Empire, the earliest from 252 BCE, although most date from after the early second century CE. They were imposing features and we might marvel at the sheer scale of quarrying, shaping, inscribing and erecting thousands of stone pillars each weighing as much as two tonnes. In Britain, many are only fragments, found buried and at the bottom of wells, or – where local stone is scarce – re-used in walls as steps or to hang gates on, even for sharpening tools. Most are now in museums, uprooted from their roads long ago. Found in the bed of a Lancashire stream, the Artle Beck, in 1803, one of the earliest survivors, dates from just over seventy-five years after the invasion. It is dedicated to the emperor Hadrian and originally marked four miles from somewhere, possibly Lancaster, according to the rough inscription.

Put up two hundred years later, one of the last milestones of Roman Britain survives as a broken block of sandstone little bigger than a paperback book. Found in 1936, built into the steps of a Welsh granary on the road to the Roman fort at Abergavenny, the few crude letters tell us that it was inscribed to the emperor Constantine II some time before his death while waging war on his brothers and co-emperors in 340 CE.

These two milestones bookend the history of Roman Britain. They stand for the thousands that once studded the island. Marking the miles as the legions marched. The true number remains unknown. If every mile of Roman road in Britannia was marked, we might expect some ten thousand

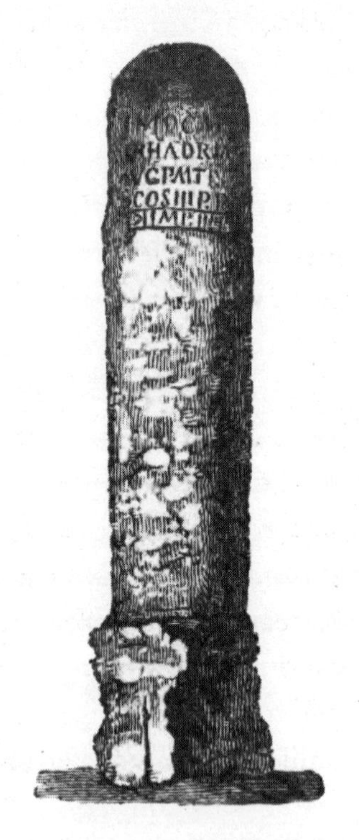

milestones to have once stood along the roadsides of the province, but since there is good evidence that many of them were regularly replaced, that number might have been much greater. In reality, it's highly unlikely that every mile would have been marked in the first place, not least because many of the stones don't even bother to mention any mileage.

Not all Roman milestones were fashioned to the same standard as we find on the Stanegate. Some may have just been impressive lumps of rock like the Hormead stone, or stumpy cubes or even timber posts. If that's true, many that we might expect to find are invisible to us because they don't look like neat pillars but boulders and puddingstones. No certain Roman milestones have been found on or near our road, nor anywhere in Hertfordshire. In a county that geology has left so devoid of building stone, they would have been re-used in church walls and such like or perhaps broken up to repair a road at some point in the 1,300 years after the collapse of Roman rule, before milestones returned to England.

A little north of where the lump of Hormead granite once sat sprouts the first of a series of sixteen beautiful milestones measured to the south-west buttress of Great St Mary's Church in Cambridge. They were placed there in the early eighteenth century by Dr William Warren, a fellow of Trinity Hall, Cambridge, and trustee of a fund to keep the road in good repair. 'I took two men along with me,' he explains, '& with a Chain of 66 feet in Length we measur'd five miles from the Southwest Buttress of Great St Maries Church Steeple in Cambridge towards Barkway.' These are thought to be the first set of milestones erected in Britain since Roman times.

A later extension of the Trinity Hall series was probably put there by the local Turnpike Trust in about 1742, coincidentally the same year that a lump of limestone that stood in the centre of London's Cannon Street was removed as a traffic hazard and placed in the wall of the nearby St Swithin's church. This is the celebrated, even venerated, London Stone, from which some say all Roman milestones in Britain were measured, making it Britannia's version of the *Milliarium Aureum*, the Golden Milestone that once stood in the forum in Rome, gilded in bronze and engraved with the names of major cities and their distances from the Eternal City. Like the Golden Milestone – now reduced to a lump of marble thought by some to have been its original base – the London Stone is but a gnarly lovable fragment of its former glory. It is rather grandly displayed in a Portland Stone shrine built into the wall of an office building on Cannon Street. Legend says that it was brought from Troy by Brutus – that it is the heart of London and must never be removed. Archaeologists have suggested that this mother of all Roman milestones in Britain originally stood in the middle of the gateway into the Roman governor's palace.

There will be many times over the miles when the stones that marked them will come to mind, and I hope to spy one on our road, in a wall, as a step, or lintel, or to catch a rumour of one in a folk memory. For centuries, a notable block of stone on Silchester Common, in Hampshire, bore the chiselled letters 'IMP', the usual abbreviation for *Imperator*. Emperor. But to the locals it had become the mysterious impstone. Legends tell of imps in these parts too.

If there was once one near here, perhaps it lies in pieces somewhere in the bank of the River Quin behind us or the

Ash up ahead. One of Britannia's most storied milestones was found in a riverbed near Carlisle. It names Carausius, the commander of Rome's British fleet who took control of the British legions and declared himself emperor in the late third century, minting coins which announced *Redeunt Saturnia Regna*, 'The Golden Age Returns', and *Iam Nova Progenies Caelo Demittitur Alto*, 'Now a New Progeny Is Let Down from Heaven Above', cryptically rendered as 'RSR' and 'INPCDAN', and only recently recognised as referring to lines from Virgil. These inscriptions on coins and milestone are not mere curiosities. They fill in the lacunae left by a history that has dismissed Carausius as a pirate: he was obviously more than this and appears to have controlled at least part of nine legions and much of northern Gaul before being assassinated by Allectus, one of his own officers. The milestone is the only structure that can confidently be associated with this charismatic rebel and confirms for us that he held authority in the north-west of Britannia. An earlier inscription on the stone has been chiselled out. Later the stone was turned upside down and re-inscribed again, this time to the emperor Constantine, whose father had retaken control of Gaul and Britain from the usurper.

Milestones, like the roads they stood along, can help tell the story of Roman Britain and fill out the lives of its emperors. One found north-west of Belgrade is dedicated to the emperor Constantius who, 'after having built the roads, remade the bridges, restored the common prosperity, he has set up across Illyria milestones every 5 miles from the River Atras to the River Sava 364 miles'. In such a way, they reveal which emperors did the most for public road-building programmes.

(Across the empire, Trajan wins hands down.) They have improved the reputation of the notorious Caracalla, who on the evidence of milestones has been shown to have rebuilt all the major roads in Spain. In Britain, the emperor most often chiselled on surviving British stones is Constantine the Great, whose name graces eighteen of them. Although milestones have been found attesting to the continued building and repair of roads right up to the end of the occupation, after Constantine, inscribed stones seem to go out of fashion.

But few in Britain are especially informative. If we are lucky, they give the emperor's name and sometimes details of who repaired the road or who was responsible for its upkeep. If we are even luckier, they give enough information for us to have a rough idea of where the stone once stood, but only a handful give place names. One says that it was fourteen miles from Lindum (Lincoln) to Segelocum (Littleborough on the River Trent). It stood two metres tall and is dedicated to the emperor Victorinus, who ruled for just one year before being assassinated in Cologne by one of his own guards. Victorinus had been having an affair with the man's wife.

The inscriptions were usually abbreviated and can be difficult for any but the specialist to decipher. One from a milestone a little north of our road reads:

IMP. CAS / M. ANNIO / FLORIANO / P.F.INVICTO./ AVG/M.P.I

Imp(eratori) Caes(ari)
M(arco) Annio
Floriano

P(io) F(elici) Invicto
Aug(usto)
m(ille) p(assus) I

For the Emperor Caesar Marcus Annius Florianus Pius Felix Invictus Augustus, one mile.

The emperor's lengthy name is rather restrained by the standards of many inscriptions. 'After AD 200,' one historian has written, 'the self-adulation recorded on milestones grew so flamboyant that titles and distinctions covered the entire road-marker from top to bottom, and one had to read through all this verbiage to find out what road one walked.' And so we read on a milestone about 'The Emperor Caesar Trajan Hadrian Augustus, son of the deified Trajan, conqueror of Parthia, grandson of the deified Nerva, father of his country, in the fourth year of tribunician power, thrice consul.' That is the emperor Hadrian, in the florid, aggrandising and sycophantic style found on a milestone, now in the Jewry Wall Museum in Leicester. The inscription ends with 'from Ratae 2 miles'. As if the carver who chiselled this in about 120 CE had suddenly remembered that it was a milestone: 'Oh yeah, 2 miles from Leicester'. Weighing over a tonne, the stone was found in the 1770s in a gravel pit alongside the Fosse Way near Thurmaston, and used for many years as a garden roller and then as a lamp standard.

As we might expect, milestones also made convenient markers when giving directions. In a letter to his friend Gallus, Pliny the Younger wrote: 'There are two different roads to it; if you go by that of Laurentum you must turn off at the fourteenth milestone; if by Ostia at the eleventh. Both of them are in some parts sandy, which makes it something heavy and tedious if you travel in a coach, but easy and pleasant to those who ride.' Such stones must have marked the whereabouts of many an assignation – 'Meet me at the eleventh milestone at nightfall' – and bore witness to affairs both great and small: in the summer of 69 CE, on hearing that he had been declared an enemy of the state, the emperor Nero took his own life at the fourth milestone on the Via Nomentana in Rome. *What mark'd events in memory's page.*

♦ ♦ ♦

Time became non-existent. To me, at any rate, it seems less real than space, though both are vague enough. The past is never quite past.

Freya Stark, *The Lycian Shore* (1956)

♦ ♦ ♦

Far from Rome now, I squat in the dark coppice of Hormead Park Wood, in the mulch, sighting along the road. Doubt and uncertainty are a good default position. Even when you know the road is there. And it is there. Can you see how the ground swells? From there to over there? It runs in a straight line at about one o'clock. Nodding. You can see one of the ditches, a slight depression, darker soil, filled with water in the winter. Yes? Nodding. This is the surviving *agger* of a Roman road, that once carried the road surface across the clay. It is about as certain a feature as can be found anywhere along the route and it is an ideal lesson in the great divide between the actuality of the road and the picture in the mind's eye of a cobbled or paved thoroughfare, like the Appian Way outside Rome or the iconic Roman road along Blackstone Edge in the Pennines (which almost certainly isn't Roman). It is nothing, a swelling of the leaf mould, a shimmer in rainfall, and yet it is completely bewitching if you let yourself believe in it.

The art historian Christopher Woodward wrote that it took his interest in the ancient world a decade to recover from a schoolboy visit to the ruins of Verulamium at St Albans. Roman ruins in Britain are an acquired taste. There is no Colosseum here, no Pantheon. Stumpy walls of stone filled with rubble are often as good as it gets. How much more amazing would it be to see the villa, the fort, the basilica they once were. A Roman road is different. It would just be a road. A road in its prime would be nothing to us today. We might even despise this thing that thrusts so imperiously across the countryside. What matters is where it goes and where it comes from and what it connects and those who have travelled along it. What it has become is far more interesting than what it once was: the humble hedgerow in spring, the earthwork hidden in the wood, the note scribbled on an old map.

You have to come at it obliquely. Start at the eastern edge of the wood and you will walk onto it before you know it. Crouch and look askew at it from different angles to convince yourself that the floor of the wood is really raised in that spot. Gaze up through the canopy to find deltas of light against the blue sky. On the ground the sun collects in tributaries like something trying to take shape. I stand on the alignment and take a thirty-five-degree bearing. North, the way I want to go, is close scrub, so I walk south instead. My sense of direction holds out along the *agger* until the hornbeam coppice gives way to the hazel one, and some pits or black ponds lie to my left and then without a compass, even with a compass, I go awry and drift off course. When you get lost in a wood and keep ending up in the same spot, is there a word for such a place – with its gravitational pull? One day I followed the *agger* three times from the same starting point and three times came out in the wrong place, the same wrong place. A friend told me that his grandma would say I was pixie-led: 'She'd recommend you turn your pockets inside out to show that you had no gold and so break the charm.'

The remains of the road were found here in the nineteenth century by a local vicar bosing the woodland floor with its mean carpet of dog's mercury. Stepping between the stools of hornbeam and hazel coppice to ring the hard surface with his pick, he listened to the quality of the sound, for the dullness or resonance of earth disturbed, the thud or thoomp of the axe head, like a doctor carefully percussing a patient's abdomen for air or a mass.

It's been said that physicians make the best amateur archaeologists, certainly the best bosers, tamping for symptoms in the landscape as they would in the human body, before taking a scalpel to the ground to excavate. Clergy on the other hand might bring an even more essential skill to the endeavour: the eye of faith.

Could you really follow the line of the old road by the sound it made when struck with a pick? Could you follow it with not the slightest doubt? He is not the first clergyman I have found to write with such conviction on secular matters. No one else had been so sure about the road for centuries. In fact, I don't think anyone else was so sure ever again.

♦ ♦ ♦

If you cannot follow the road by its music then try its flora.

On 8 April 1798, the illustrator James Sowerby finished drawing a flower that had been sent to him by the Reverend John Hemsted, one probably plucked from the ground in Wood Ditton, Cambridgeshire. It would become plate 513 of over two and a half thousand hand-coloured copper plates in Sowerby's monumental thirty-six volume *English Botany*. A carefully detailed watercolour of a delicate yellow flower with five heart-shaped petals. It was also the first publication in England of a picture of the true oxlip, a flower that botanists of the time were still confusing with the much more common cowslip and other hybrids. One of its names was 'Five Fingers', and the naturalist and local historian Miller Christy wrote charmingly in the 1920s: 'It seems, at first, particularly inappropriate; for the flowers of the plant bear no sort of resemblance to the fingers of the human hand when these are held fully extended and spread, as one usually thinks of them. If, however, the forearm be held upright and the hand bent over sharply at the wrist, with the fingers relaxed and slightly spread, the resemblance of the umbel of the Oxlip, with its characteristic one-sided droop, to the human hand becomes strikingly obvious.' Which is a lesson in botany, in analogy and in how to look.

The true oxlip was and is a rare thing indeed in the British countryside. Since it appears over much of Asia and Europe, we might expect it to be all over Britain as well, but as Christy informed the Linnean Society, the 'distribution of the plant is, with us, greatly restricted, and in *a remarkable manner for which it is not very easy to account*'. My italics.

Christy drew a map of the flower's limited distribution in East Anglia that reached almost as far west as the line of our Roman road, concluding that it only grew on certain sections of the boulder clay. Mostly in woodland. And only the chalky boulder clay. Never on chalk not covered in boulder clay. By

which we might guess that it likes the alkalinity of the chalk and the wetness of the clay. (Folklore tells a different story, that where it grows is a sure sign that wild boar once rooted in those woods because oxlips are thought to grow best in soil once enriched by boar dung.)

In the spring of 1908, a small patch of oxlips was spotted growing in Howe Wood, on the boundary of the villages of Littlebury and Strethall in Essex. On the very western edge of the wood. Fifteen years later, in 1923, more were seen in the centre of Rockell's Wood to the south. Keep these woods in mind.

By that year Christy had recorded thirteen outliers from what he called the main oxlip area, eleven of them situated on streams that flowed elsewhere, and he speculated that was how the seeds had arrived, but Rockell's Wood and Howe Wood were a mystery to him. There were no streams there, so how could the seeds have reached their location? His confusion surprises me because one autumn seventeen years earlier, Christy and the archaeologist Guy Maynard had walked and cycled past the western edge of Howe Wood and through the heart of the oxlips in Rockell's Wood. They were pursuing the course of a certain road. Further south on that line, there is only one site in the whole of Hertfordshire where the true oxlip grows. Christy didn't know about it. It's in the north-east corner of Hormead Park Wood, next to the *agger* of RR21b.

These patches of a rare flower are linked by our road and it is irresistible to suggest that their seeds travelled along it on the soles of feet, on cartwheels, stuck in the mud of hooves, finding and settling in the soils they liked.

Such botanical clues are not unfamiliar. In the late 1980s, a local naturalist rediscovered the road, which the coppice had guarded for centuries from the plough and the grubbing axe, later writing that most old routes had been destroyed by ploughing, except in 'Hormead park an ancient wood where a substantial *agger* survives and upon which subtle differences in woodland flora can be determined. These variations perhaps relate to original soil disturbance, although more likely they are indicative of the use of the highway over centuries.'

Plant habitats are not just a strange trail: they can teach us something valuable about the road, about the terrain the Roman engineers had to deal with and their achievement in overcoming it. The type of boulder clay favoured by the oxlip becomes super-saturated in winter with the water content never less than 30 per cent all year round. Little wonder that in places the road has sunk from sight, but we should rightly marvel at the engineering skill of those who built a road that in part could withstand such conditions for so long, that maintains a surface dry enough to be a friend to hornbeam and bluebells in the spring while the damp woodland floor carries ash, hazel, field maple and dog's mercury. Enough of a continuous dry surface that a little yellow, five-fingered flower could find its slow way to its favourite nesting spots.

♦ ♦ ♦

Roman roads were beautiful. They were 'not only functional, but also aesthetically pleasing,' wrote the biographer Plutarch in the early second century CE, before going on to describe the roads built by the Tribune Caius Grachus:

> They were to run perfectly straight through the countryside, with a surface of quarried stone firmly bedded in compressed sand. Depressions were filled up, bridges were thrown across every watercourse or ravine which intersected the route, and from one side to the other the roads were made flat and level, so that the work presented an even and beautiful appearance throughout. He also measured every road in miles [...] and set up stone columns as distance markers. At smaller intervals he also placed further blocks of stone either side of the road, to make it easy for riders to mount their horses.

The Romans knew their roads were special. Plutarch was not alone in singing their praises and that of their builders. The poet Publicus Statius wrote a panegyric to both the emperor Domitian and the road he had built, the Via Domitiana, in Campania, Italy. He writes that an uncomfortable journey that had once taken a whole day – the traveller holding on tightly as the ground sucked at the wheels of his cart, and *glutinous ruts slowed / Tardy travel, while weary beasts crawled / Along, under the weight of their high yoke* – now took just a couple of hours. Statius describes the men noisily building the road, draining ditches, diverting streams, felling trees. But their first task was to *mark out trenches*, then:

Carve out the sides, and by deep excavation
Remove the earth inside. Then they filled
The empty trenches with other matter,
And prepared a base for the raised spine,
So the soil was firm, lest an unstable floor
Make a shifting bed for the paving stones

Building a *raised spine* to keep the road dry was the most important thing in a Roman engineer's mind. A typical Roman road consisted of a cambered embankment, its *agger*, built from layers of rammed stone and chalk. This was to keep the soil beneath dry so that the road would never become water-logged. On the wettest sites, they might float the road on timber or brushwood foundations.

Foundations were also there to spread the load and carry the actual running surface, which was narrower than the *agger*. This was the metalled part of the road, usually grav-elled or topped with small stones where they were available. (It's a strange term, 'road metal', having nothing to do with metal – unless we are discussing Margary's road to Lewes, which was famously surfaced with iron slag from the Wealden iron industry – and was given to us by Scottish road engineers, who used the word 'metal' to mean rocks and stones.) To carry wheeled traffic, metalling needed an average depth of twenty inches. It could be more – examples as thick as ten foot have been found, built up over the centuries as the road was repaired. On Ermine Street, the average depth of the surface was thirty inches. Only Watling Street has a thicker metalling.

All Roman roads derive from the Appian way. Widely considered to be the first all-weather military road built by the

Romans, its earliest section allowed the army to march across the Pontine Marshes and keep their supply lines open during the Second Samnite War in the early fourth century BCE. It is the archetypal Roman road of the imagination, cambered and paved with slabs of stone, and bordered by ditches with retaining walls. But few of the estimated eighty thousand miles of road it had spawned by the height of the empire would have looked like this. Paving is rarely found. Cobbles would have been more common, although gravel was laid over both cobbles and paving to provide a more even platform for traffic. The attractive hard-paved surfaces might have made inferior roads to those built using the more usual mix of crushed stone, pebbles and gravel. In the north and west of England, road surfaces would more often (but not typically) be 'paved' with larger stones. Perhaps in this military frontier zone, the Roman army required a more substantial running surface, or was it simply because larger stones were readily available? (It could also be a misleading impression created by the locals in later centuries stocking up and pilfering the larger stones on southern roads, where building stone was scarce.) As a rule, the Roman engineers used whatever material was locally available.

What should we expect our road to look like when we dig into it today, 1,600 years after the Romans left? Does it come close to the ideal? A section of Ermine Street excavated a little south of here has been described as typical of the Roman roads in the area. Built of cobbles and rammed gravel on a base of clay marl, it has a hard, well-cambered surface between fifteen and twenty feet wide.

Maybe it's misguided to ask what the standard road looked like. The 'most striking feature is the wide variation in the standards of construction,' wrote Ivan Margary. 'The conclusion one draws is that very considerable latitude must have been allowed to the engineers in the actual building of the road, and that the form of it depended very much upon the judgment of the man in charge of each short section.' Even the same road could be built very differently along its length and without any obvious explanation as to why one section had a wider running surface or a much higher *agger* than another. To take Ermine Street again, closer to London it had a twenty-five-foot road surface on an *agger* nearly three times as wide at its base. The surface was formed of different materials too: a foot of flint rubble and sandstone over loam and clay, topped with six inches of flint and chalk. They were almost certainly what the Roman engineers thought were best to form a solid foundation given the nature of the soil in that location, although it might also be that some sections were left to locals and less experienced road builders to finish off.

This variety is charmingly evident in the diverting cross-sections at the back of Margary's *Roman Roads in Britain*. There are thirteen of them, hand-drawn and utterly ingenious as only black and white diagrams can be, since all the materials have to be distinguished by unique patterns legible in the tiny rectangles of the cross-section key. 'Top Soil' is offset rows of dots. 'Flint & Chalk' – an alternating pattern of triangles and dashes. 'Rammed Chalk' – offset dashes, like a proto-Morse code. 'Disintegrated Chalk' – vertical lines falling like rain. Fourteen types of construction material in all, keyed in beautiful little rectangles. The most ambitious depicts 'Limestone Slabs, Pebbles above', made of tiny circles hovering over layers of squashed ellipses.

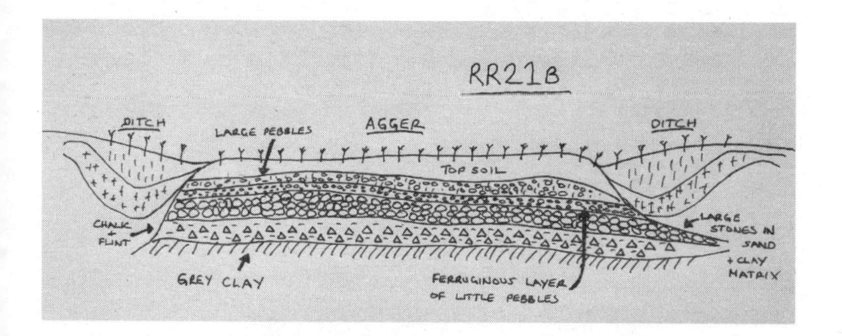

So we know not to expect our road to be paved. On a sunny autumn day in 2013 a local archaeologist finally took a spade to it in Hormead Park Wood. His notes would tell of a 'thickening of the old boundary bank' that was 'followed by a faint terrace in the wood behind it. Thick scrub impeded full investigation of this stretch, but the road reappears in the northern section of the wood as a well-preserved stretch of *agger* some 60 cm high flanked by ditches, and about 16 metres from inner edge of ditch to inner edge of ditch.' He sank a trench and found an engineered camber but few stones, concluding that the engineers had surfaced the road with rammed sand.

It was certainly built by the Romans. They had sealed a small sherd of Roman pot in the surface. Believing that the *agger* had only recently been discovered, the archaeologist concluded, 'Perhaps the most interesting aspect of the Great Hormead Park stretch of this road is the fact that it went out of use so completely that it dropped wholly out of memory.' But did it? In the 1870s, the historian John Edwin Cussans reported that it was seven yards wide and *macadamised* 'by the peculiar water-worn pebbles, locally known as "ginks", which lie scattered about throughout its length'. This may not have been a surviving road surface. People are prone to

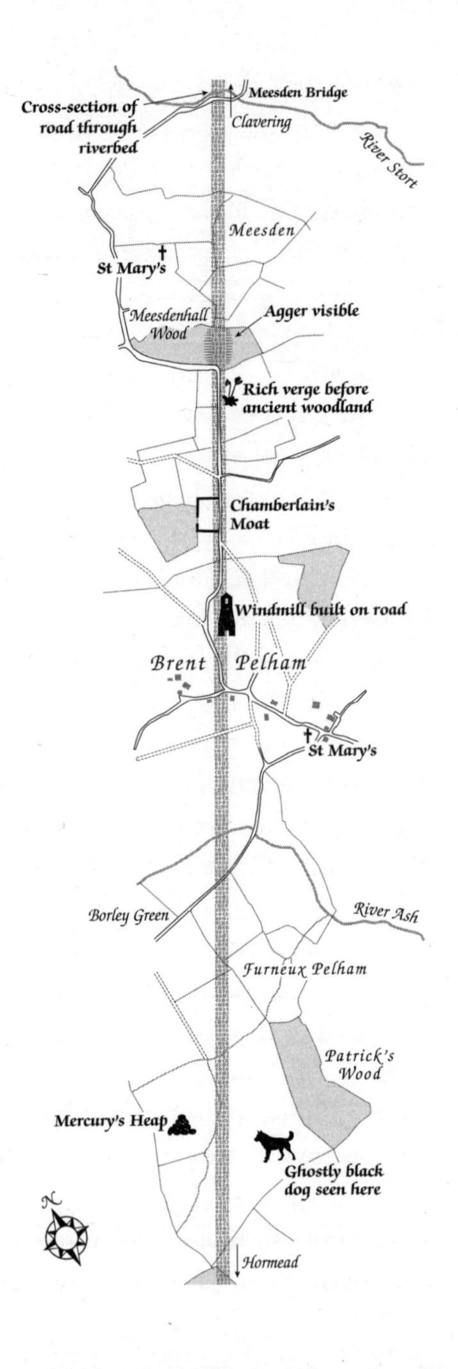

Cross-section of road through riverbed
Meesden Bridge
Clavering
River Stort
Meesden
St Mary's
Meesdenhall Wood
Agger visible
Rich verge before ancient woodland
Chamberlain's Moat
Windmill built on road
Brent Pelham
St Mary's
Borley Green
River Ash
Furneux Pelham
Patrick's Wood
Mercury's Heap
Ghostly black dog seen here
N
Hormead

confuse the foundations of a road with its surface. But either way, in this spot there was, once, more than just the sand discovered nearly 150 years later. The most likely explanation is that locals simply carried away the stones. In the 1790s the antiquary Thomas Walford saw lengths of the Ridgeway, the ancient path that runs from near Avebury in Wiltshire to the Thames, being deliberately ploughed up: 'I remember it extending thirty or forty rods more northwards, and saw the farmer carting it away.' And in 1774, at Great Chesterford, where our road is headed, another Roman road rapidly disappeared as the locals 'were removing and carrying away the stones of the pavement as fast as they could'. Many roads survived for centuries longer than was previously thought and were engineered rather differently than some of the archaeology would suggest.

♦ ♦ ♦

Every object acquires an interest quite separate from whatever significance it may have held for its previous possessors, since it is a tangible survivor from an earlier moment, putting one in touch, literally, with a vanished time. Indeed, because an object was looked at and touched by people in the interval [...] between its origin and the present, it provides a link not merely to one past moment but to a series of them. When one observes a tangible thing in this way [...] one gives close attention to all its sensuous aspects, all its physical features, any of which may proclaim something of the origin and subsequent life of the item. This sort of scrutiny, though it may subsume some understanding of the original function of an item, focuses on as many observable details as possible, whether or not they have a bearing on that function.

G. Thomas Tanselle, *A Rationale of Collecting* (1998)

♦ ♦ ♦

Beyond the wood, stones guide me along their Hansel and Gretel trail. Remarkably, in the early nineteenth century, one farmer knew the road in the fields north of Hormead Park Wood by its stones. Years later, he described it to the local vicar: 'He speaks to the portion which he *stocked up* as a wide road made with pebble gravel; of a kind not to be found to his knowledge in this neighbourhood'. Another farmer's great-grandfather remembered it as 'a grassed road but still existing in detached portions, as a road with baulks / banks & hedges on each side of it'.

He was speaking of the stretch beyond the eastern treeline of the wood, in fields through Furneux and Brent Pelham in Hertfordshire. Just beyond where the oxlips grew. Where an aerial photograph taken in the 1960s shows a clear flash of something at the junction of wood and field, exactly where we want the road to be.

The farmer's choice of the term 'stocked up' is telling, because on old maps the field is called 'Stockings', which usually means land cleared of tree stumps, but according to Thomas Codrington could also be: 'The practice of picking up or loosening the surface of a road with a pick.' The *Oxford*

English Dictionary gives us: 'To pull up (stones, a fence); to break or loosen (the surface of the ground with a pick).' And includes a quotation from 1902: 'At the foot of this artificial hill stood the castle. The people of the country have stocked up the stones to the very foundation for building and the roads.'

I walk the road north-east one summer's day, tracking the incidence of stones along it, looking for any not pillaged, hoping for a more solid marker of its course than blocks of woodland and oxlips. Stray surface stones are a clue markedly absent from Roman road books. No one says, keep an eye out for unusual stones, and no one says, ignore unusual stones, they will lead you astray. Margary mentions in passing that, 'there may be indications of the metalling if ploughing has scattered it'. It is easy to believe that there is a surfeit of stones in the fields we think the road passed through. I take to photographing groups of them. I try to pay attention to the background noise on other walks. I ask geologists, who cannot agree. Some say, yes, that isn't natural, someone has brought it there. Others say it is merely an erratic. The boulder clay is known for its erratics, stones carried by the East Anglian ice sheet some 450,000 years ago. They are chunks of limestone or sandstones; in some places they are granite, basalt or gneiss.

One farmer tells me that a particular field on the alignment is stonier than others; an archaeologist insists, 'Farmers always say that. They're wrong.'

I pick up stones that appear to have been worked or worn. I keep meeting cobblestones the size of crusty cobs. An uncommon number? This is not scientific. I raise cairns like the Romans did, Mercury's Heaps, named after the messenger god, the patron of travellers. I put stones in my rucksack to take home, fretting that I'm chipping bits off the Colosseum. We privilege these cobbles and sandstone over the flints – the sharp-cornered triangles of Margary's diagrams – which are also in the roads. The historian Oliver Rackham wrote that the lost section of a road 'came to light as a conspicuous band of flints across ploughland'. But here there are flints everywhere. They are the stones that define this landscape. I ignore them. That is, until I find a magical one.

Magical and perfectly balanced, it has a beautiful hole, the diameter of my little finger, burrowed right through it. It looks tooled as if drilled long ago – some variety of Neolithic axe head, bored over many patient months with a reindeer antler to receive an ash handle. But such holes in flint occur naturally and mysteriously and I would leave it at that, except that the cause is hardly less satisfying than the mystery. The great nodule of flint, in which my flint was once just a tiny part, formed around the bullet-shaped fossil of a belemnite, an entombed sea creature that eventually wore away, leaving behind the perfect hole. Such is one of the innumerable and ancient sculptural processes of Mother Nature. Perhaps the road crossed a belemnite graveyard – such things are known – because this magical flint is double-holed. A much smaller hole is next to the main one and on the other side are two smooth stone peninsulas marking the position of what must have once been a third hole. Flint Trismegistus. It could be a Henry Moore sculpture, Reclining Figure Pierced, and Moore, who worked not far from our road, would have taken inspiration from flints as vertebral as this one: as votive, fecund, Venusian. There are no recent breaks. A dirty fleecy white has leached into some of the flint's curves like scar tissue over the wounds where it departed the mother lode, but it is also treacle-coloured in parts and deceptively bone-like in others. Such flints masquerade as human remains and transform fields into vast ossuaries. Look very carefully and there is purple colouring on the flat white areas of my flint and, underneath, marks not unlike the percussion marks of the Stone Age flint knapper. No doubt easily explained by the natural historian, but sometimes we must be thankful for ignorance: to me they are organic stains from long ago made by one of the Trinovantes grinding pigment to colour their clothes or their skin. Their makeshift pestle tossed aside or lost as they came down the road.

Dimpled and pitted and pressed into shape by a giant's fingers, it is a hag stone and we might hang it in a stable to protect against night-mares – horses hag-ridden to exhaustion under cover of darkness. Others hid them in walls, hung them from bed ends or tied them to latchkeys to keep witches from their chests and ward off other terrors of the darkness such as bad dreams, nightmares in the more modern sense. The inventiveness of those who treasured these stones and were determined to find meaning in them is endless: you could look through them to see the world of fairy, they stopped milk curdling, and in another place I read that ale poured through a hole by a midwife ensured a safe birth. It is not hard to see why holed flints and other stones fashioned from the remains of other fossilised sea creatures should come to form the geology of supernature. The stories we told about hag stones teach us about our own preoccupations. Are they a reaching after

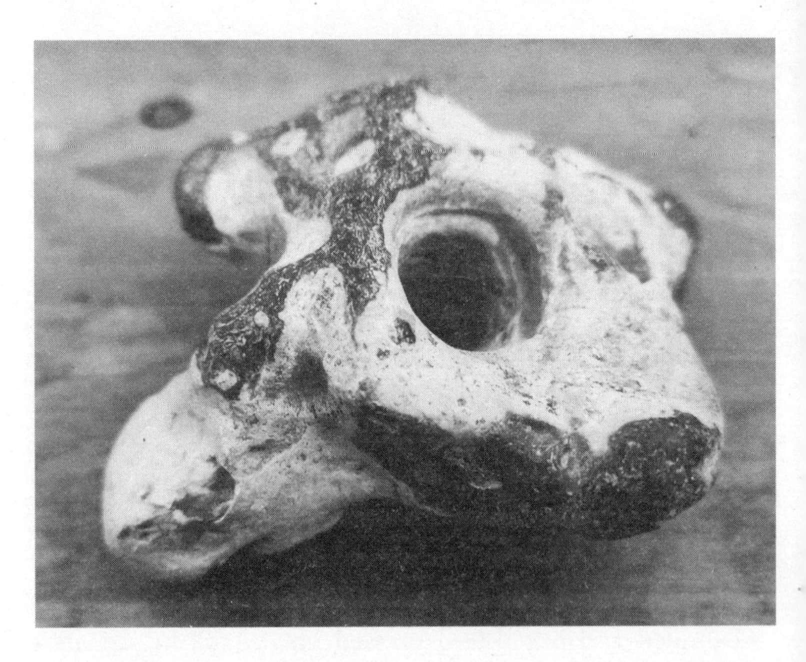

an aesthetic? A justification for taking them into the home, for the satisfaction that comes from holding them tight. Lacking the vocabulary of the art critic, we instead called them magical and ascribed powers that made them useful. Today they should make us rethink what 'useful' means. Mine has wings that, now I hold it up to find more things to say about it, give it a primitive cruciform shape; it is a crossroads. Like all stones, it is an entire landscape in miniature – perhaps the very landscape we are walking through, and I must take it into the field with me and peer through it to find the road and perhaps its travellers too.

♦ ♦ ♦

Ha ha! Why, how much better to be silly, than as wise as you! You don't see shadowy people there, like those that live in sleep – not you. Nor eyes in the knotted panes of glass, nor swift ghosts when it blows hard, nor do you hear voices in the air, nor see men stalking in the sky – not you! I lead a merrier life than you, with all your cleverness. You're the dull men. We're the bright ones. Ha! ha! I'll not change with you, clever as you are, – not I!

Charles Dickens, *Barnaby Rudge* (1841)

♦ ♦ ♦

Bracketed by cratered fields and a tumbledown wood, Cut-throat Lane is a wide, lonely gravel track leading east out of the Ash Valley to a remote reminder of Roman Britain. If its name is not enough to keep you away after dark – and bearing in mind that a holloway known as the Coffin Walk branches off it – a note scribbled in 1935 by Archdeacon George Cameron might prove good counsel: 'N.B. There is a superstition that a dog howling and dragging a chain may sometimes be seen in Cut-throat Lane at midnight.' We should not be too surprised to find shades of the uncanny here. Furneux Pelham, the third parish on the route of RR21b, is remote and on the edge of Black Shuck country. I can imagine great black dogs coming down the road along with other goods. The first-century Roman historian Strabo famously said that Britain was known for exporting 'hides, slaves and dogs suitable for hunting', adding that the Gauls used the British dogs in warfare. Is there an echo of one of those creatures right here? A ghostly ur-Mastiff. This one chained to guard something by owners who never returned. Still guarding it.

NO TRACE ACROSS 'LEVEL' AREA, LARGELY UNDER PLOUGH, wrote the Ordnance Survey investigator. A Roman quern stone was found just north of here; slivers of rich Samian ware too. Cropmarks suggest the ghost of a Roman field system just beyond the next block of woodland, where fragments of *tegulae* – roof tiles – litter the soil. My eye searches for tall patches of barley thriving over buried ditches or tell-tale depressions in the crop where the road has been laid waste, but there is nothing much to see. This is a vast and disorientating field. Cameron would have come here to explore the road. Was he hoping for a glimpse of a hunting dog? He might have allowed himself to imagine he could see ancient Britons approaching on foot or in their war chariots. He would have known what they looked like: 'The men of Britain are taller than the Gauls and not so yellow-haired. Their bodies are more loosely built. This will give you an idea of their size: I myself in Rome saw youths standing half a foot taller than the tallest in the city although they were bandy-legged and ungainly in build.' So reported Strabo, adding helpfully that Britons were not good farmers and couldn't make cheese.

The Venerable George Henry Cameron had been imagining the past of Furneux Pelham since his arrival in the village two years earlier, after thirty years of missionary work. What would this former chaplain of Baku, rector of Eshowe in

Zululand, and archdeacon of Johannesburg find to do with himself in this quiet corner of Hertfordshire? It had been described as 'dull enough in the eyes of such as love excitement rather than peace' by Herbert Tompkins in his classic 1903 guide to the county. 'These are villages,' he wrote of the three Pelhams and the surrounding countryside, 'whose inhabitants live very similar lives, and who take little interest in the history of their parish, one is sorely puzzled to know how to discover the hiding places of that romance or history which surely lurks in every hamlet or village, only waiting for the arrival of that wanderer who, deeming nothing beneath his notice, shall bring it forth once more into the light of common day.'

At seventy-one years of age, and after his wanderings, Cameron had arrived to shine his own light. He might have been forgiven for treating his new incumbency as a retirement, but he intended to put his twilight years to good use: taking up Tompkins' challenge to uncover those hiding places of romance and history. One evening in the spring of 1935, he sat in his vicarage at Furneux Pelham and doodled. He was designing a cover for his new history of the village. What to put on it? Perhaps the thirteenth-century church, an angel from the roof of the nave, or just a detail from the William Morris window. Too obvious? What, then? What picture came to mind? What a shame there were no great henges thereabouts. A ring of standing stones would be easy to draw. Then again, who was to say there was not, long ago, a megalithic wonder on Tinkers Hill, or perhaps a giant pagan figure, painstakingly scoured into the chalk slopes of the Ash Valley by the ancient Britons of Pelham? Some such idle thought must have made the archdeacon adorn his cover with the Long Man of Wilmington. The 230 foot-high chalk giant, clutching a pole in each hand, was only a hundred miles away in East Sussex.

For Cameron, the Long Man with his poles was an ancient surveyor of roads. A dodman. When he first came to the village, the vicar had noticed a preponderance of Roman snails, which excited him since Cameron had read that long ago such snails had been nicknamed 'dodmen', because their antennae had supposedly reminded our ancestors of the sighting rods of the surveyor-magicians who laid out the roads. Even the surname Dodman was 'not unknown in this parish although corrupted to Dedman,' wrote the vicar hopefully. He was especially interested in ancient tracks like Cut-throat Lane and roads such as our lost one that came from Braughing en route to Great Chesterford. While the snails may or may not have been vestiges of the Romans, the real dodmen were much older, thought Cameron. He believed that the Romans had had little to do with the old ways. No. The Britons had planned and built them long before the invaders came.

From the very first page of his history, Cameron tackles the mysteries of the past with astonishing rapidity and some remarkable leaps of logic. Within a few pages he has ancient Britons raising mounds to the sun god; soon the emperor Constantine is ordering Christians to build churches on these very mounds. Despite his enthusiasm, Cameron readily admitted that the part of his story dealing with the prehistory of the Pelhams was 'highly controversial'. But, he writes hopefully: 'Those who can piece together these facts, traditions and legends, will have the material for a story of our past which will provide an interesting background for many parish histories.'

Facts, traditions and legends were one thing, but he knew that he lacked any tangible evidence for his personal vision of an ancient Pelham. That nagged at him. We know because over the next five years, as his health deteriorated, George Henry Cameron would return again and again to the same themes, often clutching at straws as if in a race against time to discover the beginnings of the soil he had chosen as his final resting place.

Much of Cameron's thinking was muddle-headed and based on a strange diet of authorities: scholars such as Professor Lawrence Augustine Waddell, author of *The Phoenician Origin of the Britons*, with whom Cameron had corresponded as early as the 1920s when still archdeacon of Johannesburg, enquiring about evidence for the use of the Aryan alphabet on ancient monuments; evidence that Waddell thought proved that the Phoenicians brought the secrets of bronze to Britain and were mining tin here as early as 2800 BCE. It had a profound effect on the archdeacon, not least in his adoption of the tone of Waddell's work in his own writing: utterly uncontingent, one that brooked no doubts.

The *Dictionary of National Biography* warns that Professor Waddell, once a distinguished orientalist, had turned to the study of early civilisations in 1917 and proceeded to write a number of books, which 'containing much painstaking research and impressive to many, did not win the approval of experts'. Waddell belonged to a historical tradition that has been termed by one archaeologist as the 'search for respectable ancestors', eager to overturn the prevailing view of ancient Britons as blue-painted barbarians roaming the wildwood, or bobbing around in coracles, while waiting for the Romans to come and civilise them.

Cameron was participating in a long tradition, but whereas others had sought ancient Britain among the myths, he wanted more concrete evidence, turning that spring of 1935 to the holloways and causeways that he hoped would lead him back in time. He was sure that the path across a field called the Warren concealed a dead straight line of cobbles. When his ancient villagers were not raising temples and mounds, they were building roads for which, he complained, the Romans would later take credit. Cameron was now reading Alfred Watkins, who in the 1920s had begun to imagine the British landscape as one giant dot-to-dot puzzle, finding straight lines between churches, burial mounds and lumps of rock, which he claimed marked lost trackways.

On page six of his Pelham history under the heading 'British Roads', Cameron tells us that 'Hertfordshire was one of the chief centres of Ancient British civilization', and so we should expect to find 'that it abounds in British track-ways and roads'. He cites Julius Caesar on British chariots and says that we must have had roads for them to travel along, before turning his attention to our road and its course, noticing that it passes near to an outlying settlement known as Rotten Row, which he insisted meant 'a road for wheeled traffic, "rotten" being the old plural of the British word rota, a wheel'. He adds that the idea that our road is Roman 'is not borne out by the names of the places along its supposed route'. Here the juggling of place names, as so often, leads Cameron to some strange conclusions as he finds lines of moats, mounds, leys, ends and burys.

'There is however, I think sufficient evidence to prove that there once existed an absolutely straight road made by our British forebears, which, except where here and there, for half a mile or so a modern road follows the line of the old one, has completely disappeared,' Cameron writes of our road.

By 1939, as the war approached, Archdeacon Cameron discovered that he was dying of cancer. Evidence had emerged of Roman activity in the fields bordering Cut-throat Lane with its ghostly guard dog. A labourer called Albert Sparkes had admitted to finding things in a gravel pit there: two *sesterces* – bronze coins – of the emperors Hadrian and Marcus Aurelius, a rare Roman hammer, various bits of pot and a knife that was identified as Anglo-Saxon by Sir Thomas Kendrick at the British Museum. Further digging in the pit unearthed a skeleton 'extended roughly north to south', with two more knives and a spearhead. The remains were shipped to the Royal College of Surgeons, where they were examined by the eminent pathologist A.J.E. Cave. On the basis of – now outdated – skull osteometrics and, presumably, the association with the knife, they were identified as 'Anglo-Saxon'. All context was lost, but the possible meeting of Romano-British and Anglo-Saxon culture is always beguiling.

By then Cameron was growing too unwell to minister to his flock and had just a few months to live, so it was a great kindness that someone directed him to an issue of the *Archaeological Institute Journal* from 1853. In its pages lay the evidence that he had been looking for all along – so he made an excited announcement in the parish magazine for

September 1939: 'We have lately learnt that about 80 years ago, the late Lord Braybrooke, of Audley End stated at a meeting of the Society of Antiquaries that he had in his possession a collection of bronze implements that had been dug up at Furneux Pelham. This supports our contention, which had so far lacked concrete evidence, that there was a British settlement here in prehistoric times.' Cameron was overjoyed. And where had these bronze implements been forged? 'The site of the foundry was no doubt that of our present churchyard.'

No doubt. No doubt.

♦ ♦ ♦

In the Roman empire the ease of intercourse and communication was proverbial ... For specific illustrations it is enough to recall the voyages of Paul of Tarsus; the vogue of Antioch, Athens, and Alexandria for western students; the Phrygian merchant who made seventy-two journeys to Rome; and the man of Cadiz who travelled all the way to Rome and back merely to set his eyes on the historian Livy.

Charles Homer Haskins, *The Spread of Ideas in the Middle Ages* (1926)

♦ ♦ ♦

If we can resolve 'Plautius's Dilemma', we might decide if the archdeacon was right that the Romans took credit for roads that were already here when they arrived. The dilemma is a conundrum put before the Roman commander Aulus Plautius by the author and archaeologist Mike Bishop. When Plautius arrived on the shores of Britannia in 43 CE, with forty thousand troops, did he quickly build a road, did he march across open country or use an existing trackway? Let us pause to consider the practicalities. As the Romans advanced along what would one day be called Watling Street, were the engineers up ahead frantically laying down a road? How fast could they have built a penetration road into the interior? Bishop has argued convincingly that permanent all-weather roads could not have been constructed fast enough to keep up with the army; instead the legionaries would open up existing trackways as campaign roads, which would be sufficient in the summer months and could then be consolidated over a much longer period. The British army's Royal Engineers have estimated that a thousand men could have built a basic 'tactical' road from the Kent coast to the Thames in London in fifteen weeks. To turn that into a fully engineered strategic road would have taken over three times as many men ten times as long. Others are sceptical of these calculations, suggesting that their recipe for a tactical road would not have survived wheeled traffic for long, proposing an intermediate type of road with light metalling and drainage ditches that could be built in the campaigning season. The important point was to have supply roads quickly in place and enough link roads for the army to hold territory by marching quickly between strongholds.

How long did it take to build different types of road in different terrain under different levels of threat? How long would the road builders march to a day's work before it became so inefficient they would need to build a temporary camp? How many men were on a road-building team? We might be drastically underestimating how many men worked on such a squad. What if 10 per cent of the forty thousand-strong invasion force were used? And this is to ignore the possibility that the local population, prisoners and slaves might have been press-ganged into road-building duties. In his *Agricola*, Tacitus has the British chieftain Calgacus at the Battle of Mons Graupius describe how the Romans have made slaves of the Britons, 'our goods and chattels go for tribute; our lands and harvests in requisitions of grain; life and limb themselves are worn out in making roads through marsh and forest to the accompaniment of gibes and blows.'

While the epigraphy of some roadside stones tell us who had the roads built, there is little solid evidence as to who provided the labour, but in Holland in 2019 archaeologists excavated a series of oak piles that once supported a stretch of Roman road near Valkenburg: one of them carried the simple inscription 'COH II CR' – Cohors II Civium Romanorum – a Roman army auxiliary cohort, and has been taken as evidence that those soldiers built the road.

However fast they worked, they wouldn't have kept pace with the legions, so the main roads, built in the early years of the advance, probably followed existing Iron Age tracks, at least to some extent. Assuming the Roman army needed roads for the advance. Might the legions have dispensed with the local ways and simply marched over suitable terrain and open ground, using trackways only if they made sense from a military standpoint?

There is a difference between an engineered Roman road and a general route. It is unsurprising that many roads built in Roman Britain followed, or stuck closely to, much older routes, they obeyed the diktats of geography. Undoubtedly, in some cases they followed existing trackways that the surveyors would have incorporated into their alignments where appropriate: military roads might head dead straight across country before picking up a bit of Iron Age track, kinking and then returning to the planned line.

In all this, we may be underestimating the Britons. Did they have the know-how to have built engineered roads themselves? Might there have been Roman-style roads that pre-dated the invasion? In 2009 archaeologists working on the route of a known Roman road surviving as a cropmark near Sharpstone Hill in Shropshire, Margary's RR64 from Wroxeter to Trefeglwys, discovered a metalled surface of river pebbles floating on a brushwood matting made of elder. Carbon-dated, it proved to be from the Iron Age, a century before the Romans arrived. And careful excavation revealed that the road – probably a salt road – had known three lives in the Iron Age alone, growing wider and acquiring parallel ditches. It had continued to be used and repaired into the

Roman period and beyond. The evidence, including wheel ruts, cattle prints and finds within the road surface, suggested that it might have started life as a Bronze Age droveway and was still being repaired as late as the early nineteenth century.

If one test for a Roman road is that of checking for known Roman activity or settlements at its beginning and end, likewise many routes are known to link settlements that were active in the Iron Age or seem to be associated with hillforts and prehistoric monuments. This is true of our road, with ample evidence of Iron Age activity along its route. But it doesn't necessarily follow that they were linked in the same way by some *old straight track*. We also have to be careful about marking simple boundaries between historical periods. Where is the Roman-Iron Age boundary? It is not as obvious as we might imagine, especially in a county like Hertfordshire where the evidence for activity in the Iron Age comes predominantly at its end, that is the century between Caesar's brief foray and the Claudian invasion. 'If we did not have the written record of the "conquest" in AD 43 – describing events which take place elsewhere – it would be very difficult to say when the "late Iron Age" became "Roman",' one archaeologist has written. The so-called Romanisation of Britain was not universal. The roundhouse, not the villa, remained the main form of habitation for most people well into the Roman period.

There is another possibility. The luxury imported goods found in Braughing and elsewhere in Hertfordshire suggest that the southern and eastern peoples of Britain had been clients of Rome for years, perhaps paying tribute and enjoying extensive trade, at least since Julius Caesar's second visit in 54

BCE. At Folly Lane in Verulamium, St Albans, the grave of what is thought to be a local chieftain was found in an elaborate ceremonial enclosure and among the expensive grave goods were the fittings of a Roman cavalry officer. The burial has been dated to just a few years after the conquest, and possibly even before it. Was he the son of a local chieftain of the Catuvellauni taken as hostage to Rome, serving as an officer in the Roman army, before returning to his hereditary lands with a taste for the Mediterranean lifestyle? With such close contacts, is it not possible that engineers and surveyors experienced in Roman road-building were not already aiding local elites in Britain before the invasion?

While the Wroxeter to Trefeglwys road is an intriguing case, until more examples emerge, it is hard to conceive that anyone but the Romans engineered most of the roads credited to them. In the conscious decision to go to the cost, in both time and resources, to engineer them to a standard high enough to take heavy wheeled traffic, in all weathers, to provide stone bridges and to allow freedom of movement along them with very few tolls, the roads built across the Roman Empire were unparalleled in the world until modern times. The classicist R. Bruce Hitchener has expressed this idea most forcibly: 'Roman roads annihilated distance to an unprecedented degree in antiquity' – a statement made with more than a nod to the eminent historian Fernand Braudel's claim that throughout history, distance was humankind's number-one enemy.

Whether or not our road or its route has earlier origins, RR21b looks exceptionally Roman. If it picks up trackways along the way, it is not obvious. It is far too straight for too long a distance to be on a prehistoric alignment. As the writer

John Higgs observed in his book on Watling Street, 'For a Roman road to follow a pre-existing native road was to fix a straight, clearly defined line through a meandering, fuzzy, constantly evolving route.' And RR21b is nothing if not straight, at least so far.

♦ ♦ ♦

The road persists, stubbornly straight, although nowhere are there the long, corridored, diagnostic views that drivers have of such modern roads as still follow the lines of Roman ones. No vanishing points. It is segmented into history's subdivisions. Tenanted by meadow and arable land and wood. Compartmentalised by hedgerow and furrowed lacunae.

I'm thinking of quennets, Raymond Queneau's experimental verse form so brilliantly deployed in 2016 by the poet Philip Terry to describe the East Anglian shore. Thinking of the quennet's potential to evoke and organise the pieces of the road in words. To accommodate the road's absence too. In the same collection, Terry tinkered and turned the form into a column of words that attempts to channel W.G. Sebald's journey across Suffolk in *The Rings of Saturn*. This tubular quennet is the perfect container for the road: a verse arranged like our line with its interrupted views, flanking ditches, found fragments, all corralled into strict stanzas.

Hooked Wood
Parched Mark
Hollowed crop
No Trace.

A line of road built from uncertainty and doubt. A test core, or borehole of strict phrases. Couplings of adjective and noun, heaped like strata excavated from the archive and the field.

Such is my way through farmland, across the road at a place called Borley Green, collecting rumours, memories and faint traces captured from the sky. Adrift until I discover a keloid scar puckered into the land by laserbeam. The LiDAR way.

Developed as long ago as the 1960s to detect submarines, and now the eyes of driverless cars, LiDAR maps our world in three dimensions, bouncing laser pulses off objects and measuring their reflection; using that data to render delicate, accurate models of the world. For the archaeologist, light beamed earthwards from an aeroplane can measure as many as a hundred thousand points per second and produce an intricate, exact model of the ground, revealing the slightest disturbance or wrinkle of the land at a precisely located point. The results are overlaid on standard maps, resurfacing them with structures long lost: walls, earthworks and roads invisible to the eye and camera. Now imagine firing laser pulses at woodland. The first reflection will come from the canopy, others from the branches and understory, the final returns from the ground. Clever software that can separate these different reflections penetrates the ground cover, erasing grasslands, stripping away crops, scrub and entire coppices to reveal structures that ripple the woodland floor.

Ours is an age of indelibility. Science and technology make more things indelible and ever more so by the day. Things we thought erased or written over – whether on parchment or solid-state drives – can be read again using chemicals or ultraviolet light or ingenious code. Our indiscretions are mostly indelible now, recorded and circulated on the internet until the end of time. We can read pollen in the gut of Palaeolithic corpses to pinpoint a birthplace ten thousand years ago. The flight paths of birds chart long-lost trees and woodland once known to their avian forebears. The distinctive patterns of wear on early metal type can unlock the printing history of Shakespeare's *First Folio*. Even something already as indelible as a tattoo on human skin is now more permanent, not only beyond the life of the tattooed, but beyond the existence of the tattoo: traces of ink in a murder victim's lymph nodes remember the swallows and butterflies on a missing body part.

LiDAR is Alan Garner's Moon of Gomrath made real, its numinous light revealing the secret path. LiDAR maps are strange, sometimes mono-coloured, silver-grey, lurid green or unnatural-looking rainbow colours. They bead the land with virtual papier-mâché relief, outlining walls and barrows and roads. Maps online, modelled by the Department for Environment, Food and Rural Affairs from data originally collected to detect areas at flood risk, demystify the earth, revealing its deceptions and secrets – the works of humankind it had tried to erase. Where Hormead Park Wood grows, the map is made treeless, lasered down to the mulch, showing a clear embanked road and the exact spot where it disappears and leads us awry on the ground. Now we can see why. A series of circular pits cluster across the line at one end, like bomb craters: the remains of extraction pits, for charcoal burning or ponds dug to soak hazel sticks?

Trace the line lasered north-east and there is a ruck in the fields that has not been smoothed out by the centuries, by ploughing and stocking up. It runs through Stockings to meet

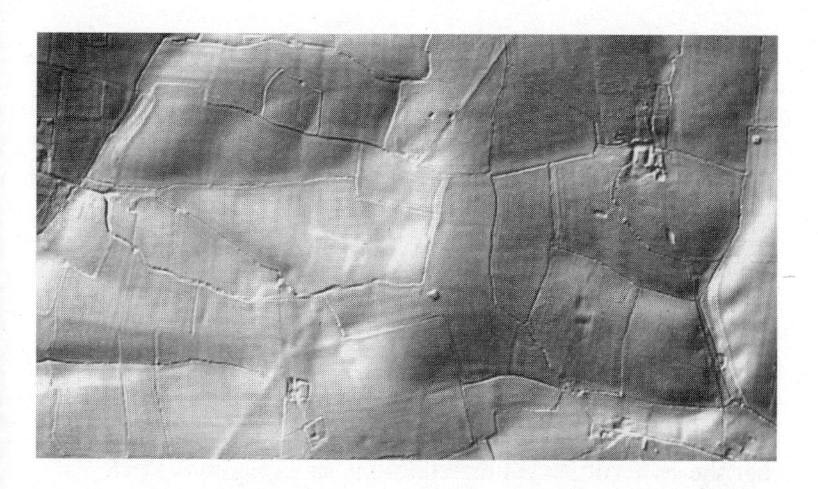

cropmarks, across the watercourse, across Borley Green Road, a faint ridge between pylons and trees to Chapells and Brook Mead, between two houses, across another road and field, and here is an *agger* now on the ground targeting a rusted red tower.

♦ ♦ ♦

> There are primal things which move us. Fire … two voices outside at night … A roof … A tower far off … the least obvious but most important is The Road. It gives a unity to all that has arisen along its way … It knows upon which side an obstacle can be passed, where there is firm land in a morass, and where there is the best going … The Alps with a mule-track across them are less of a barrier than fifteen miles of forest or rough land.

Hilaire Belloc, *The Old Road* (1904)

♦ ♦ ♦

'The Parish of Brent Pelham is far removed from any great thoroughfare and is in a retired situation.' So wrote the Tithe Commissioner, with unknown irony, in his 1830s report, unaware that the village sat on a once great highway. It was still there if you knew where to look: see that ridge line running towards the windmill and disappearing beneath it to bear the full weight of the oak frame, the weatherboarding, brickwork, pulleys, axles, belt drives, stocks, sails, ropes and millstones.

The sails and machinery are long gone. A two-storey, rusted corrugated-iron dalek now sits on an octagonal brick base, with red-brown metal cladding the original wooden batter of the smock mill. Don't be surprised if Caractacus Potts from *Chitty Chitty Bang Bang* walks out the door to announce that it is ready to launch to the moon.

It is hard to tell from early maps but the existing road looks as if it was diverted round something before the mill was built. Some think it is perched on top of a grave mound that might have been used as a survey point by the Romans when they laid out the road. In the 1830s, the twelve-acre field here was recorded as Elverley – could this be the lost medieval Elfringmead? Was this elf ring the mound? If so, the LiDAR ridge and the hump on the ground runs straight into it and burrows under the mill.

The labourers who raised the mill found the road when they were digging its foundations. They were still talking about it thirty years later. Such encroachments were not uncommon. When lengths of Roman road were parcelled off as lots in the enclosures of the eighteenth and nineteenth centuries, some became closes where houses were built straight onto the *agger*. Writing of those who used old roads for their own devices, one author tells us: 'Most flagrant of all was to build a house, or even a church or chapel, right on top of the *agger*, using it as a foundation. In such cases the secret is to look not at the ground but at the roof, to observe the tell-tale curvature.'

There is nothing obvious in the tin man cap of the windmill tower today (perhaps any curvature was straightened out when it was struck by an RAF Gauntlet on a night mission in the spring of 1937, tragically killing the pilot, twenty-year-old Sgt John Alfred Wardle). The mill had been silent for over half a century by then. The last miller had been Walter Watson in the 1880s. Did he know his mill was built on a Roman road? Did he hear marching on the wind beneath the thwump and groan of the sails and gears?

◆ ◆ ◆

Beyond the mill we no longer need poetic licence or pictures painted with light. There is a road; a real modern road with the occasional car curving around the windmill and onto the alignment. SUNKEN LANE ON LINE, writes J.R.L. on the file map.

To my annoyance, it is not marked as a Roman road on modern Ordnance Survey maps. I trawl old ones. There it is in the 1960s: ROMAN ROAD, but they are infuriatingly fickle in their judgements. In 1978 it's gone, only to reappear in 1982. Then gone again. A Brigadoon road. A state secret.

This is where most previous explorers have begun their descriptions of RR21b. In the 1920s, Miller Christy – he of the oxlips – described the road as running nine miles from

Brent Pelham to Chesterford, writing, 'About half-a-mile of straight road, starting from close to the Brent Pelham windmill [...] indicates the line of the old Roman road.'

For so long now we have studied how the road disappears and changes into something else; at last we can wonder at how it survived and remained a road. Oliver Rackham observed that Roman roads were not one day reinstated after having not been used for some years: that would have been impossible. In disuse, they would quickly have become unpassable. 'A gravel road neglected for five years gets overgrown with bushes; after ten years it becomes a thicket more impenetrable than if it had never been a road. Blackthorn has a nasty habit of growing on disused highways and powerfully induces passers-by to go round some other way.' So the road must have been kept open and passable for well over a thousand years, fit for carts and mules and packhorses, for going to weddings and funerals, for the business of the nearby Chamberlains' manor, whose tenants would have battled that blackthorn. Oddly enough, a French diplomat and belletrist Jean Jules Jusserand best imagined others who came this way in his 1884 book *English Wayfaring Life in the Middle Ages*: there were, he wrote, 'quacks and drug-sellers, glee-men, tumblers, minstrels, and singers; then messengers, pedlars, and itinerant chapmen; lastly outlaws, thieves of all kinds, peasants out of bond or perambulating workmen, and beggars ... preachers, mendicant friars, and those strange dealers of indulgences called pardoners. Lastly there were palmers and pilgrims, whose journeyings had a religious object.' All passed the mill, in the footsteps of their Roman forebears, on towards Meesden and the Stort valley. Didn't they?

In 1695, the road appears on a map for the first time, drawn by John Oliver, who boasted that it contained the 'Miles, Furlongs, and Poles between Place and Place on all the Roads in the SURVEY exactly measured'. Our road is shown between Brent Pelham and Meesden Bury. As contour lines showing elevation were yet to be devised, Oliver depicts high ground with little shaded mountains. It looks like any traveller along our road is about to scale an Alp, and over the county boundary in Essex, the Himalayas await.

In the reign of King Charles II, the village of Brent Pelham was brought before the quarter sessions – the court that sat every three months – because 'the inhabitants ... have not repaired the highway leading from Violate Lane towards Meson [Meesden]'. Since the Tudor Highways Act of 1555, parishes had been responsible for the upkeep of roads. Wealthier parishioners had to provide 'one wain or cart furnished after the custom of the country ... and also two able men'. Poorer labourers simply had to do four days' work on the roads every year, overseen by the parish surveyor, a job that nobody wanted and so had to be shared around the village. With minor changes, this was how highways were looked after until the mid-nineteenth century and even later in many parishes. The surveyors' books for Brent Pelham survive and show the accounts from year to year throughout the 1700s. Here are payments for labour, for levelling, for ditch cutting, for picking stones, for digging gravel. These must have been tasks carried out for a thousand years or more to keep the road open. In June 1770, 'For a whelm 16 feet long and 2 wide', the surveyor paid 10s/6d and for 'laying it down', 1s/8d. A whelm was a wooden drainpipe, a hollowed-out tree trunk, '"whelmed down" or turned with the concavity downwards to form an arched watercourse'. It is why we are underwhelmed and overwhelmed.

That same year, the surveyor collected £13/19s/10d and paid out £15/8s/8d, which was reimbursed by his successor. Loads of stone were by far the most common expense, especially in winter when little other work was available. The artist George Clausen painted local stone pickers clearing the fields in spring and summertime, with wild flowers dotting the grassy hills. One canvas in St Albans Art Gallery shows a man in rags, holding a tin pail and pausing to wipe his brow; at his side sits the hillock of stones he has collected. More arresting still is a painting in the Laing Art Gallery, in Newcastle, of a young woman on a hillside wearing a hopeless stare after emptying her apron of stones. Clausen painted both pictures near his home in Hertfordshire. Stone-picking was a well-attested job for children, to clear the fields before ploughing, but also to gather materials for building and road repairs. We might imagine it always had been, back into the Roman countryside and beyond.

In Brent Pelham, John Bradford is paid 1s for one load of stones. Keen gets 6d for half a load. James Rule's boy, 6d. Mary Smith is paid a healthy 9s 6d for stones and a staggering £3/16s/6d on another occasion for a massive seventy-four loads of stones – she must have been running quite an operation. We might wonder if those were dug out of those sections of our road that had been abandoned. Remember the stocking up that the farmers recalled.

The system worked relatively well so long as you didn't have a busy road leading to a major town running through your parish. As early as the fourteenth century a 'grant of pavage' was made to Puckeridge for repairing Ermine Street and in 1390 the 'bailiffs and constables of Standon, Puckeridge and Buntingford were allowed a similar grant for the road: 'It was particularly liable to get into a bad state owing to the springs of water arising in the swallowing clay and sandy places.' People have always complained about the state of roads. One of the better known tablets from the fort at Vindolanda is a late first-century letter from one Octavius to his brother Candidus. After asking him to send a large sum of money urgently to pay for some grain, Octavius mentions a wagonload of hides at Catterick, writing: 'I would have already been to collect them except that I did not care to injure the animals while the roads are bad.' The Elizabethan poet and mapmaker John Norden imagined – incorrectly – that the three Pelham villages got their name from an ancient word for springs. Nathaniel Salmon poked fun at this: there were few springs in the Pelhams, but plenty of potholes: 'If he could have made out anything from Sloughs, he might have found enow hereabouts, especially in Brent Pelham.' A slough was a pothole filled with mud. A century later, little had improved on our road: 'Presentment that there is an ancient highway leading from the village of Meesden … through the village of Brent Pelham … containing in length 2800 yards and in breadth five yards, is in decay, and that the inhabitants of the parish of Brent Pelham ought to repair the same.' This was brought before the justices in 1816.

Eventually, in a piecemeal fashion, throughout the nineteenth century, various acts of Parliament did away with parish responsibility for their roads. It was one that the locals in Brent Pelham had exercised, with their varying degrees of diligence, since the Romans left. Recall Oliver Rackham: 'Every few years, through the darkest of the Dark Ages, there has been somebody from Duddenhoe End and Brent Pelham to take a billhook to the blackthorn on two short stretches of Roman road, which stand out by their straightness amid the maze of lanes.' The old system had the virtue of only maintaining roads that were used. No effort would be wasted on a road for the sake of it. It has survived the years, the depredations, the neglect, the sloughs, because it was used. The road persists. Today it is part of the C10, which at over seventeen miles is the longest Class III road in Hertfordshire, a mishmash of routes running east to west with no historical reason to be lumped into one road.

Walking here you'd never know it had been laid out by a Roman. It doesn't look straight when you are on it. It meanders around headlands where plough teams turned, avoids puddles long dry and trees that fell centuries ago. It runs past the oddly oversized moat known as Chamberlains, where the family of that name had their manor house in the thirteenth century. A local farmer tells me that the *agger* is in there among the trees, where a Roman brooch was found and oyster shells have been dredged up in their thousands. I'm imagining marching camps or auxiliary forts again. The site is big enough. Further on, past Westley Farm, not quite half a mile since the windmill, the C10 turns abruptly right. How paradoxical that this first section of actual road is the least Roman piece we have collected; while remaining a road, it has changed the most. It is why a lost road can tell the story of Roman roads far better than those that have survived. Far more interesting than the half a mile of modern tarmac is the ancient alignment, which keeps straight ahead, disappearing into the shadow of a treeline.

♦ ♦ ♦

You tell me this has all been proved a myth. Of course it has. Do you know of any story, romantic and picturesque, from the Noachian Deluge to the Thundering Legion, that has escaped a mauling from prosaic hands? Alas! even science seems but a quicksand of conjecture.

Herbert Tompkins, *Highways and Byways in Hertfordshire* (1902)

♦ ♦ ♦

Let us go simpling in the straggling grasses of the verge before the road disappears again into the dark of an ancient woodland. For an especially 'rich kind of verge related to woodland grassland, is often found where an ancient road approaches an ancient wood'. Here is a defiant herbal of astringents and tonics, poultices and teas. Tiny pink angels of wild basil partner chalk knapweed with its purple thistles beginning to flower. *Hypericum perforatum*: the golden radiant crown of St John's wort known to the Romans as an ingredient of the legendary *mithridate*, a cure against all poisons. Yellow rods of agrimony too, for soaking tired feet on the march. The tiny florets of yarrow carried by Achilles in battle. The white bonnets of bindweed, the thunder weed, unwanted, but persistent – like old roads and those who would follow them into the thicket. Once, such flora would have taught us how soon we will die or whom we will marry, staunched our wounds, soothed our eyes or provided a posy against enchantment amid the twisted trunks. Instead, we need a panacea against all doubts or a potion to open our third eye, to see the road laid out before us and men and women emerging from the dark band of Meesdenhall Wood.

I don't know if the rich verge is real evidence of the onward march of our road, although it is certainly richer in grasses and flowers the closer you get to the trees, but I do like this edge effect, how flora from one habitat meet in a living Venn diagram of woodland, grassland, roadside and arable field. And if spatial, then temporal too: Iron age, Roman Britain, the Middle Ages, this June day in the twenty-first century, when I face the thicket where there is supposed to be another *agger* to see. I say June day, but my notes are confusing because they contain bluebell buds. It was another time of year, another year when I first came to follow what one of the locals called 'the foss' through the scrub like the Roman of the popular imagination hacking his way into the darkness, clearing the land to make way for his great thoroughfare.

'And this also,' said Marlow suddenly, 'has been one of the dark places of the earth.' So begins Joseph Conrad's *Heart of Darkness*. Marlow is 'thinking of very old times, when the Roman first came here ... Imagine him here – the very end of the world, a sea the colour of lead, a sky the colour of smoke.' And he paints an uncivilised land of marshes, forests and savages. 'Here and there a military camp lost in a wilderness, like a needle in a bundle of hay – cold, fog, tempests, disease, exile, and death, – death skulking in the air, in the water, in the bush.' Conrad is working his way to a comparison with the jungle where Marlow's story will take him. Britain was jungle then: 'Land in a swamp, march through the woods, and in some inland post feel the savagery, the utter savagery, had closed round him, – all that mysterious life of the wilderness that stirs in the forest, in the jungles, in the hearts of wild men.'

It is a powerful and vivid mythology that doesn't only belong to fiction. Half a century later the pioneering landscape historian W.G. Hoskins would write of the dense clayland forests of Britain and he too would imagine the Roman forcing his roads through the dark heart of the wildwood. But historians now think that even the unyielding claylands had been cleared for agriculture in the Iron Age. Britain was no jungle. The wildwood had long gone when the Romans came.

Thank goodness that Conrad didn't know this or he may not have written the brilliant opening to his masterpiece. But we must stop thinking it, insisted Christopher Taylor who glossed a later edition of Hoskins with: 'We shall never understand the history of the English landscape until we remove from our minds the concept of the primeval woodland that our prehistoric ancestors had largely removed from the landscape by 1000 BCE.' Such a shame. Conrad's soldier, so vivid and delineated in his torment, has to fade before our eyes as if vaporised because a careless time traveller has tampered with the past.

While it might be questionable how wooded the parish of Meesden was in Roman times, there is no doubt about how impenetrable the scrub is in Meesdenhall Wood today. It was not so formidable at the beginning of the twentieth century, when a field stood between road and wood. One walker noted, 'At Black Hall the modern road swerves sharply to the left, but the mound of the ancient road is distinctly visible in the field between the modern road and the wood, carrying on the line to the edge of the wood.' Half a century later, John Holmes reported seeing an *agger* running through the wood, as did Ivan Margary a few years afterwards, but by the 1970s the wood had overwhelmed the field and disfigured the *agger*. J.R.L. is blinded by them: NO SIGN IN CLOSE SCRUB AND COPPICE.

Another half century on, it takes the eye of a zealot to see the *agger* as you enter the wood from the south. The scrub is now so dense that no progress can be made along the alignment through the hazel and maple coppice. I can pace out where I think the spread of camber ends. It is about fifteen or twenty metres across, depending on where you guess the ditches are hidden.

My image of a Roman forcing a way through the wildwood ahead of me may have been erased, but if not a legionary, allow me an English settler on the road here. At least for a moment or two. It is some time in the fifth century. These are the early years of what would become the Anglo-Saxon settlement.

My Anglo-Saxon was first conjured onto the road by landscape historians too. Hoskins wrote: 'The real importance of these roads comes out in the Anglo-Saxon period, for they were, together with the larger rivers, the ready-made routes by which the English colonists penetrated more swiftly and safely into new country than if they had had to hack their way in yard by yard from the edges.' Hoskins wrote perceptively that the trackways kept to the high open ground and the light soils, but the Roman roads 'thrust through the heavier and more fertile soils that offered greater possibilities to the Old English farmers'.

In his classic 1977 book *The Hertfordshire Landscape*, Lionel Munby elaborated on the idea, suggesting that our very road appears to have played a role in the settlement of Meesden in Anglo-Saxon times: 'The area was, in fact, much more accessible to English settlers than it is to modern travellers. They could have worked their way up the valleys of the Stort or Ash, or along the Roman road from Braughing.'

For Ivan Margary, the newcomers were wild invaders: 'The roads must have constituted a dangerous factor in the coastal districts by providing a ready means of penetration for the raiders, and nothing adequate could have been done to prevent this, for even the deliberate destruction of bridges would have been of little avail against such wild people.' But for others the newcomers were more benign, not invaders but settlers in an unfamiliar land using the best routeways to find a new home.

Here stand two traditional sides of the *Adventus* debate. The *Adventus Saxonum*. The arrival of the Saxons. One contends that sometime in the first decade of the fifth century after the legions were withdrawn from Britain, leaving no one to defend the northern frontier and the so-called 'Saxon Shore', the Picts from Scotland and raiders from the continent arrived in hordes. In one version of the narrative, they joined with Germanic mercenaries already in Britain who turned upon their paymasters. Throughout the century, the Britons were pushed into the west despite the valiant rearguard actions of a Romano-British commander who became known to legend as King Arthur.

Set against this idea of a violent rupture from the Romano-British past is a school of thought that argues for greater continuity with what went before, a gradual and mostly peaceful integration of newcomers with the local population.

For various reason, a number of historians now contest the use of the term 'Anglo-Saxon' at all. It is true that the English had far more diverse origins than Saxony and the German-Dutch homelands of the Angles, but 'Anglo-Saxon' is entrenched in the literature and the imagination. It remains a useful shorthand for the period from the early fifth century to the Norman conquest in 1066 and for the people from north-western Europe, whose culture and especially language came to replace the Romano-British world in an area roughly equivalent to modern England. How that happened is the mystery.

This was the Dark Ages: another unfashionable term, and one fiercely rejected by most students of the Early Middle Ages, but it still seems a useful way to describe the fifth century, not to diminish it, because it is so dimly lit; the archaeology is inconclusive and the history is based on scant documentary material, mostly from many years after the events they describe.

We have raced ahead to the end of Roman Britain, but this is the moment we have arrived at on the road. It begins in the decades leading up to the sack of Rome by Alaric and his Visigoths in 410 CE. There is an undeniable economic collapse in the late fourth and early fifth centuries. Britain had been insulated from some of the continental chaos as the Roman

Empire tottered throughout the century, but when things did start to go wrong on this far-flung island outpost they went wrong quickly; at least that's what the archaeology suggests. It has been called one of the most marked 'mass extinctions' in the archaeological record in British history.

Things began to unravel here when the legions in Britain mutinied over pay and appointed their own emperor, soon to be replaced by another, until finally Constantine III gained control and in 407 CE withdrew what remained of the British field army to fight for the survival of the empire on the continent. Not only did this presage military and administrative collapse of a state that could no longer guarantee the security of its citizens, but the army that had always been the mainstay of Britannia's economy.

In many parts of the country, villas were abandoned and occupation levels plummeted. Pottery and newly minted coins disappear from the strata. On the other hand hordes of precious metal reach their peak, suggesting that people were not only hiding their money, but also not returning to claim it, especially in East Anglia. Roman buildings were used as rubbish dumps and building works stopped for good. Where forts and villas remained occupied it was in very reduced circumstances with timber structures replacing stone ones. At Roman Cirencester, one of the largest cities in Britain, repairs were made to Akeman Street, the road to St Albans, and after that nothing was built and nothing was repaired ever again.

Hard pressed across the Western Empire, despite some military successes that pushed back the invaders, the Roman military administration never returned to the province at the end of the world. For a while, Britain became a backwater, with an economy and infrastructure in rapid decline. The elites were undone. Pockets of Romano-British culture remained for a generation or two. Most people continued to work the fields and raise their livestock and might not have noticed much difference, but power gradually fell into the hands of Germanic warlords whose culture and peoples usurped that of the Romans. There were striking regional differences in how and when this happened and the extent to which the locals mixed with the new arrivals and adopted their customs, but as I write, the latest study of ancient DNA has proven that there was migration from continental Northern Europe on a mass scale over a long period of time beginning towards the end of Roman Britain.

One legacy of the near four-hundred-year occupation survived. If you want to find continuity, look at the roads. In fact it is the one thing we know for sure about the fifth century, arguably the most important fact we know about Roman roads, the most important thing they can tell us: somebody used them. Somebody repaired them. Many of the things that had made Britain Roman faded into the past, but the roads endured.

Throughout those centuries, thousands of miles of road were maintained. We know this because, as we have already learned, it is universally accepted that once a road goes out of use it doesn't become a road again. At the very least, somebody kept walking on them. With a general decline in the market economy, the roads became less important for trade, but they were not wholly neglected.

In a brilliant study of Roman roads in East Anglia, the landscape historian James Albone has concluded that many lost roads weren't neglected until the eighth and ninth centuries, calling that the 'first period of major road-loss, or at the very least a period when the initial breakdown of parts of the Roman road network occurred'.

Is that when the trees returned to Meesden? We know that they did because of Domesday Book, in which woodland is measured in pigs, or more precisely, in pannage: the number of pigs that would be able to pasture there. Braughing, where our road begins, was five times the size of Meesden in 1086; it had woodland for just six pigs. Great Hormead, at six times the size of Meesden, had sufficient for twenty-four. And Meesden? Little Meesden had enough woodland for four hundred pigs. Perhaps it had been cleared of trees in the Iron Age, but in 1086 it was easily the most wooded place on the whole alignment. Did our Saxon stop here with his family and settle? Did he let the trees close up behind him and block the way he had come?

Meesden had another dark age. It was a 'dark and miserable place' in the mid-nineteenth century, according to one Reverend Upton, who had nothing good to say about anywhere. The owner of the land then took an interest in antiquities, presenting a 'Roman millstone' to the Society of Antiquaries in 1835. Did he probe the road hereabouts? A black pond on the far side of the wood might be the remains of an excavation. I speak to a local who as a young man put up a fence next to it and remembers being mystified at how hard it was to dig postholes until someone told him he was digging through a Roman road.

It is bright on the summer's day when I step out of the trees and the small pond is collecting sunlight in its water. I move on determinedly, stubbornly following my imaginary settler. The church, rectory and moat at Meesden have been said to belong to the earliest stage of settlement and are built between the modern road and the disused Roman road. They sit in the supposed clearing in the woodland, hacked out by those industrious incomers. Writing in 1921 of the journey he made many years earlier, Miller Christy observed 'in the middle of a meadow, a stretch of from 200 to 300 yards of well-preserved old roadway, with a bank and a hedge on each side. This I take to be a short stretch of the old Roman road.' It is still there.

Following it is a walk of whitethorn and blackthorn; hawthorn with its little pink flowers and bramble with its white ones. Dog roses and ivy. Elder too, which children once hollowed out to make blow pipes or pop guns with a stick of hazel for a ramrod. But it was risky business, unless you asked the tree's permission for its wood. Elder is an unlucky tree, a witch tree.

A track descends towards the valley and to the last field in Hertfordshire, one of wheat now with an oak on its southern edge, then another further south near the end of the hedgerow, marking the alignment. We still have aerial photography and LiDAR to encourage our observations, and they show the alignment clearly, a ripple in space-time, heading straight for the road and a river beyond. But they won't help us for much longer.

♦ ♦ ♦

For when light begins to glimmer, day to break, on the Dark Ages ... what is the first thing we see? I will tell you what is the first thing I see. It is the Road ... I see the Roads glimmer up out of that morning twilight with the many men, like ants, coming and going upon them; meeting, passing, overtaking; knights, merchants, carriers; justiciars with their trains, king's messengers riding post; afoot, friars – black, white and grey – pardoners, poor scholars, minstrels, beggar-men; pack-horses in files; pilgrims, bound for Walsingham, Canterbury, or to Southampton, to ship there to Compostella, Rome.

Arthur Quiller-Couch, *Studies in Literature: First Series* (1918)

♦ ♦ ♦

One day in the spring of 1950, a field investigator walked north along the alignment until he came to the River Stort in its infancy, not far from its headwaters, where it marks the county boundary between Essex and Hertfordshire. He had just followed a 'slight, but marked elevation of the arable field' to a road and the river beyond, and now he dropped down into the riverbed and must have smiled to himself.

'There appears to be a section of the road exposed in the North bank of the river Stort,' wrote G.W. Ridyard, as he signed himself on the 495 index card, in tiny but immaculate handwriting. If he carried a trowel or small shovel he took it from his knapsack, because he now 'cleared away a small section of the bank directly in the centre of the projected line of the road'. As he scraped away the vegetation, the strata revealed themselves: six layers that he lettered (a) to (f) in a sketch that thankfully has been preserved in the Essex County Council Historic Environment Record.

At the bottom of the road was the natural grey clay. Above that came a thin base of paddled chalk packed with small flints, supporting a thick layer of large pebbles. All was held together in a matrix of sandy clay. 'Paddled chalk' is a term that evokes an army of navvies hard at work tamping or compacting the chalk with their heavy wooden paddles. On top of this layer were six inches of a 'ferruginous' mass of small pebbles and flints, topped with another six inches of large pebbles. The entire structure measured just over thirty inches thick and lay buried under eighteen inches of top soil. Here was plenty to rebuild a road with. It was substantial engineering, equivalent to that found on major roads like Ermine Street.

The Stort is the fourth river crossed by the road, after the Rib, the Quin and the Ash. It is the largest, but at this point nascent, narrow and often dry. All four belong to the precious 160 English chalk streams (of only 210 in the world). The Hertfordshire chalk is dissected by them; by the likes of the Bulbourne, the Mimram, the Ver. These are the ones we can see, but they are with us always in the landscape. A chalk landscape bored by mute waters beneath our feet, cleansing, channelling, alternately scouring and furring up the arteries of the ground. Auden knew it when he wrote his encomium to limestone, his 'secret system of caves and conduits', the timelessness of his 'murmur / Of underground streams' in a 'limestone landscape'. Chalk everywhere on our journey. Chalk paddled into roads, sprinkled into Roman coin moulds so the alloys wouldn't stick, and carved into walls and statues that would one day be broken, burned to lime again and returned to the land.

The rivers must have run with more urgency and life in Roman times, but many were winter bourns pouring from the chalk once it was saturated and the aquifers filled. This presaged disaster. They were woe waters or woo waters. The Bulbourne to the west is the best known of them. In his *Chronicle of the First Thirteen Years of Edward IV*, John Warkworth wrote of the woe waters that ran before death or pestilence or a great battle. Today, only their dryness presages doom – the disappearance of these clear streams. Too much water is sucked daily out of the chalk aquifers. The streams are dying.

♦ ♦ ♦

'I did discover that the strata did not occur 20 yards away either up or down stream and [are] therefore almost certainly not natural,' wrote Ridyard of his discovery in the riverbank. It was a sound double-check and one that might also have helped determine the width of the road, but the outer ditches were untraceable and the *agger* itself spread and razored.

It is sometimes assumed that Roman roads were built to a standard width, even that this width – via a process involving the consistency of ancient wheel ruts and axle lengths – continues to dictate railway gauges today. It is an attractive theory, but untrue. The dimensions of the running surface, the *agger* and the whole road zone varied widely, even along the length of the same road and for no obvious reason: in Hormead Park Wood, our road spans sixteen metres from ditch to ditch; at the Old Vicarage in Braughing, only twelve.

The more prestigious the road – the more traffic it carried – the wider they made it. The whole road area could cover as much as a hundred metres, if we include the further zone of land cleared beyond the outer ditches to ensure there was nowhere for bandits to hide. At the 2019 excavation of Dere Street – the Roman road that ran from York into Scotland – by the Roman Roads Research Association, preliminary investigations had suggested that the road might have three carriageways, but two of them turned out to be wide, lightly surfaced verges beyond the *agger*, presumed to be for horse riders and foot traffic. As the centuries pass and the road surface deteriorates, it is these outlying parts of a road that might become the new holloways, followed and worn by medieval traffic.

An average running surface would probably have been somewhere between six and seven metres wide. Roman law stipulated that for a way to be considered a *via*, two vehicles must be able to pass each other. By measuring the ruts in the gateways of Roman forts, and by assuming that many goods vehicles would have needed to be drawn by two animals yoked abreast, we can estimate that many Roman wheel tracks must have been a fraction under a metre and a half wide. Two such carts could have avoided each other with about the same distance to spare in the dark of the surviving *Crypta Neapolitana* tunnel on the *Via Domitiana* from Naples to

Pozzuoli. We might expect the minimum possible width to have been cut through a hillside; the average width of metalling is thought to be a more generous six and a half metres in the UK. Watling Street has an expanse of over ten metres. Wider than two modern motorway lanes.

♦ ♦ ♦

The river has wandered over the last two thousand years; it is not obvious where any original bridge footings might have been. The story of Roman bridges in Britain is really the story of their absence, of their disappearance and destruction. We look in vain for a symbol for them in the key of the various editions of the Ordnance Survey period map of Roman Britain. There are currently fewer than a hundred sites where remains of bridges have been found, while even at a conservative count there are over 560 places where a Roman road crosses a river. Many of these theoretical bridges may have been fords, especially if the crossing was far upstream, although the whole point of a well-engineered all-weather road is that it should be usable even when a river was in full flood.

We are more likely to find the fragments of bridges in the north, thanks to the availability of stone. When I think of Roman bridges, I think of Piercebridge in County Durham where great blocks of stone lie scattered incongruously in a field. They once carried Dere Street over the Tees, but the mighty river has slithered northwards, leaving the dismembered abutments behind for children to clamber on.

For their stone bridges, the Romans used the ingenious device of cofferdams to construct the piers, driving timber piles into the riverbed to form a box which would be made watertight with clay. They then bailed or lifted out the water with an Archimedes screw before filling the empty boxes with stones and rubble cemented together.

The legions were adept at bridging rivers rapidly; it is a safe bet to think the first Roman bridges in Britain were constructed during the invasion in 43 CE as the invaders pursued the Britons into Catuvellaunian territory. More permanent bridges would have been made mostly of timber in Britain and so would inevitably succumb to time and the elements. The best-known remains are the wooden pier found in Pudding Lane, London, in 1981, which supported a bridge over the Thames, built as early as the late first century.

Another oft-cited trace can be found at Aldwincle in Northamptonshire, where a timber bridge that carried the Leicester to Huntingdon road across the Nene was found during quarrying. The timber abutments have been compared to log cabins filled with earth and rubble; formidable iron-capped timber uprights twenty by twenty inches had been driven into the riverbed to carry the stone road surface on a timber platform.

Once Roman administration collapsed, the 'wooden bridges would be the first to go,' wrote Ivan Margary, 'and if some local owner did not carry out the repair the road would be broken at that point unless a ford was available nearby'. They may have been deliberately destroyed. Even the emperor Trajan's spectacular bridge over the Danube below the gorge known as the Iron Gates, with its arches and twenty vast masonry pillars, had a relatively short lifespan, because the emperor Hadrian ordered it destroyed as it made an invasion

60 LAYS OF ANCIENT ROME.

XXXIV.

Now while the Three were tightening
Their harness on their backs,
The Consul was the foremost man
To take in hand an axe:
And Fathers mixed with Commons
Seized hatchet, bar, and crow,
And smote upon the planks above,
And loosed the props below.

of the province of Moesia in the Balkans too easy. Cassius Dio saw what was left of the bridge in 190 CE when it was over a century old and only the stone piers were still standing. He was awestruck. There were twenty piers, each 150 feet tall and 60 feet wide, 170 feet apart, and connected by arches: 'Brilliant as Trajan's other achievements,' he wrote. 'This stone bridge surpasses them all ... they [the piers] seem to have been erected for the sole purpose of demonstrating that there is nothing which human ingenuity cannot accomplish.' The same architect built Trajan's remarkable early second-century column in Rome, on which we can still see a sculpture of the bridge today in one of the 155 scenes – each a metre or more high – spiralling round the column in relief.

Perhaps Hadrian had in mind the story of Horatius Cocles. After all, the destruction of the first and most famous Roman bridge was a central part of the nursery history of Rome. It tells of the heroism of the republican soldier and his two companions, who in 508 BCE held the *Pons Sublicus* against the invading Etruscans while their compatriots retreated across the Tiber.

> But meanwhile axe and lever
> Have manfully been plied;
> And now the bridge hangs tottering
> Above the boiling tide.
> 'Come back, come back, Horatius!'
> Loud cried the Fathers all.
> 'Back, Lartius! Back, Herminius!
> Back, ere the ruin fall!'

That's how the Victorian historian Thomas Babington Macaulay told it in his *Lays of Ancient Rome*. At the other end of Roman history, some nine hundred years later, as Alaric, King of the Visigoths, descended on Rome in 410 CE, the retreating legions also destroyed the bridges behind them – to little avail as the city was soon sacked.

♦ ♦ ♦

The first field in the county of Essex lies on the other side of a hedgerow of hornbeam, field maple, oak and ash that hems the River Stort. A willow here with its velvety leaves and catkins. Coppiced hazel too, its leaves appropriately riparian, patterned in relief by gossamer tributaries offset along a central vein. In the barley is a hollow where a deer has rested and to my surprise a stretch of *agger* is here too, quite clear to my eye, a swollen embankment modelled in the corn aiming across the crop. My eye is keener now I have the confidence of Ridyard's report and his sketch of the layers in the riverbank that places the road where I expect it to be. J.R.L. hadn't seen Ridyard's work nor did he spot the *agger*, but he was there in February with no crop to guide him. UNDULATING AREA UNDER PLOUGH, he prints on the map. NOTHING TO IMPEDE CONTINUATION OF LINE TO NORTH, BUT NO EVIDENCE. Which seems to be saying nothing, but by J.R.L.'s cautious standards is a strong statement.

The OS strip map shows other speculative courses. The alignment has become three. Two contingencies as fainter red-dashed lines flank the centre line, bulging out to converge again a mile north-east of the river. They follow sections of parish boundary and footpath through fields. They are not unconvincing, but unnecessary when there is a road buried in the riverbank and *nothing to impede continuation of line to north*.

Several months after Ridyard, Major John Brinson, an experienced archaeologist and the Ordnance Survey's local correspondent for Essex, agreed: underneath Ridyard's statement, his opinion places the road on our line. Which would settle it, except the swelling in the crop runs for a few yards out of the valley and stops abruptly. Perhaps we should not be surprised to lose the road near a river crossing at a natural territorial boundary. Any bridge would have fallen fifteen or sixteen centuries ago. Locals would have forded it upstream and built a new bridge downstream, and the ways were several, which explains those other possible routes, not an engineered Roman road but trackways and driftways, alternative routes that might eventually find their way back to the original alignment.

Landscape historians talk about the functional continuity of roads, where the original line has been lost for some distance or diverted around something or to somewhere, but eventually returns to the old route, so that one way or another the road still travels between the start and finish intended by the Roman surveyor. One historian speculated that the early English settlers chose to go other ways: 'It does look as though the first English settlers turned off the Roman road one kilometre south of where it crossed the Stort and made their own track to a different crossing place further upstream.'

The result is that today, functional continuity requires a diversion of one and a half miles along surviving roads circling east and west. None go north and south, only narrow tracks with appealing bucolic names: Cooksaldick and Nancy's Lane. You feel these are old enough, but meant for very local traffic. They don't want to be on the way anywhere at all. That short length of *agger* in the crop, leading from the riverbank, ends in a hollow, a bowl in the earth, as if here someone long ago dug across the road, sank their mattocks and grubbing axes into the land and tore it up. Bringing down the bridge wasn't enough to sever the way and the dangers it might bring.

Margary wrote pessimistically: 'A trunk road is a highway for armies. At least two armies out of three will be either hostile or unfed; main roads are dangerous neighbours.' Was the road destroyed at this gateway into Essex? We know that Roman roads were deliberately blocked in the Early Middle

Ages. It was a tactic that had precedents even before the Romans left. During the troubles of the fourth century, when raiders from the north and the continent descended on Britannia, the massive three-mile-long Iron Age earthwork Bokerley Dyke, in Hampshire, was rebuilt across the Ackling Dyke Roman road from Old Sarum to block access to the settlements in the south. Excavations have revealed that the road was opened again before being blocked permanently a century later. It has been argued that in the years after the Romans left nearly *all* the major Roman routes were deliberately blocked off by earthworks. The terrible plague of the Byzantine Emperor Justinian's reign, which ravaged Europe, North Africa and the Near East in the middle of the sixth century, would have been reason enough to pull up drawbridges everywhere.

The earlier a section of road was taken out of use, the longer it has had to vanish. Whether time is the culprit or the route was deliberately severed, the result has been the complete erasure of the road. A few steps into Essex, the land of the East Saxons, there is nothing, nothing on the ground, nothing on aerial photographs, nothing on LiDAR, nothing. The road has gone.

PART III

LOST AND FOUND

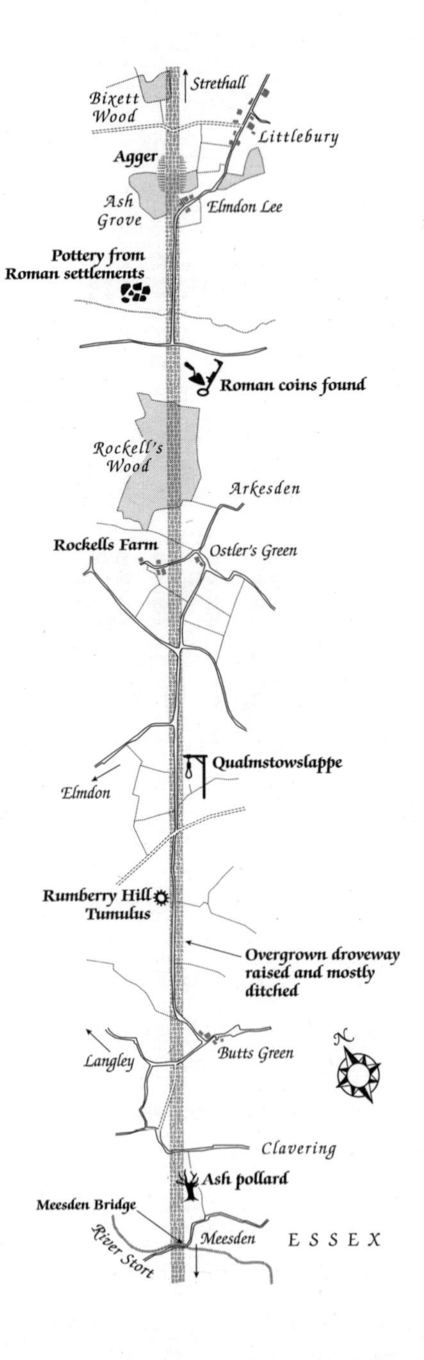
Strethall
Bixett Wood
Littlebury
Agger
Ash Grove
Elmdon Lee
Pottery from Roman settlements
Roman coins found
Rockell's Wood
Arkesden
Rockells Farm
Ostler's Green
Qualmstowslappe
Elmdon
Rumberry Hill Tumulus
Overgrown droveway raised and mostly ditched
Langley
Butts Green
N
Clavering
Ash pollard
Meesden Bridge
Meesden
ESSEX
River Stort

In the river valleys, the old ways disappear. I struggled to follow the road out of the Quin valley and it is hiding from me north of the Stort; but on the clay plateaus and wooded hilltops it is there, as paths and roads or hidden beneath the soil, occasionally betrayed by cropmarks and LiDAR and other clues. It has been argued that when roads stopped being used as long-distance routes, the sections across plateaus would have still carried local traffic, since they were the shortest ways between the valleys. Once people started heading down slope towards the rivers, they would have used the most convenient way between the road and the settlements. Sometimes that was still the original road, often it wasn't. Where it wasn't used, a road was lost. The chalky slopes of the valley sides refused to harbour neglected roads. Farmed away, washed downhill and buried so deep as to be beyond all but the detective powers of our imagination.

If the buried won't help us, perhaps the invisible can prove the way. Where the road has lost all substance we must call upon the boundaries of the land it travels through, because 'a genuine ancient long-distance road is nearly always a parish boundary at least in places,' claimed Margary.

Early maps show an *Ash Pollard* on the northern edge of the first field in Essex. An ash tree, its branches lopped, a boundary mark. It defines a short stretch of the parish boundary between Clavering and Langley, and it grows right in the middle of the alignment. If the road is there, the tree was growing on it at the time it was surveyed in the late nineteenth century.

I return to those fields north of the Stort and walk south against myself. Following hedgerows, crossing the alignment at some point near where deer have nibbled away the ears of corn. Sighting where I know the road crosses the river below me, I find that old ash in the hedgerow. It is not the first time I have thought that trees on the edge of boundaries rise out of the road surface to mark its course. The writer Bernard Berry thought the same when he explored *A Lost Roman Road*, in 1963: 'Now, seeing several of these ancient trees in some alignment,' he wrote, 'it just occurred to me that even the positions of some or all of them might still afford a true but most unusual guide to the course of the Roman road.' Berry, not unreasonably, thought that the trees might have stood along the road when it was still there to be seen. His theory convinces him because, like me, by this point on his journey he has already seen several trees that seem to be on the alignment. He now sees trees everywhere. A little further on, his line points directly at an oak in a hedgerow; next he sees an ancient maple on it, then two oaks separated by what he takes to be the width of a Roman road. His final tree is a stubby oak he spots from a distance and he makes for it, 'illogically,' he concedes. But resting under the tree, Berry notices from his map that he is sitting on the parish boundary that his road has followed for many miles. He has found a boundary tree and found his way again.

Standing by my ash, looking back into the valley, I can see the land rising behind me, back towards Meesden, and it is clear that although there is no sign at all on the ground and competing routes on the Ordnance Survey strip map, there is no reason that the road would diverge from the alignment. It must cut straight across towards the tree. Trees like this one might once have carried boundary marks carved into their trunks, simply the letters 'B.M.', or a cross. The ash marks a right-angle turn in the boundary, which now heads north for 150 metres, echoing the line of the road, although there is nothing to see on the ground. It is undefined, its moorings already loose when the boundaries were surveyed in the nineteenth century, but the local meresmen remembered, they knew it was there, had been there since time out of mind.

◆ ◆ ◆

Terminus was both a boundary stone and the very god of boundaries: a deity who protected the stone and lived in it. The Romans considered him one of the oldest gods in their pantheon and an altar to him on the Capitoline Hill in Rome was already ancient when the temple to Jupiter was built around it in the sixth century BCE. Other altars were moved, but not that of Terminus – some say the god himself refused to give way to the king of the gods – and an opening was made in the temple roof so that Terminus could be in the open air. Moving a boundary stone became punishable by death.

The Terminalia, the feast of Terminus, was celebrated on 23 February each year, when neighbours met at a boundary and dressed its markstone with garlands. In later times, parishes in Britain beat the bounds at Rogationtide, just before or on Ascension Sunday, when boundary trees were scored with crosses and villagers struck sticks against the stones and against young children too to ensure they would never forget where their parish ended and another began. If houses sat on boundaries, young men clambered over the roofs; if ponds lay in the way, they tethered themselves together to wade through; and they took to boats to follow the course of rivers that described the limits of a place. Parishes formed the most important unit of peoples' lives for the next thousand years, until the nineteenth century. They dictated where you were buried, where you could get poor relief, where you paid your tithes, what rights you had in and over land, and – as we have seen – which roads you had to repair. Knowing where your parish began and ended was essential to knowing your rights and where you belonged. In turn, boundaries were made sacrosanct by ceremony. This protected roads that were boundaries. Once a mere, it could not be removed. Terminus was a powerful god.

Parish boundaries have come to be seen as the oldest things in the landscape because of the assumption that many parishes are based on even earlier land divisions, delineated in Roman times if not before. Boundary lines on maps today are still traceable on the ground, in all their unusual shapes and protuberances. They might mirror not only Roman roads, but

Mesolithic fights over territory, and agreements made in prehistory to ensure that each camp had sufficient arable land, pasture, woodland, water and waste (uncultivated communal land for hunting and gathering). It is an appealing link to the deep past, to permanence. We like to find ancient constructs, ideas, beliefs, the small details of daily living for our ancestors, underpinning our own world.

The historian of Roman Britain David Mattingly listed the *termini*, those things that might have been used to mark a boundary in Roman times: 'stone or timber pillars, or upturned amphoras, or marks on standing trees or natural features such as hills, slopes, water courses, watersheds, or built/dug features such as wall, ditches, *roads* and so on ...'

My italics because roads were already being used as boundaries by those who built them. Roads may have played a significant role in the division of land in Roman Britain. And there is something quite striking about our one. There are three Roman roads in Essex that appear to run diagonally across the county from south-west to north-east in parallel with one another. One of them is RR21b. Some have seen this as evidence of something called 'centuriation'. It is a controversial topic in Romano-British studies: centuriation was the Roman practice of parcelling out land by establishing a grid of squares carefully marked by boundaries that were often roads. It was most associated with *colonia* for military veterans. We know the Romans used centuriation in other provinces on the continent, but was it ever a feature of land division in Britannia? It may have been used very early on in the occupation in the area around the first *colonia*, Colchester in Essex. Quite conceivably, our road could have been part of this.

The edges of manors, estates, parishes, townships, hundreds, wapentakes, counties and kingdoms came to be defined by Roman roads, but only if the road were still in existence when the boundary was made. They were not only practical divides, but their very antiquity granted authority and legitimacy. Boundaries might align with some of the divisions of Anglo-Saxon estates. The earliest descriptions of these appear in whimsical detail in old charters, proto-maps drawn with poetry: '*Thonne of hindehlypan on thone wylle aet tham lea ufeweardan.*' 'Then from Hind's-leap to the well at the clearing's upper part.' '*Of dam wylle on daet heorotsol. Of dam heorotsol nord on geribte on done beorg …*' 'From the well to the hart's wallow. From the hart's wallow due north to the hill

...' This Northamptonshire perambulation from the mid-tenth century appears in a grant of land by King Eadmund, now held in the British Library, and concludes with a section of the bounds defined by a Roman road. The greatest of the Great Ways. The Anglo-Saxons' *Waeclingastraet*. 'Then due south along Watling Street on the road to Weedon boundary.'

Where a Roman road still exists, but the boundary ignores it, this is a clue that the boundary may be older than the road. In the rare cases where there is no road, path or surface trace left today, as here between the trees in the field north of the River Stort, and yet the boundary still doggedly follows the alignment, the road must have been a significant feature when the parish boundaries were established. It probably went out of use fairly late in the day when the power of the old gods like Terminus was fading.

This is supported by an interesting example back the way we've come, in the Hormeads, where until the modern tidying up of the boundaries, sections of Little Hormead were islands in Great Hormead and vice versa. These exclaves, or so-called 'detached' portions, were created in the Middle Ages when the parish boundaries were set down and it proved difficult to draw neat lines that ensured each parish had its fair share of resources. These anomalies are gone now, but can be seen on early nineteenth-century estate maps of the area where two short sections of boundary follow the line of our road for a few yards. Another clue that the road went out of use relatively recently. Back in Hormead, the road was still carrying travellers when the parishes were divided in the twelfth century.

I like it when history is hidden in such abstractions, when things we hold today as concepts – administrative boundaries

– were once material, not only in the sense that you could touch them, hit them with a stick or feel the crunch of them under foot, but also in the way that they affected people's lives, involved toil, had consequences that could be a matter of life and death. Colours that were once pigments teased from sea snails, beetles and plants; upper- and lower-case letters that came from a literal wooden case containing lead type; buildings long gone that had to be avoided and survive only as kinks in a line on a map; boundaries that today remember uprooted hedgerows and trees and stones. The county boundary that follows the River Stort where I crossed it exists only on maps as an unruly squiggle. It leaves the modern course of the river and meanders into the field for a short stretch. Why? Because it is the ghost of the river's old course, of what was once true on the ground we tread.

◆ ◆ ◆

For those who value imagination above discovery, what can be more evocative than to walk a leafy lane whose former glories have evaporated into the mists of time. In the eyes and ears of the mind, one may walk besides the creaking haywain of an Iron Age stockman, shelter from the martial tramp of foreign legionaries on the move, eavesdrop on the gasps and chatter of a band of pilgrims or follow the basket-swaying progress of a bygone packhorse team.

Richard Muir, *Shell Guide to Reading the Landscape* (1981)

◆ ◆ ◆

Let's take a walk in Roman Britain, following the field edges and footpaths northwards. Ahead after a lost mile, a holloway curves for a few yards, then straightens, right where we want it to. For over a mile it divides four Essex parishes: Clavering from Langley, Elmdon from Clavering and finally Elmdon from Arkesden. This is Beard's Lane and its adoption as a substantial parish boundary could be the secret of the road's survival.

G.W. Ridyard was still following the road in the 1950s and wrote that in places along this green lane there was a definite *agger* visible. When J.R.L. was nearing the end of his survey in the 1970s here, his customarily guarded comments become slightly more expansive than usual: OVERGROWN DROVEWAY RAISED & MOSTLY DITCHED BOTH SIDES. Ivan Margary found it overgrown too and locals remember it as being almost impenetrable fifty years ago.

'Droveway' would have been used deliberately rather than as just a picturesque term for a sunken lane. Butts Green at the southern end is thought to have been a pasture for live-stock travelling to market and maybe that is why the road has survived as a route here, not just as a boundary. Was it one of the old droveways that for centuries had crossed the country, allowing the movement of animals to market from as far away as the Scottish Highlands?

One hot August bank holiday morning. The sun has not long risen. The land is silent but for the far-off hum of planes and the kazoo of crow calls. Glimpses over the fields at breaks in the hedge line are of golden green sinuous lines, all shade and shadow burned out of the long-ago waterworn folds of the land. I search for views without buildings or power lines to see what those who came before us saw.

Where the lane curves to the right to meet the alignment I root around, registering, rightly or wrongly, traces of an *agger*. Or is it just a spoil heap? Walking up and down the ditch to no avail. It is here that modern Ordnance Survey maps now print the words 'Roman Road' for the first time. There is a pond, a patch of ground – small, enclosed and abandoned – a ridiculous sense of being the first to arrive here for many centuries. A cuckoo silently flies by.

The lane meanders and is perhaps nine to ten metres wide between ditches. Is this Ridyard's *agger*? There are great ruts in the surface, gouged into the road by 4 x 4 vehicles. In winter, it is churned into mud that sucks off your shoes in protest at your passing, broken by puddles deep and widening to ponds. Dried out in summer, deep welts reveal strata of flints. Then ahead the lane has straightened. It is flanked by field maple and hawthorn and blackthorn and brambles; the sloes are fattening already. Best of all are the large ash trees, hollowed and gored like hag stones where limbs once grew. The way is wider now, its eastern edge a wide platform of coppiced hazel.

There are teasels and old man's beard – wild clematis – is winding into the hedgerow, as if sheep have been driven this way and snagged on the hawthorn. But Beard's Lane gets its name from elsewhere, from the medieval Bayardesfeld. On a map from the late eighteenth century it is Bayard's Lane.

'This could refer to bay horses: a similar field-name elsewhere relates to medieval tournaments and later horse-racing,' wrote a local historian. There is an Ostler's Green at the northern end of the lane where travellers' horses were looked after. When someone from the county's Historic Environment unit walked the road in the early 1980s, it was in good condition, banks and ditches used mostly by horses. And we summon centuries of them, messengers at full tilt, Roman cavalry, heavy horses working the fields, packhorses, carthorses, reeves on geldings cutting across the plateau to visit estates, the horses' hooves keeping weeds at bay. The ring of crotal or rumble bells sounding across the years.

One November noon I encounter David Ahn, a farrier who has ridden the lane all his long life. I'd had a simple phrase running around in my head as if I'd read it somewhere: 'An old road once came this way', and now seeing David, I half-expect him to pre-empt any enquiry with the words, 'Ah, so you've found it at last.' As though I'd quested many miles, over many years, following rumours, traces and shadows glimpsed in search of this old road. Not only the road, but also its oldest wanderer, perhaps its toll keeper. He might have guarded it since the legions left. Don't we all have these thoughts when we walk the old ways? David was like a wizard out of time. I saw him from a distance coming down a track at the back of his cottage, an apparition conjured into view. Or had I dreamed him up in my less lucid musings about old roads? He was coming from Cooper's End and pulling a barrow – having been to tend to his sick horse Lily in a nearby paddock. David is bent over, a wiry man, I think, but padded against the cold with various layers of coat and cardigan and scarf.

There are different ways to time travel, but encounters with the odd immortal is one of my favourites. David is timeless. Anywhere between sixty and six hundred. Most striking are his white beard and white hair that frame a face straight out of Enid Blyton. Here is Mr Pink-Whistle. Not a wizard of another world like Gandalf, but of ours like Uncle Merriman or, even better, like Cadellin. A magical guardian of Beard's Lane. He won't mind me pretending that he was a farrier at a way station of the *cursus publicus*, providing hipposandals to Roman cavalry or trimming the shoeless hooves. Was he here when the parish boundaries were laid out or the drovers came this way? Medieval and Roman harness pendants have been found along the road. David probably made them.

♦ ♦ ♦

'The Veil is just a name for the one of the places where the walls between worlds is thin,' the bard began. 'The druids conjured what they thought of as bridges through blood sacrifice, prayer, fasting and very complicated rituals. I don't know if the new magic works the same way, but I was taught that the aim of the sacrifice is to pay the toll.'

N.M. Browne, *Warriors of Alavna* (2000)

♦ ♦ ♦

If David Ahn were guarding something, it would be the mysterious Rumberry Hill. A 'TUMULUS,' wrote the cartographers above a five-pointed corona drawn next to our road. A swelling of the land. Since 1816 the Ordnance Survey's standing orders insisted, 'All Tumuli and Barrows shall be noticed in the plan where they occur', but oddly, this one was overlooked until the 1960s. You might easily walk by today unaware of its existence.

Rumberry Hill, a rotund and bulbous name from the Old English *rūm* meaning 'spacious' or perhaps 'unoccupied'. It is a likeable, avuncular name but 'unoccupied' speaks of loneliness, of abandonment, or perhaps the name came to disarm any superstitions about who did occupy it. The second part of the name is common enough for a barrow, from the Old English *beorg*.

Tufts of grass and teasels, once used for carding, or combing out wool, cover its surface. To call it a hill is misleading. It is a slight heaving of the ground. A 'low' might be a more appropriate word. It is a wide and gentle mound, once circular in shape, but now its base has been neatly squared off by the plough. At fifty metres across, it is has an exceptionally large footprint. Round barrows rarely exceed forty. It must have once been quite imposing, but now its domed apex rises to only a metre in height.

When the archaeologist Guy Maynard was putting his papers in order in the 1950s, he put some scraps into a used brown envelope and scribbled 'R. Roads in N.W. Essex' on the front as a clue to the content. They were torn from a notebook he had kept back in 1906 as he cycled along our road. There is a simple sketch of the tumulus, labelled as eight to nine foot high and fifty paces across. This means that in the last century it has lost over a metre in height, but the width remains much the same. With that in mind, we might be right to picture it as significantly more imposing some 1,600 years before. The centuries have been unkind. Not only has it been ploughed down by the farmers, it had 'apparently been disturbed. Very likely it was one of those opened by Lord Braybrooke ... but of this I can find no proof.'

Find Audley End House, a palatial Jacobean mansion near Saffron Walden in Essex. Make for the parterre garden, face the little circle of dahlias with your back to the cast iron fountain and walk to your right – towards the south-east corner of the north range. If you cup your hands to the glass, and the shutters are open, you can peer into the fourth Baron Braybrooke's cabinet of wonders.

But you've arrived too late.

For nearly three-quarters of a century now, it has been a museum of nail holes and fading pencil marks. That pencil line on the west wall, two feet from the ground, marks the position of a shelf that was once laden with funerary jars, amphorae and Samian ware. That circle of holes to the left of the hearth recalls a wheel of weapons. This is all that's left of Braybrooke's great passion; here we have only a room of shadows more ethereal even than our road.

Richard Cornwallis Neville, who became fourth Baron Braybrooke in 1858, built the collection. His father had been a keen scholar, writing a history of his house, once the largest in England – and editing the first published edition of Samuel Pepys' diaries. He encouraged his eldest son in his natural history and antiquarian pursuits, buying him a cabinet for fossils in 1832 when he was just twelve years old. By the late 1840s, this one cabinet had become many – mostly filled with stuffed birds – and Neville had transformed a dressing room into an archaeological museum, stocking it by excavating barrows, cemeteries and Roman sites in the countryside around Audley End. The fourth lord died young, in 1861, but the family preserved his collections and the *Saffron Walden Yearbook* for 1866 described a 'museum abounding with relics, antiquities, and curiosities'. Some thirty years after Neville's death, the *Illustrated London News* recorded, 'the little museum that is also a smoking-room. Here are great Roman vases, arms, jugs – not unlike our modern claret jugs – heavy chains and implements of iron; with primitive British ornaments, bracelets of mere pebbles (and then, a little later, of bits of coloured clay), and bone knife-handles, and – a ghastly survival – some human skin of a Dane once nailed to a neighbouring church-door.'

An anonymous nineteenth-century watercolour of the room shows brightly coloured rugs and tiles and wallpaper as the backdrop for shelves and brackets stocked with vases, beakers, amphorae and flagons. On the walls hang medieval weapons. The centre of the room is dominated by a long

display case, its contents hidden from view. We live in an age that has little time for the amateur archaeologist from the Big House, but Neville had his admirers among the professionals. In his prefatory note to his 1923 *The Archaeology of the Cambridge Region*, Cyril Fox wrote: 'To the Hon. Richard C. Neville, afterwards Fourth Lord Braybrooke, a debt of gratitude is owed by all archaeologists ... That most of the objects found in the course of his investigations have been preserved in the Museum at Audley End House enhances the value of his work.'

Some twenty years after Fox passed judgement, these prized objects were gone. From April 1941, the army, and later the Polish branch of the Special Operations Executive, were stationed at Audley End. During the war, the eighth Baron Braybrooke began negotiations to sell up and the house was finally secured for the nation for £30,000. In 1948, the Ministry of Works moved in, stripped the museum room bare and turned it into an office.

So what happened to the treasures when they took down the shelves?

We must follow them to a world of Polynesian canoes, North American totem poles and more than two hundred objects from Captain Cook's voyages around the Pacific. This is the Cambridge Museum of Anthropology and Archaeology, where alongside the world's earliest stone tools from Tanzania are tools of stone, bronze and iron from the countryside hereabouts. Many were acquired in 1948 when the Ministry of Works flogged off R.C. Neville's collection, among them the socketed axes from a Bronze Age hoard found in the Essex village of Elmdon. Neville tells us about them in the opening pages of his 1848 *Sepulchra Exposita: Or an account of the opening of some barrows*. Two of his workmen had spotted the remains of the hoard of axes at the local blacksmith's. But we are interested in what those men were doing in Elmdon. This was March 1847, and they were 'quartered' there 'for the purpose of making excavations in a mound supposed to be a barrow'. The workmen visited the blacksmith to have their spades and mattocks repaired. While the fabulous hoard that the blacksmith had been giving away as curiosities to his customers took the limelight, it is the barrow, mentioned only in passing, that is far more interesting.

We normally associate barrows with an earlier or later Britain, with prehistory or, thanks to Sutton Hoo, with the Anglo-Saxons. Most plentiful are the burial mounds we call long barrows and round barrows. According to Historic England, almost every parish contains at least one and often more, although they are usually unknown and little more than a wheeled stain in the soil. Those not burgled over the centuries might contain evidence of cremations or skeletons, crouched within a chamber in the centre.

Before they were distracted by the Bronze Age hoard at the Elmdon blacksmith's, Lord Braybrooke's workmen had found several objects in the mound and submitted their report. We know because at a meeting of the Essex Archaeological Society at Waltham Abbey in 1857, Neville read some 'Notes on Roman Essex', a jumble of short anecdotes about his finds in different parishes near Audley End. After detailing the discovery at Arkesden of a Roman terracotta figure of a female with infants, he recalled: 'Further west, a tumulus existed of considerable size, which proved, on my opening it, to have been disturbed before. It was clearly of Roman origin, from the broken pieces of brick, glass, and Samian ware, near the centre, the remnants of the sepulchral deposit.'

There is no obvious entry for them in the catalogue of the old museum room, now at Cambridge. Nothing listed under the right parish or having come from a burial mound. There are many broken pieces of Roman glass though, several with no known origin. Could it have been: 'Central fragment from the base of a glass dish or bottle'? Or 'Glass phial full of earth, in two pieces' or 'Fragment of neck with handle, from a glass bottle'? One entry that is closest to what we are looking for describes a cinerary bottle, for ashes: aquamarine and with a squat globular body, partially broken, a heavy moulded neck and two handles, and its base illegible. Still more promising is the one piece of Samian ware in the whole collection that fits what we know: a dish with a flat base and flared sides found somewhere in Essex, and crucially in 1847. If this is the pottery from the tumulus, it gives us a date because it bears the stamp of a potter from Lezoux in central Gaul, modern-day France, who is known to have been working sometime in the early to late second century.

It is not much to go on, but we are used to that on our journey. However, Cyril Fox was convinced, calling these fragments of Neville's: 'Ample evidence for a primary cremation interment of Roman date.'

Rumberry Hill is one of those rare things: a Roman barrow.

♦ ♦ ♦

Bell barrows and disc barrows, bowl barrows and ring barrows: my old Collins field archaeology guide shows silhouettes in profile of them all. At the bottom, as an afterthought, sits an outlier, a steep-sided cone with a flat top that is labelled 'Roman'. It looks like the motte of a Norman castle. As a spotter's guide, the diagram is no use to us because Rumberry Hill today looks nothing like this ideal of a Roman barrow. They often had a ditch around them, but if ours ever did it has long been filled in. The best evidence remains its location alongside a Roman road.

The Twelve Tables of Roman law forbade citizens from burying their dead within a settlement, so the Romans liked to place their departed alongside roads. We can date the better-known Six Hills Roman barrows near Stevenage in Hertfordshire because they lie along a Roman road, although as one archaeologist has quipped: the road running past the mounds is said to be Roman because of the Roman tumuli, while the tumuli are said to be Roman because they are alongside a Roman road.

At nearby Bartlow Hills stand the largest surviving Roman barrows north of the Alps. For them, the word 'hill' is appropriate: the largest is forty-six metres high and just over twelve in diameter. Their contents were acquired by Lord Braybrooke, but lost in a house fire. A description and drawings are all that survive of iron lamps, brasses, coins, glass jugs and bottles, Samian ware pottery and chicken bones. These give us clues as to what was in our mound. One at Bartlow contained a glass cinerary urn, a gold ring, a coin of Hadrian, a wooden tankard and a wicker work bottle filled with incense. In the largest mound lay a wooden chest with a glass bottle holding the

The Bartlow Hills, raised over the Slain, after the Victory obtaind here by Canute King of Denmark, over King Edmund Ironside, in the Year 1016.

cremated remains of a small adult, possibly a woman. Her grave goods included bronze strigils, for scraping the skin clean, an iron folding chair, containers filled with a wine and honey mixture, flagons and a gilt bowl enamelled in blue, green and red. Were the broken glass and brick and Samian found in Rumberry Hill all that was left of a cist? A burial chamber with a glass bottle that had once contained the burned remains of the dead?

It amazes me that any barrows are left with anything in them. A number have Old English names that mean 'the broken barrow' or 'the barrow that has been burst open'. One archaeologist has written of a Hampshire charter with a '"*beorh thae adolfen waes*" = "the barrow which had been opened"', suggesting that many barrows had been opened before or during Saxon times. The Middle Ages saw various attempts to plunder them for treasure. King John himself excavated a barrow at Corbridge in 1201. Henry III issued a licence for his brother to open barrows in 1237. When rumours reached the royal court, the king's seneschal and marshal set out to investigate if treasure had been discovered at a barrow known as Golden Lowe in Dunstable. The Romans themselves were not shy of proto-archaeology or, rather, treasure-hunting, opening prehistoric barrows to plunder them. Perhaps that is what 'unoccupied' might mean in the name Rumberry – whoever was in there had gone, long ago, along with their grave goods.

We might assume that the burial was a cremation, as the workmen found no skeleton. This would place it in the early period of mound building when it was still common for Romano-Britons to cremate their dead. There is evidence that mourners ceremonially burned the body on the mound, perhaps after it had lain there on display for some time. They then gathered the bones under bricks or timbers, forming cists, before sealing the entrance. However, the absence of a skeleton doesn't mean there wasn't one originally. As well as treasure, bones could be removed from mounds too. In the early twelfth century, monks at St Albans opened a barrow near Redbourn called the Hills of the Banners and removed the skeleton. They claimed it was the early martyr Amphibalus, murdered by the Romans in the reign of Diocletian.

If not a fourth-century saint, perhaps a different kind of religious figure lies within Rumberry Hill: druids and druidesses, archdruids no less, or bards, priests and priestesses. At least that's what William Stukeley imagined. Other antiquaries assumed that barrows were the burial mounds of people killed in battle. This fits with William Camden's sixteenth-century observation about the Bartlow Hills: 'The country people say that they were reared after a battle there fought against the Danes. For, Dane-wort which with blood-red berries, commeth up here plenteously, they still call by no other name than Danes-blood, of the number of Danes that were there slaine, verily believing that it blometh from their blood.' A picture drawn in 1776 shows the Bartlow Hills with dwarf elder trees growing incongruously and palisaded on their conical summits. Dwarf elders were known as dane-wort.

Who really sleeps within? Most of the Roman barrows in England are in Hertfordshire, Essex and Kent, and are thought to have been built mostly in the second century. Scour the map of Roman Britain and we can see them often associated with Roman roads. But little more is known for sure. Maybe their owners were copying the barrows of Britain's past, the majority of which were raised in the Bronze Age, but there were Iron Age examples that might have made quite an impression in the second century. The most notable could be seen at Lexden near Colchester, a late Iron Age barrow long thought to be the tomb of Cunobelin or perhaps Prasutagus, Queen Boudicca's husband.

Others see such barrows as a nod to Rome, a provincial attempt to copy the great tumuli there. They have been called the 'lesser counterparts' of the great circular tombs of Roman Italy, 'humbler' versions of those beside the ancient Appian way south of Rome with their stone retaining walls. They were mostly raised during the first and second centuries CE, in Britain and Belgic Gaul, modern-day Belgium, where barrows already formed part of pre-Roman traditions and so allowed people to find 'a means of blending a new taste for Roman fashion with something older and more familiar to them,' wrote one historian.

Who is in there trying to ape grand Roman fashion? A magistrate, a merchant from Belgic Gaul, a local client ruler, a wealthy landowner, an aristocrat, perhaps someone in the provincial administration? One clue might be that folding iron chair with leather straps found in the largest mound at Bartlow. It sounds suspiciously like a curule seat. A *sella curulis*. A symbol of authority in ancient Rome. Magistrates and other similar offices that exercised imperium over a military unit or a province were entitled to a curule chair. It is something you might well take to the afterlife with you.

The cluster of comparable barrows in Belgic Gaul near the modern-day city of Tongeren might tell us more. One compelling theory has it that the mounds in Britain were raised by Tungrians serving in the Roman army. Originally a thousand-strong auxiliary force, the First Cohort of Tungrians had certainly arrived in Britain by the late first century CE, serving with Julius Agricola and fighting at the Battle of Mons Graupius in the Scottish Highlands. There are also Roman barrows near Hadrian's Wall, with which the Tungrians are associated and from where they speak to us through tombstones and altars. A Vindolanda writing tablet even attests to their unit strength having been significantly reduced after large contingents were posted elsewhere. To East Anglia perhaps. Did veterans settle in the area after the Boudiccan revolt?

Some of what we know of the Tungrians comes from other ways in which they honoured their dead. A now lost sandstone tombstone found near Housesteads Roman fort on Hadrian's Wall reads: 'To the spirits of the departed (and) to

Hurmius, son of Leubasnus, soldier of the First Cohort of Tungrians, beneficiarius of the prefect: Calpurnius, his heir, had this set up.' And at Birrens fort north of the wall: 'To the spirits of the departed (and) to Afutianus, son of Bassus, centurion of the Second Cohort of Tungrians, Flavia Baetica, his wife, had this set up.'

Stone altars, perhaps originally forming part of roadside shrines, were dedicated to both fortune and victory or to the well-known gods and goddesses of the classical world like Minerva, Jupiter and Hercules; to local British ones too, such as the now forgotten Silvanus Cocidius (a god of warfare and woodland); and to continental gods like the harsh-sounding Germanic goddesses Viradecthis or Ricagambeda, who must have come to these shores with the legions. An altar found near Housesteads fort in the early eighteenth century reads: 'To Jupiter, Best and Greatest, and to the Divinities of the Emperors the First Cohort of Tungrians, under the command of Quintus Julius Maximus, prefect, (set this up).'

We certainly shouldn't be surprised to find continental burials and funeral rites in Britain. When a Roman military cemetery of some two hundred cremation burials was found at Brougham in Cumbria – dating from around the beginning of the third century, 150 years after the invasion – archaeologists originally assumed that most of the inhabitants would have been local Britons. They looked like 'Celtic' burials, yet the grave goods and the burial rites have left researchers with little doubt that the people buried there in the Upper Eden valley came from modern-day Hungary and Austria. Roman Britain was a multicultural society.

♦ ♦ ♦

Landscapes gather … They gather topographies, geologies, plants and animals, persons and their biographies, social and political relationships, material things and monuments, dreams and emotions, discourses and representations and academic disciplines through which they are studied. So landscapes are mutable, holistic in character, ever-changing, always in the process of being and becoming.

Christopher Tilley and Kate Cameron-Daum, *An Anthropology of Landscape* (2017)

♦ ♦ ♦

Rumberry is solitary, a secret, a quiet power, hoarded over millennia in its spacious, unoccupied landscape. Today it is hard to imagine that this low platform alongside Beard's Lane was ever anything as soaring and impressive as the Bartlow Hills, but it has far more power than those showy monuments fenced into their little garden, hemmed by modernity. I return one morning at sunrise along the lane, because of all the places on the road this is the one that most demands return. The weight of it under the dew as the mist burns off, heavy on the land, a shield pinning something to the earth. What has it been to people? A memorial, a sepulchre, perhaps once with a carved stone or post on top. What rituals and rites has it witnessed? Was it the lost moot of the Clavering Hundred, where people came to pass judgement? The site of a fair, a dancing place where long shadows moved in rhythm at certain times of the year? Something to give directions by. Certainly a boundary mark to divide the land, perhaps even in Roman times if the boundaries are that old. A place for neighbours to honour the god Terminus at the Terminalia in February, gathering on the mound to feast and garland it, to pour libations and shed the blood of a lamb.

Listen to the silence as you walk round it, first clockwise then anti-clockwise, challenging the forces of folklore. I have been overwhelmed here by a desire to see out my days, down there in the fold in the valley, in peace, undisturbed. Someone in the days of Trajan must have felt the same thing and perhaps acted upon it. If not a platform to meditate on the English countryside, what is it to us? Perhaps a desire for a place for our own rest. That's how the English antiquary John Aubrey felt: 'I never was so sacralegious as to disturbe or rob his urne: let his Ashes rest in peace: but I have oftentimes wished that my Corpse might be interred by it,' he wrote of one barrow, adding sadly that, 'Lawes Ecclesiastique denie it.'

The views north across a rift in the plateau are long and wide even today, but it may have been the views *towards* rather than *from* the tumulus that dictated where it was built. Architects and archaeologists talk about a monument's viewshed: the area from where it could be seen. People were meant to be in awe of it from afar. Those drawn to the esoteric have had other theories of course: the historian Cussans left a note about a Mr W.H. Black who 'had mapped out nearly the whole of England in equilateral triangles of different but proportionate areas, and he insisted that at each angle the Romans put a large stone or tumulus'.

Maybe so, but Rumberry Hill doesn't need to be a node in a network to generate power. Its solitariness is potent enough. That's not to say its position isn't deliberate. It is no accident that a few yards further on is a ford across Beard's Lane where the last stream flows south towards the Stort and on via the Lea into the Thames. A mile ahead the next stream is the Wicken Water and here the land drains north into the Cam, the Ouse and out into the Wash at King's Lynn. Rumberry marks a major watershed. An auspicious place, a marvel that wouldn't have been lost on those who built it. And it's no accident that it is alongside a road: the Romans saw death as a journey. At St Albans, a child was found with a coin of the emperor Septimius Severus in its mouth, Charon's obol, to pay the ferryman of the underworld. Grave goods often included iron hobnails from Roman sandals so that the 'dead may go well shod on their journey overland to the future life'. Along the roads.

The road brought others towards it. Recent thinking on barrows suggests that we see them less as burial mounds and more like churches, perhaps used for many years before reaching their final state. Visitors helped to build their church. We have already met the late Iron Age burial at Folly Lane in St Albans of what appears to be a British princeling with strong connections to Rome. Soil scientists have shown that the grave shaft was packed with distinct turves brought from far afield: 'This material had been stacked in readiness and drawn from a wide area including stockyards, pasture land (possibly a hayfield) as well as heath and marshland.'

Something similar happened at Six Hills in Stevenage, where 'the grass around the burial mounds is of considerable age. It includes species such as bird's-foot trefoil, mouse-ear hawkweed, harebells, whitlow grass and slender clover, which are not found in the more modern grasslands nearby.'

And so at Langley out of the early morning mist I see mourners coming along the road from north and south, east and west. They bring with them baskets of earth from their own fields, and turves to lay carefully one at a time on the mound growing over the honoured body within.

And then more sinister travellers came.

♦ ♦ ♦

Barrows are the work of the devil, associated with a pre-Christian past, pagan and evil, a nest for dragons, for fire-drakes, like at Drakenhowe in Norfolk. 'Witches resort to crossroads,' wrote Abbot Aelfric in the tenth century, 'and also to heathen burial sites with their evil rites, and call upon the devil, and he arrives in the form of the person who lies buried there as if he had risen from death.'

Surely not here in this silent place, and yet the mind wonders if those beneath all that earth were weighed down for good reason. If not the original occupants, then later ones; intruded into the mound to bury them once and for all. Barrows and boundaries are liminal places for suicides and pagans. For the deviant dead.

Across Beard's Lane from the barrow, at the ford, is a field that locals once called, improbably, Constant Slap Station. Tradition says it hid the entrance to a tunnel built by the

Romans that led to Great Chesterford, which of course is a garbled account of the road itself. But that strange field name caught the ear of landscape archaeologists. I wrote about field names extensively in my book *Hollow Places*, the poetry of them, the stories they condense, the histories they hide and how they morph into familiar words once their original meaning has been forgotten. No one could fathom Constant Slap Station until someone noticed a record of an old field name Qualmstowslappe. A sinister name. A name that might change for ever how we feel about Rumberry Hill and the countryside about.

The 'slappe' part was not too difficult. 'I'm tending to think the "slap" element may be a corruption of "slipe" which is a commonly used term in Uttlesford for a small field,' says landscape archaeologist Simon Coxall, referring to the district of north-west Essex today named for the old Uttlesford Hundred. He was even more interested in the first part of the name: Qualmstowe. The field appears on an early eighteenth-century estate map of Fitzwilliam's farm in Clavering parish as a small parcel of land wedged between two other fields: Clarks Field to the south and Little Bassell to the north. Nearly two hundred years earlier during the reign of Queen Elizabeth I, there was a description of a field adjoining Bassell's Field. It was called Quamstowe Pightle. An even earlier deed mentions a Quamstowe Slat next to Clarks Field. Coxall had proven the link with Constant Slap Station. The fields were part of the old Fitzwilliam farm estate. Why should we care? Because with one exception all of the estate is on the east side of Beard's Lane: the only field on the west of the lane is Rumbergh.

Quamstowe and Rumbergh linked together in the same ancient estate on either side of a Roman road, part of the same territory, with an ancient barrow, a major watershed, a hundred boundary, a crossroads, a dramatic perspective, a theatrical viewshed, a liminal place where four parishes meet, far from where people lived, an edgeland where the dead are buried and worse things happened. It is exactly where we would expect to find a Quamstow or Qualmstowe, an Anglo-Saxon *cwealmstow* – unambiguously, a killing place, a site of judicial execution.

What happened here? What is waiting to be found? That word 'unoccupied' comes to mind again. What did the locals know? What is the numen of this place? Do we feel the weight of history or the weight of suffering? Is this why so many of these godless mounds were razed to the ground?

The condemned may well have been buried in the mound. Barrows on boundaries away from the community would be perfect places for burying the executed, says Nicola Whyte: 'Physically and symbolically, cast out of the community.' At South Acre in Norfolk a cluster of six barrows at the meeting of hundreds gave up 116 Saxon execution burials. If there was no barrow, then victims might be buried directly in the *aggers* of Roman roads. Were they preparing the dead for a journey along the road to the afterlife? Or inviting travellers to trample on the unfortunate and damned?

♦ ♦ ♦

'But it's not so much deep space that concerns me as deep place. Once place is lost, you fall into history.'
'And there's no way out?'
'There's no way out.'
'Mm.'

Alan Garner, *Boneland* (2012)

♦ ♦ ♦

They feasted here once, savouring wine from southern Italy carried along the road in the distinctive Campanian amphorae, flecked with black sand from the coast at Pompeii. Fragments lay in a ditch among the bones of horses, cows and goats. A few feet away stands a waymark for the Harcamlow Way – a long-distance path through Cambridgeshire, Essex and Hertfordshire – a fallen ouroboros, a figure of eight, that crosses Beard's Lane here, only to return again and again for ever.

Kernels of wheat and green unopened hazelnuts skitter underfoot. Time has caught up with J.R.L. and we must go our separate ways. I'll miss his company. METALLED LANE ON TRACK, is his very last word on RR21b and here it is, after a farm drive, the lane tarmacked, an unpleasing, narrow black veneer of modernity, like lino laid over quarry tiles. A squirrel emerges from a hedgerow medicinal with rosehips, hesitates in staccato then patters off along the hard road.

The lane emerges onto a second stretch of modern road, into a silent hamlet called Coopers End. A silver birch and beech and apple trees too. A twisting willow grows in a moat in front of a timber-framed farmhouse, its high branches cork-screwing into the sky, and I covet a length of it.

♦ ♦ ♦

With its folds and little ravines and the lanes that meander constantly, the land confuses the eye and any sense of direction. A straight road boring through all of this must have made sense to anyone who didn't want to arrive late or not at all. Ahead, along our road, lies Rockells Farm and its three-acre coarse-fishing lake – you would have no idea it was there if it wasn't on the map.

In the grounds, men fish quietly in the sun among the weeping willows. The surface of the lake blisters with bubbles made by the carp. The freshwater fish found in coarse fisheries – carp, roach, rudd and chub here at Rockells, but perch, pike and eel are common too – rarely feature in modern cooking, but the Gallic and German soldiers in the legions would have had no such scruples. There is evidence for freshwater fish ponds in Roman Britain and studies of fish bones at Roman sites have shown the eel to have been the most favoured fish by far. Pungent fish sauces like *garum* and *muria* were immensely popular and trade in them, along with preserved fish, was only surpassed across the empire by those in wine, oil and grain. Near the road, archaeologists have found rare amphorae that once contained mackerel from Spanish waters.

At the eastern end of the lake, water pours dramatically into a hole in the surface as if we have found the entrance to something here. The road is down there somewhere. In 1973 when the then owner dug the lake, he found it. According to the local newspaper, 'three archaeologists' were called in, but they left no report of what they found. The press clipping is the only evidence that remains. It is very precise, recording a Roman road surface sixteen feet wide, paved with flat stones, topped by compacted gravel and resting on a deep stone foundation. Drainage ditches on either side measured about six feet deep. That's impressive engineering and, if accurate, it was the best preserved section of the road.

Between the end of a grassy bank and a small building, a low hump of land heads for the water on the alignment, aimed precisely at the angle of a twin arrowhead drawn by the lake's edge. Going the other way, it meets a walnut tree at the boundary line. It's tempting to think the stony surface here between some trees is the section of road that the owner told the newspaper he would leave exposed. But I think it's out there in the water on a small island that rises above the lake's surface just where it ought to be.

Some years ago I came this way on a February day and encountered the farmer, a white-haired, white-bearded Dutchman who had taken the farm in the 1980s and knew nothing about the excavation and what was or wasn't found. 'There is nothing to see here,' he insisted several times in our brief conversation. Friendly but wary, he thought I was mad and seemed worried, as if I were from some ancient inspectorate of roads, come from Rome to check that it was being maintained, bearing a proclamation from the emperor about the terrible penalties for those who dug lakes through them. Perhaps he had had enough of archaeologists, since Rockells Farm also sits on top of a lost chapel and manorial site known as *Wigghepet* in Domesday Book. He knew the road was there, though. The field immediately to our north is heavy with cobbles, he said. Stones that are much harder than flint and damage the plough.

A century earlier, a Hertfordshire surveyor named Urban Smith presented a report to the county council about its Roman roads. A thinly disguised panegyric and manifesto on their behalf. He wanted to:

> place on record a statement of the present-day conditions of the roads where their course is defined and recognizable, but also to endeavour as much as possible to ascertain the facts relating to those portions of the roads where the traces have almost or quite disappeared, and where in consequence their course can only be fixed by correlation to the position of other portions of road whose course is defined, or by the evidence of printed records, or by local tradition ...

Urban was far-sighted and concerned that if the roads weren't traced and recorded, the public would lose their right of access to portions 'not now metalled'. He wanted to set up information boards at regular intervals and protect them for the future, especially:

> those lengths which are overgrown with grass and other vegetation, and which from their sylvan aspect and historic interest form exceedingly delightful resorts, adding much to the attraction of the neighborhood in which they are situated and tending greatly to maintain the high reputation which this County deservedly bears for the number and charm of its shady lanes and leafy glades.

Despite sharing his unusual name with an early bishop of Rome, Urban failed to win many converts to his worthy cause and his proposals went no further. Thankfully, today many sections of Roman road in Britain are scheduled monuments with all the protection that brings, but no part of our road has been so lucky. Urban Smith didn't seem to know about it. If he did, he left it off his map.

From the far side of the lake, looking back at the willows and squinting, you can sight the line over the grey water, from the walnut marking the far boundary where we've come from and into the future, to the corner of Rockell's Wood across the hedge northwards. Can we see any hint in the field with its treacherous cobbles? Of course not.

◆ ◆ ◆

Let's plot the ups and downs of the road. Google Earth will do this for us: the road cardiogrammed with its peaks and troughs. It descends into valleys and tributaries and out again to blocks of ancient woodland, because you find that almost all of the high points collude with the trees to conceal their secretive *aggers*. The zenith of RR21b at 144 metres is hidden back in Hormead Park Wood after a long fractured climb out of the valley. The next peak, about ten metres closer to sea level, comes in Meesdenhall Wood. The third, across the Stort Valley, is today treeless near Butts Green, but the fourth climbs here to Rockell's Wood. Is it just that the woods are on the points that are furthest from the valleys? Furthest from the settlement, too far to take the oxen to pull the plough, on the worst arable land? Oliver Rackham wrote: 'Woods are not on land that was good for growing trees, but on land that was bad for anything else.' Or is there something different going on at these points where the road was most likely sighted by those who surveyed it and set it out?

The land climbs steadily to the ancient ash trees that dominate Rockell's Wood. Ivan Margary wrote that no *agger* was visible in there. Did he enter it? Miller Christy followed a woodland ride into the wood that was 'on or near the line of the Roman road'. But he commits himself to nothing more concrete. This is a mystery, because it is here. Rackham knew it was here. In his *History of the Countryside*, he describes an *agger* now used as a woodbank: 'Rockell's Wood has for centuries blocked [the road's] course … now surviving … as an *agger* through Rockell's Wood.'

In the shade of the trees, the *agger* is an obvious raised platform on the alignment amid the tangled briars of woodland.

Ash marching along it as coppice and standard. Further in, further north, here it is again bisected by a track – even more obvious now with oaks standing sentinel along it, their bark spotted with dark patches of fungus.

In the late seventh century, one Anglo-Saxon law code proclaimed that if 'a man from afar, or a stranger' should pass 'through a wood off the highway' and he 'neither shouts, nor blows a horn, he shall be assumed to be a thief, [and] may be either slain or put to ransom'. Trespassing in here, I have no horn so I shout hello, expecting an echo, but my voice travels away not to return.

Remains of the *agger* persist quite clearly at the northern edge of the wood, substantial and raised above the woodland floor, still there on the other side of the trees in a triangle of land, but requiring the eye of faith. The modern track northwards is not on the same line.

I scramble out of the trees and look over the valley towards Elmdon Lee. The field immediately north of the wood swells out in a patch of uncultivated scrub where the line would be. Walking down the steep slope towards the tributary of the Cam, I pick up stones in the field, lots of squared pieces of sandstone. From a road or from a building? Halfway down the track a red marker is sticking out of the ground: HIGH PRESSURE GAS PIPELINE. It is the line that runs between Cambridge and Matching Green, in Essex. When it was laid in 2002 archaeologists were in the vanguard. They put a trench here, across the line of the road. Of course, they found absolutely nothing.

♦ ♦ ♦

Roman burial customs might almost have been invented to give as much help as possible to present-day archaeologists – just as the Roman habit of losing coins in every conceivable and inconceivable place is remarkably useful.

Geoffrey Boumphrey, *Along the Roman Roads* (1935)

♦ ♦ ♦

Listen. What does a Roman coin sound like? A *denarius*, say. With its solid silver ping as the metal detector sweeps over it. What is the sound of a brass *sestertius*? A copper *as*? Is that the ring of an *antoninianus* buried next to the road for one and a half millennia? Dig there.

From the clod one September morning protrudes a damaged circle of silver and bronze. On one side is a bird with open wings, its beak in profile, an eagle standing but looking like it is in flight, its neck outstretched, twisting on the wind. On the other, the obverse, a head facing to the right, bearded and wearing a spiky radiate crown, the head of the soldier emperor Claudius II. Known as Gothicus after his crushing victory over the Goths at the Battle of Naissus, Claudius died of plague on another September day 1,750 years ago. The metal was hammered into shape and issued after his death, probably as a gift, a *donative*, to the legions who had supported Aurelian as his successor. It is just one of the coins to have been pulled from the earth here in the field between Rockell's Wood and a modern road.

Rockells Field is the name given on the colourful plan that the metal detectorists have outlined and numbered. It is number nine of twenty-two fields they are planning to explore over the coming months, but today is the first day, a beautiful day for it, and the fields are perfectly ploughed and the stubble pulled through ready for seeding. 'You get a nice solid sound with a hammered coin,' explains Klaine, a millwright by trade, as if ignoring the fact that it's the twenty-first century. He helped organise the dig with his partner Zoe. 'You balance the detector, send a frequency into the ground, settle the machine until it makes a sharper tone; you can just catch it on the corner. Centre the sound, then dig.' He says that you must dig behind it, giving it three inches clearance, half a width of your spade. Some people get so excited they put the spade right through the find. Instead you cut out a large sod, carefully break off a handful and wave it over the coil of the detector to pinpoint what's been hiding inside, perhaps for two thousand years.

The fields either side of where the road should be were unusually 'Roman'. 'Every era came off there, but it was busier for Roman than anywhere else we've ever seen,' says Klaine, who has been detecting for decades. If they had to guess, they'd say they were finding the leftovers of a roadside Roman market.

The field slopes down towards a modern road in the valley of a nameless stream. It is the steepest slope on the journey, although still less than 12 per cent so it is hard to imagine that the road needed to stray from the alignment and dog-leg down the hill. Yet there is no sign of it and none in the gas-pipe trench. Is it just lost again to centuries of arable farming on the valley sides: ploughed out, washed away and buried?

Wherever it has wandered, people have travelled this way. Someone has found a brooch, greened and verdigrised; someone else, half a hammered coin. A coin folded to make a love token, stirrup ends, musket balls, thimbles – 'lots of thimbles, because the women embroidered while the men worked in the fields,' says Zoe – an old bonnet badge from a car, a Land Army girl's matchstick holder, a falconry bell, lead weights, and a medieval ring inscribed in Latin, IESVS NAZARENVS REX IVDAEORVM, 'Jesus, King of the Jews'.

Here was all of life alongside our road for over a thousand years. All with their stories to tell, but few objects tell the story of trade and travel along roads as neatly as a coin. The historian Peter Frankopan recognised this when he wrote: 'We can imagine the life of a gold coin two millennia ago, struck perhaps in a provincial mint and used by a young soldier as part of his pay to buy goods on the northern frontier in England.' Frankopan imagines the coin back in Rome, in the coffers of a tax collector, then in the hands of a merchant heading east, who buys good at Barygaza. In the Hindu Kush, it is copied by an engraver and used to strike a new currency.

Coins travelled as physical objects, but also as ideas and concepts, as illustrated by a small black disc decorated with wavy lines found by one of the detectorists: an Iron Age potin, from about 50 BCE, cast from a tin-rich bronze alloy, possibly used like a modern coin, to pay for things, or perhaps not, no one knows for sure. It is an idea as much as it is an object, all the way from the Mediterranean, based on Greek coins made in Marseilles.

Chance finds along the road, mirror chance losses across two thousand years. In 2009, a bronze unit of the British chieftain Tasciovanus, dating to about 20 BCE, was found very near the road in Arkesden. It looks like a little coin, but archaeologists call these tiny discs 'units' because they don't know what the ancient Britons called them or even if they were used as coinage. Further along, a walker picked up a tiny and intricate golden *stater*. The image on the back is a mysterious geometric design, a beautiful abstraction of the head of Apollo, interpreted by an artist at the mint of the Trinovantes.

Fascinatingly, British Iron Age coins are all based on a single gold *stater* that was minted for Philip of Macedon, the father of Alexander the Great, in the second half of the fourth century BCE. The original showed the head of Apollo on one side and a two-horse chariot on the other. The increasingly fanciful interpretations of these images can be traced through the Iron Age. After Julius Caesar's visit, a marked difference appears between some of the tribes – those who continue with the same imagery and those who adopt completely new designs, aping the Roman ones. These new coins are made of a different type of gold too, perhaps from somewhere in the empire, and they begin to bear the name of the chieftain who had them minted, anointing him with the Latin 'Rex' for 'King'. They are so influenced by the classical imagery on Roman coins struck during the reign of Augustus, in the late first century BCE, that there is no doubt the British tribes came into close contact with Rome before the invasion. Their princes had probably spent time in Rome too. The great king of the Britons Cunobelin distributed over a million such coins, most famously sporting his ear of corn to represent Britain's agricultural output or, as one historian has suggested, British beer – in opposition to his rival king Verica, who on many of his coins opted for a far more Roman vine leaf. Some historians have contended that these provide evidence that the kingdoms of the south and east were client states of Rome before the invasion – it had been Verica, king of the Atrebates in Sussex and Hampshire, who appealed to Claudius for help and so prompted the Roman onslaught.

At Puckeridge near the road hub, a fake gold *stater* of Cunobelin was unearthed. The coin expert Mark Curteis suggests that the coin was votive, intended for the gods: 'Some people didn't want to sacrifice a real coin so they used forgeries – maybe they thought the gods wouldn't be able to tell the difference.' That's not to say that some wouldn't have presented real coins at the temple. When we find gold coins from the Iron Age or Roman Britain, they would usually have been a deliberate deposit. 'If you drop a £100 note by accident,' says Curteis, 'you're going to try very hard to find it. So when an archaeologist finds a gold coin, they look hard at the location.'

If they tell us nothing else, coins reveal that there was activity along our route in the late Iron Age and early Roman period. Today we have LiDAR images, dendrochronology (dating tree rings), macroscopic analysis of seeds in ancient rubbish, luminescence measurements in buried quartz, geophysical surveys and no end of scientific aids to archaeology, but numismatics, the study of coins, is one of the original forensic techniques. Coins were and still are essential to understanding the past. The dating of the Claudian invasion of Britain was based largely on the discovery of a single coin that was minted in Alexandria sometime between August 42 CE and August 43 CE with an image of Claudius's son, identified as 'Britannicus Caesar' – the name given to him to celebrate the victory. There are few things better to find than a coin encased in a layer of a road. They are usually datable and so give us a *terminus post quem*. The earliest possible date of the road surface. An earliest possible date, but not necessarily a very precise one. How long had a coin been in circulation before it was dropped or buried or cast into a sacred spring? Wear and tear offers a clue to how long it had been exchanged in antiquity before it found its way, either deliberately or accidentally, into the ground. And copies, forgeries or unofficial mintings (to make up for a shortage of supply from official sources) can play tricks on us, because sometimes these versions didn't appear until a considerable time after the official issue.

We are particularly interested when early Roman coins are found that pre-date the invasion. Two weeks after their first excursion, Zoe and Klaine's detectorists returned to the field immediately to the east of Rockell's Wood: Wood Field, or T-shirt field as they called it, because of its shape. Here lay a coin dating from the Roman Republic, before Julius Caesar's arrival in Britain. Were Roman coins being used in Britain that early or was it brought here by someone much later? A few years ago, a silver *denarius* that had been minted in Rome in 42 BCE was found alongside the road in Elmdon. It shows an Apollo on one side and the goddess Diana holding two torches on the other. Because of the high silver content of republican coins, they were a useful store of value. 'They stayed in circulation much longer than others,' says Curteis. 'You find lots issued by Mark Antony because he had hundreds of thousands minted to pay his troops after the Battle of Actium.' It's assumed that large numbers of these republican silver coins came over with the legions and their distribution has been used to track the movement of troops. There were probably some here before the Romans came, having arrived as gifts, and as the stored wealth of merchants. However, coin hoards dating from the 120s onwards – the *terminus post quem* established by other coins found in them – still contained many earlier, republican *denarii*. So if you find one of those in a road surface, it would give you a fairly imprecise timespan of over a century and a half.

We can imagine coins minted far away in Rome coming over here in someone's pocket, or rather in a purse worn on their arm. Coins from closer mints in Gaul probably arrived in huge official batches. At Arkesden, someone found a Roman copper alloy coin, a *nummus*, from the reign of Constantine. It was minted in the early fourth century, in Trier, in modern-day Germany, and most likely arrived in Britain as part of a large consignment of coins to pay the army.

Coins are useful for dating the sites where they are found, for placing events and rulers, for studying the Iron Age tribal groups who minted them, for tracking the movement of goods and armies, for studying the beliefs and propaganda efforts of emperors. Numismatists also analyse the distribution patterns of coins, by period, by region, by site type – is it a villa, a farm, a fort, a temple, a roadside settlement? Since the 1990s, all coin finds have had to be reported as treasure and so find their way into the database of the Portable Antiquities Scheme. In recent years, this has made it possible to study the spread of coins with less guesswork and to show when sites were occupied and at their busiest. Over 2,500 hoards, 180,000 stray losses and more than 450 assemblages from excavations have turned up in Britain. Most coins found in the north can be linked to military sites and it's been estimated that in the first century alone, the Roman army in Britain would have needed over 1.5 million *denarii* a year to pay salaries (and it was mostly the silver *denarii* that soldiers trusted and wanted). In the south, coin finds are much more widespread and turn up in a far greater range of denominations.

The story of Roman Britain is here along our road. Told in the coins that litter its corridor. Not every emperor perhaps, but the heads of a great many lie in the fields we are walking through, from Augustus to Theodosius, the last emperor of a combined empire, and the father of Honorius, the Western Roman emperor, he who is traditionally thought to have told Britain to look to her own defences. Here at the roadside in Furneux Pelham lies Septimius Severus, reminding us of the role the most northern outpost of the empire played at the heart of Roman affairs because he died at York in 211 CE, three years into an imperial expedition to exterminate the Maeatae in Scotland and end a long period of unrest in the province. It is a *denarius* from the first period of Britannia's Roman coins, when they were true to their value, when silver coins were mostly made from silver.

The thirty years after 260 CE saw a rapid debasing of the coinage as Rome weathered one crisis after another during the period of the radiates, so-called because of the spiky radiate crowns worn by the emperors in their portraits. The coins are called billons and were eventually mostly bronze with a silver wash. Many more of these have been found making us ask: was there more activity in the late third century or were people simply taking less care of vast numbers of low-value coins? It's been suggested that such coins may have been so worthless that they were weighed out rather than counted, with spillages accounting for some of the finds. The various crises of the time may also have led to more caches being buried that were never recovered. The *antoninianus* radiate of Claudius II found in Rockells Field is supposedly worth two *denarii*, but by that time was barely worth one and a half. Worse still were the so-called barbarous radiates. Two were dropped alongside the road, one a copy of the Claudius II coin. Historians don't know if these are forgeries or were minted by the local administration to make up for a lack of official coinage from the empire needed to pay the troops.

Of all the emperors buried alongside our road, Constantine the Great – elevated to the purple at York in 306 – has given us the most modern coinage, the most likely to have been used as small change. In Elmdon, a *nummus* of Constantine minted in Rome shows a legionary eagle between two *vexilla*, or military standards. It is inscribed 'S P Q R OPTIMO PRINCIPI': from 'The Senate and People of Rome to the Highest Princes'.

The majority of finds along RR21b and across the island belong to the period between Constantine's final years and the unravelling of Britannia. The end of Roman rule is encapsulated in three very rare silver coins found back along the road. These are *siliquae* from the fourth century, struck using a high

percentage of silver in an attempt to restore faith in the currency. The first is a *siliqua* of Constantius II cast at Arles in the middle of the fourth century as a *donative* payment by the emperor. It might well indicate the site of an elite villa waiting to be found. The other two were also *siliquae*, this time from the short reign of the usurper Eugenius. Both have clipped edges, where people have pinched tiny snips of silver; a crime that carried the death penalty. These only appear in hoards deposited at the beginning of the fifth century and were probably clipped after the end of Roman Britain when there was no central authority left to enforce the law. Clipping has been seen as evidence of what the fifth and sixth-century Greek historian Zosimus described when he wrote that after 409 the Britons ceased to obey Roman laws. 'The result was the end of the coin-using economy in Britain, for clipping brought the collapse of the silver coinage,' wrote one historian. 'Thus, in one aspect at least, Roman Britain suddenly ended in 409.'

Coins mark the road's course through the countryside and through history: through that of Roman Britain and beyond. Braughing, the starting point of our journey in both time and space, has produced an unusual number of coins from the early days of Roman rule, attesting to its importance in the late Iron Age. Our destination at Great Chesterford is one of only two towns in the East of England that doesn't see a rapid decline in coin finds in the fourth century. The end of the Romans didn't mean the end of the road, nor the end of those carrying coins along it. Here in Rockells Field the detectorists have found a nice little short cross. The classic silver coin of the Middle Ages. Another turned up at the roadside in Elmdon. In Arkesden, a traveller dropped a silver penny, another a silver cut halfpenny from the reign of Henry III. People were still coming along the road, careless as they ever were.

♦ ♦ ♦

They are browns and reds, white and blacks, but mostly greys, dulled and abraded, the colour of soil and overcast skies. Clays tempered with grass and flint and sand. Here, sitting clearly in the plough soil, is the most diagnostic of them all: a grey durable piece of pot. It is only the arc of a rim, flecked bright with ground fragments of shell that were worked into the wet clay in the fourth century to save it from shrinking and cracking in the kiln. Rebuild it in your mind into a portly storage jar, thrown, rilled and fired in a Bedfordshire kiln, loaded onto a mule cart and sent east, now coming up the road here, brought to a Romano-British farmhouse and one day broken, perhaps carelessly, perhaps in the hurry to clear out; one of many grey sherds settling into the plough soil on the edge of the wood here, turned and tumbled for sixteen centuries, but remaining as a clue for field archaeologists to spot. Here is one now, striding along. It is 1984, and he might be looking for that jar as if he knows it has been mislaid, but instead he is painstakingly walking many square miles of countryside to find out how old it is and who lived here, and other improbable things to read in the soil. Our road runs right through the middle of it all.

The Roman pottery industry, like their roads, was hardly surpassed in the West until the Enlightenment. Like coins, pots and bits of pots can be studied for their own worth, their beauty and form, to understand the technology that made them – if they were thrown on a wheel or shaped by hand, the source of clay and temper, the working of the kilns. Bits of pot are also useful for studying changing tastes in food and cooking, for telling the long story of trade and transport, and for dating sites. On the basis of a lip, just a fragment of the rim, experts can identify not only when it was made and what sort of pot it was, but where it was made, sometimes even who made it, if other examples have been found with potters' stamps. And like coins, pottery, lots of pottery, can have other uses for the archaeologist engaged in field-walking.

The brilliant landscape archaeologist Tom Williamson defined field-walking as the 'systematic examination of the ploughsoil for the spreads of pottery and other debris indicating the location of settlements'. It was Williamson who field-walked the countryside either side of our road in the 1980s, mostly because he wanted to establish if the land had been settled and which soils its settlers might have favoured.

He walks neat transects, eyes trained on the ground for fragments of the everyday from the Iron Age, Roman Britain, the Anglo-Saxon and medieval worlds. And what he finds changes our picture of the past. There are large clusters and small ones, a penumbra of sherds around them thinning out, not to nothing, but to single sherds that each tell a story. He is finding pot where he isn't supposed to find it. We thought the Romans settled and farmed the light, easily workable soils of the valley sides. Surely the heavy clay on the plateaus between the river valleys was too unyielding? As we learned back in Meesden, the traditional view held that such clay-lands weren't cleared of natural woodland until centuries later. Just two years before Williamson scours the fields, one archaeologist wrote that when you find pottery on the clay it 'need mean no more than a temporary shelter made in a woodland clearing by some cowherd or swineherd'. He argued that the Boulder Clay plateau should probably be seen as a source of fuel, browsing, pannage and venison, instead of as ploughland. But Williamson finds pot and rubble so dense as to leave no doubt that people were living out there away from the valley, next to our road. They were farming there too.

In the countryside that the road bisects, there were as many as 3.3 Roman settlements per square mile in the middle of the first century and that hardly changed for over three hundred years. The density of pottery can only be explained by permanent settlement – people lived there and they generally shunned the valleys. The wealthy who left behind a sliver of fancy Samian ware preferred the margins between the valley sides and the clay, while others built smaller settlements on the denser but more fertile soil of the plateaus. There, the ground had poorer drainage, but that made it perfect for digging ponds that held water. While harder to work, it was richer, better arable land.

Hold up a potsherd to the light and in your mind's eye watch it form into a wide-brimmed bowl. There are thousands of them, so dense here that they render entire isolated farmsteads, surrounded by grass for grazing, wood for fuel and clay for pottery kilns. And over the years as the settlers manured the heavy land with the contents of their middens and farmyards, broken pottery was scattered to become single sherds that one day an archaeologist would find and so map which fields were once cultivated.

I reach here one day, walking through one of the imaginary quadrilaterals that Williamson mapped out to define his study area. Leaving Rockells Field and its thimbles and coins behind, the route climbs steeply out of the valley along a third stretch of modern road, following the line for half a mile. It seems to sit immediately to the east of where the *agger* ran – now a wide scrubby embankment. The chalk here is exposed on the valley sides as I approach Elmdon Lee. To my right is Littlebury Green, once called Streetly Green – the 'clearing on the Roman road'.

A settlement abutted the road at Ash Grove overlooking the valley of the Cam, where the clay meets the chalk of the valley slope. Between Ash Grove and Lee Wood, a wide grassy avenue comes up from the south, a raised piece of scrub. Ivan Margary called this a green lane continuing the line of the road for a distance. It is marked as a right of way on the Ordnance Survey maps, as a track on older ones, but is now overgrown and nearly impenetrable. How usual is it for a lane to sit proud of the fields either side of it? Not a holloway but a causeway. Some 250 metres long and 16 metres wide – the remains of the *agger*.

The fields beyond are a graveyard of flints. These are false friends to field walkers: from some angles and for a fleeting moment they look like the rims and handles of earthenware, of amphorae or mortaria, what Pliny the Elder called in a beautiful phrase, 'a kindness of Mother Earth beyond description'.

I have strolled the countryside with experienced field walkers. Every few minutes they stoop to pick up something and rub off the soil with their fingers before dating it. Their eyes are tuned to the frequency of medieval tiles or Roman potsherds and they rarely pick up flints in error. If they do, it is to examine the stone for percussion marks, those tell-tale signs left on a flint core from which some Neolithic craftsman had chiselled a sliver to make a knife or scraper.

Spend enough time with field walkers and every ploughed field becomes carpeted with history. Here is a piece of Tudor brick or Roman roof tile, there a hand-axe or a cobble from a Roman road that must have passed through this very field, a fingernail-sized portion of red Samian or a marble-sized fossil, an *Offaster pilula*, which are not uncommon in the chalk, but may have been dropped by a Roman, who carried it for good luck.

If the coins and the querns and the tumulus hint at a landscape for our road to pass through and bring travellers along, the fragments of pot are peopling it. Williamson found evidence of twelve Roman settlements in the parish of Littlebury alone. Many of them on the heavy clay. Some dense clusters emerging from the edge of woodland indicated that

there were even more amid the roots of the trees that grew back when the population declined after the legions left. And so our road passes by Roman farmhouses, perhaps even a villa like that two miles away at Wendens Ambo, now beneath the M11. But we must be careful not to populate the Roman countryside only with villas. Roman-style villas account for a tiny 2 per cent of known rural archaeological sites and are probably outnumbered at least twenty-five to one by settlements that look like they belong in the Iron Age. Williamson didn't just find Roman settlement here, but Iron Age too: thirteen main concentrations of pottery tempered with flint and sand or vegetable matter. Five Anglo-Saxon sites, five Saxon-Norman settlements. Even more back down the road. Even more up ahead. This was one of the most highly populated area of Essex in the Middle Ages but, cautions Williamson, these findings may not be normal: the density of settlement is probably due to the gravitational pull of our road.

♦ ♦ ♦

the historical sense involves a perception, not only of the pastness of the past, but of its presence.

T.S. Eliot, *Tradition and Individual Talent* (1919)

♦ ♦ ♦

The field-walking grids make me think of the windows to the past and future in Richard McGuire's extraordinary graphic novel *Here*, a book that, better than anything else I know, conveys the *thinness* and *immanence* of place – the sense that the past might leak through to the present, and the present to the past, like ink through tissue paper. Each of its double-page spreads shows a picture of the same space: a corner of a room. In 2014, we see a beige wall, a sash window, a fireplace, a blue sofa and little else. Turn the page. It is 1957, the same room, different decor. Page by page we are gradually taught the grammar and possibilities of the book. Inset panels appear showing the past and future, multiple pasts and futures in this exact spot. Events in one moment are obscured by patches of the past and we can only guess at them, perhaps by glimpses of things yet to happen or things said long ago. A family poses for a photo on the sofa, first in 1959 over a full page and for the last time in 1983 in a small panel seen from 3450 BCE.

It is 1957, but at the bottom left of the page is an inset showing a cat walking across the room forty-two years later. Turn the page and the room becomes an autumnal swamp in the early seventeenth century, yet two windows are open: one to 1957, the other to the cat licking its paw seconds after we last saw it. From 1955, we spy the cat reaching the edge of the room, never to be seen again. We hear a joke begin in 1989. We can overhear it in 8000 BCE, in 1009 BCE, in 1873. Sequences play out over different pages. The resonances grow, as do poignant narratives. The significance of tiny moments is only discovered in their thematic relationship to events centuries, even millions of years apart. Stories are nested in stories across time and space. In 1609 a native American man sitting in the woods appears to be telling a story to his lover about a wild beast, and the reader can see a window to 1975 in which a child walks across the room dressed as a bear. On another page, the native Americans pause in their love-making in 1609 when the man says, 'I heard something.' It is a startling moment. Has he heard the doorbell ringing in 1986, where an old woman lies on a sofa just a few feet and centuries apart? The time gaps seem insignificant. It is like Offa in the eighth century overhearing himself described as the 'overlord of the M5' in Geoffrey Hill's *Mercian Hymns*. What do we hope to overhear, what might the dead hear us saying? What might we learn from them about a field scattered with ancient pot?

I am reminded of the bizarre and much-celebrated account from the early twentieth century of two Oxford scholars who claimed to have experienced the memories of Marie Antoinette while searching for the Petit Trianon at Versailles (on a date that they later discovered was the anniversary of the sacking of the Tuileries in 1792). The elder of the two, Charlotte Moberly, principal of St Hugh's College, was not only sensitive to eighteenth-century apparitions. In 1914 at the Louvre, she encountered a giant of a man in a crown and toga. At first she thought he was Charlemagne, but later decided she had met the ghost of the emperor Constantine.

Ghosts, immortals, time-leaks, spiritualism, previous lives, retro-cognition. Thought experiments on the road. Simultaneity, echoes, continuity, change, prophecy even. Things begun in one period are completed in another. A rider on the road glances left to see a slave throw a broken pot into the midden; a different pot lands in the same spot on the earthen floor of an Anglo-Saxon church, its crack heard by a passing mule driver. A woman pours from a flagon, and another woman 1,800 years hence bags a sherd from it. Fragments, clutched at, fragile, often friable, all we have left. Windows in time. Ways to the past. What am I doing but trying feebly to prise open these windows with pieces of pot and pencil marks on maps?

◆ ◆ ◆

The eastern extremities of the Chilterns channel us northwards, through country scattered with potsherds from settlements reaching back to the Iron Age. The land heaved and smoothed. There are lovely little drawings of this countryside by a local artist, Mary Seymour, that strip it down to its sketchy secretive self, its folds and irregular fields; the misleading randomness of their curves forming the most natural shapes; the ground before me creased like a much-used old map, folded and refolded against itself over a lifetime. Emerging at a five-ways junction and taking the track north,

climbing a slight slope and skirting the eastern edge of Bixett Wood with its distinctive woodbank, I come to the other side of the trees where the land dips to the meeting of two fields: a ley and a mead.

For over nine miles now the spirits and the more corporeal have walked straight ahead, following the line of the hidden road. We have been able to prove it from the ground and from the air, with only sections on the valley slopes hiding from us, but with little reason to suspect that they are anywhere else or any reason to assume the engineers needed to change the route.

Before the Romans, roads grew organically over the centuries. Twisted and crookbacked, lordotic, beautiful esses that surely we prefer to the imposed tyranny of the straight line. G. K. Chesterton's rolling English road. Why should we attack the thuggishness and boredom of the modern straight road, but find delight in the Roman road? The cultural historian Joe Moran points out that 'straight roads have been a symbol of political coercion'. From William Blake to W.G. Hoskins, British commentators have despised them. We might pause for a moment to wonder if this animus is a folk memory of the Roman road inflicted on the land of our forebears, cut ruthlessly and unrelentingly on, deliberately ignorant of tradition. The Roman road as the superhighway of its time with all the good and bad that offers. Armies and plagues perhaps, but also commerce, ideas and stories, an opening up to the world beyond any comforting, stultifying insularity.

The straight road doesn't have to be seen as an act of vandalism and brutality. The American straight road Route 66 is a romantic icon, a symbol of freedom. I want to believe this, because while my favourite road in all the world is an ancient winding country lane near my home, with its spiritual litany of switchbacks that lift my soul on an early morning, I am rather invested now in this straight road built two millennia ago. Its straightness is arresting and fascinating, mysterious and mystical. Its wonder in this particular countryside is in its difference to every other line drawn by the landscape. It is the contrast of the road as it runs against the grain, not sitting above the shallow gentle river valleys, chalk streams and tributaries, not forcing a straight line alongside a rolling riverine one, but dissecting them, rising to wooded heights and dropping down into the valleys, a making-strange, offering the best views of this landscape, revealing vistas that look like the open pages of a hefty gospel book, the road running across its gutter, across the cockled vellum. An ancient crib that allows us to decipher the curves we so love in a way that a winding road does not permit, for all its other charms. The Roman road is a point of view, a narrator visiting this countryside with no middle distance, only long views, because the fields fold the middle ground into themselves. And if none of that convinces, then consider what the road has become, not what it once was in Roman times. Maybe this is the road's redemption.

◆ ◆ ◆

Let us contemplate, as briefly as possible, the straightness of Roman roads. It is a subject both baffling and sometimes tedious to all but a few enthusiasts, but we can't ignore it because it is essential to understanding the roads the Romans built on this island and is indubitably at the heart of what is fascinating about them. It is what everyone knows about Roman roads. That they are straight.

It has become a truism in recent years that Roman roads are not as straight as we used to think or were taught to think by *1066 and All That*, where, 'The Roman roads ran absolutely straight in all directions and all led to Rome', which is itself obviously meant to put us on our guard against that very claim. Roads built by Romans are rarely completely straight from beginning to end, but they are often built in straight sections. They make detours from a surveyed line to respect the topography; they wend around the landscape where they must, and sometimes they wiggle along lengths of older tracks, before returning to their original line; but it remains true that they are remarkably straighter than other roads.

This is not news. 'In an open country like much of the south of England,' wrote Thomas Codrington long ago, 'the general course of the Roman roads is often wonderfully direct, perhaps not deviating more than a quarter or half-a-mile from an absolutely straight line in 20 or 30 miles, but it does divert to avoid rivers and steep inclines if necessary.'

It is assumed that the surveyed line was a straight one between two distant points and unless there was an overwhelming reason to stray from it, a hill or river say, the engineers built the road on that line or at least parallel to it.

Still, it is hard to stop wondering at the straightness, in part because we aren't sure how they managed it. Oliver Rackham gave an example of what we should be marvelling at: 'The surveyor of Peddars Way starting at the north-west corner of Norfolk, knew to within half a degree which way to go to reach a certain ford of the Little Ouse, 42 miles away. The road twice deviates very slightly, each time on a hilltop, but returns to the original line on reaching the ford.' The most famous example of this is usually cited as Stane Street between Chichester and London. 'In no way on the ground then or now could one place be seen from the other,' wrote Richard Bagshawe in his 1970s book *Roman Roads*. 'Yet from Old London Bridge as far as Ewell the alignment was directed at Chichester's east gate ... Nobody knows how it was done.' In other words, the road is not straight all the way, but right at the start it points exactly at the gate in Chichester before changing alignment to avoid various obstacles. This – at first glance at least, we will take a second glance in a moment – is an extraordinary thing. It is undoubtedly part of the wonder of Roman roads. How did they do it? How did the Romans get them so straight without modern technology? There is something teasingly aliens-built-the-pyramids about it. We might invoke the Trigan Empire from the children's magazine

Look and Learn – a civilisation that looks suspiciously Roman in dress and architecture, but with lasers as well as swords and flying cars to hover around in. Presumably they built straight roads with pickaxes and GPS.

No description of surveying methods has come down to us from the Romans that answers all our questions, so we have to make educated guesses that don't involve spaceships. Let's take that alignment from London Bridge to Chichester's gate. There is no need to assume they were able to align a road on a gate over fifty miles away. There are two sensible possibilities to consider. Was the gate already there and they measured north, thus reaching the banks of the Thames at a point where they then built a bridge regardless of whether it was a good crossing point? Or did they build a bridge at the best point for crossing the river and then measure south in the general direction of a nearby Iron Age settlement that only later became a place of importance? Eventually they built a gate there, since that was the end of the road.

The magic of Roman surveying loses a tiny bit of its lustre if we stop imagining that they were able to plan a single straight line over many miles between two fixed points; but only a tiny bit. Even if the gateway at Chichester was constructed later, it is still extraordinary that the road – or at least its alignment – was so straight. It is helpful to understand that the surveyed lines may well have been independent of the road. It appears that the Roman surveyors established long-distance survey lines in the landscape for roads or to parcel up territory, or for both. Some of those lines were then used to build roads either on the line, parallel to it or at particular angles from it. But how did they survey the line in the first place?

Among the more entertaining solutions is Hilaire Belloc's idea that a team of hundreds or even thousands of soldiers held hands, shuffling forwards and backwards to get in line. Or that homing pigeons were sent off in the right direction with the surveyors hurrying after them. Sadly the process was disappointingly less wacky. 'There can be no doubt that the Roman engineers made use of a method well known to surveyors for laying out a straight line between extreme points not visible from each other, from two or more intermediate points from which the extreme points are visible.' This is Thomas Codrington again. 'By shifting the intermediate points alternately all are brought to lie in a straight line.' And this neat explanation has remained broadly unchanged ever since. He is asking us to imagine a surveyor, or rather a team of surveyors setting out from Pentlow Hill in Braughing, where they would set a tall visible marker or beacon, and perhaps using the sun or stars, start walking in the general direction of the destination to the next high point, where they would set up another marker. Once they had done this for the length of the line and reached their destination, they would be able to line up these beacons or markers using a simple device called a groma. It looked like a weather vane on a pole with plumb lines hanging from the four ends. Standing where Hormead Park is today – the highest point on the whole road – they would plant the groma at the marker there and align two of the plumb lines with another marker or beacon lit on another relative high point to the south-west, then they would turn 180 degrees to the north-east and see if the strings of the plumb line lined up with yet another marker up ahead. If it did, they would have three markers in line. If not, they would measure how many degrees out they were and reposition their own marker, or simply signal to another surveyor to move theirs until it lined up. Having done this for all the main sighting points, they would lay out the centre line of the road using hundreds of stakes, lining each up with the groma. This is the usual explanation seen in no end of TV programmes and YouTube videos. It is a tiresome thing to explain and must have been a tiresome thing to carry out, and prone to significant error over long distances. And yet they made so few errors, which makes the explanation not entirely convincing.

The real method probably employed more of the simple magic of Pythagoras and Euclidean geometry and involved measuring base lines before establishing right-angled triangles on the ground. The Roman road expert Hugh Davies has proposed that the surveyors must also have had maps or at least plotted out the roads in sand pits. Others think they must have had an archive to record the long-distance alignments for future use.

One thing everyone agrees on is that the roads always changed direction on hilltops. Which is why it is odd that when we must change direction on our road we find ourselves in a hollow between two high points. After nine and a half miles travelling true, RR21b finally leaves the straight line on the map, changes bearing and adopts a heading that will take it all the way to Great Chesterford.

PART IV

BEGINNINGS AND ENDINGS

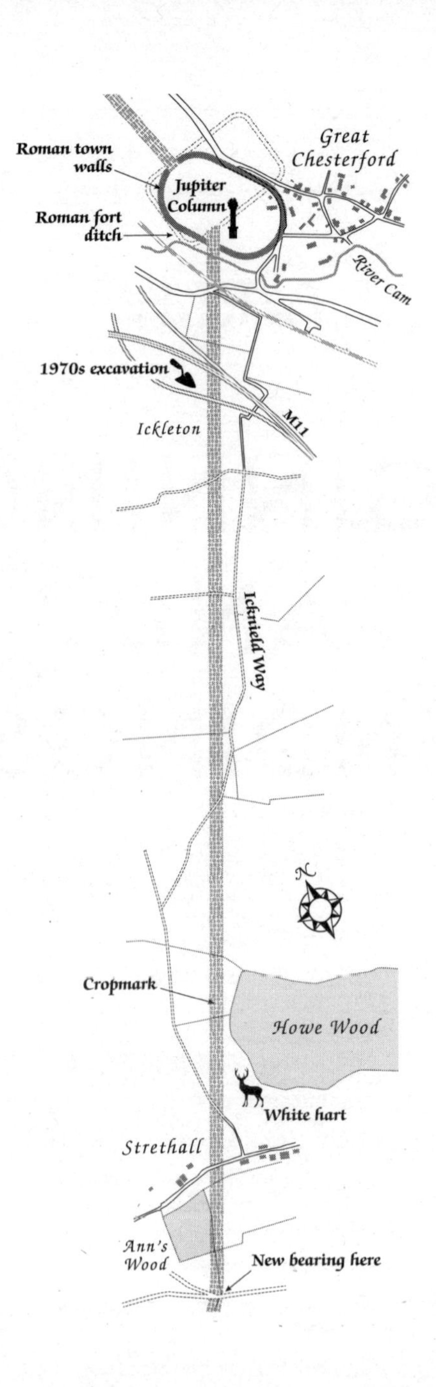
Roman town walls
Great Chesterford
Jupiter Column
Roman fort ditch
River Cam
1970s excavation
M11
Ickleton
Icknield Way
N
Cropmark
Howe Wood
White hart
Strethall
Ann's Wood
New bearing here

You might be forgiven for thinking this tangle of paths where the road changes direction is here to confuse and misdirect. Which way to go from the dip north of Bixett Wood if you insist on walking in the footsteps of Romans? The field investigators were never sure, although they knew the road changed its bearing somewhere near here; if it didn't it would miss Great Chesterford entirely. They settled on a straight line from the high ground of the wood – where conventional wisdom says the road should be – but then it would have to change again to hit the Roman town. From the meeting of the five ways in the hollow – where conventional wisdom says the road shouldn't be – it would get there in one efficient and elegant straight section.

Old maps offer the proof. Here in 1805 a track is shown approaching from the east. It widens and stops in the middle of nowhere at precisely the point that RR21b changes direction. Even more compelling are today's fields. Right up to the dip, they are all aligned on the original bearing. Immediately after that point, they tilt to the north-west in the direction of the new line of travel, long before the high point on the road.

Field boundaries reorienting themselves to the diktats of Romans on the march.

Why was there a change of direction at all? As we have seen, the Romans were capable of building roads completely straight over long distances. Was it an adjustment of the original plan, a change of destination, a surveying error corrected? Perhaps two construction teams working towards one another on slightly different bearings. The most likely assumption is that the exact point of the road's end was unclear when they started building the road. The main length from Braughing may have followed an existing long-distance survey line and then changed direction to make for the precise end point. If the road and its destination were being built at about the same time, this would make sense, even the change of direction in the dip. Unless it was important to pass through that place where the five ways meet.

What was once here? What is the spirit of this place where the road veers? What the Romans called the *genius loci*. I love the idea suggested by one writer that psychogeography – briefly defined as the study of the effect place has on us – might be 'an unconscious attempt to encounter this *genius loci*'. So it might be better to ask, not *what* but *who* is the spirit of the place? An unnamed god perhaps? These deities had shrines dedicated to them, like the one found in Cirencester in 1880, standing in a niche beneath a pediment, crowned and holding a *patera* to pour libations over a carved altar and in its other hand a cornucopia, a horn of plenty. Among the many altars surviving from Roman Britain, it is not the scrolled and pedimented ones confidently carved and dedicated to gods like Mars or Neptune that I like best, but those in honour of these unnamed gods. A thin slab of red sandstone from Tilston in Cheshire, scored and worn and looking home-made, is the sort of stone I imagine stood north of Bixett Wood. Crude lettering graffitied into the surface reads: '*Genio / loci fe [liciter].*' 'To the spirit of this place, may there be luck.' Or was our place where five ways meet dedicated to the *Lares*, the Roman spirits who guarded boundaries, homes, fields, roads and particularly crossroads? Did they stand guard over this meeting of the ways in the dell?

The most striking of the British travelling spirits stand shoulder to shoulder on a rectangular stone found in a shrine near Housesteads Roman fort in Northumbria. It frames three cloaked figures, *genii cucullati*, the hooded ones. They look like travellers on the roads, cocooned in long hooded cloaks

to protect them from the winds and rains of Britannia, their mouths grim set, their eyes hooded too.

Climb away from the five ways towards the next block of woodland, Ann's Wood. As you look back, it is clear that the hedges behind you follow the original alignment before the lie of the land shifts, pointing up the slope. The absence of something is profound in this strange place between Bixett and Ann's Wood. Tracks and paths come from all directions, north and south of the wood. Coming to what?

Does the road change direction in the dip to avoid something? Was there something of importance here? Not for the first time I want to find an explanation and significance beyond the prosaic. I want to dress the surveyor in priestly vestments and picture him choosing this place to change bearing because of some great energy or spirit way that must now be followed. After all, the surveyor was a sorcerer, who had the power to alter the nature of space itself, who knew the secret of making lines in the landscape so straight and permanent they cut through hillsides, parcelling up the world like rivers, forests and mountain ranges did, striking awe into the local population. And still do two thousand years later.

I follow the new line across the land, alien in its straightness, a road forcing settlement and community together, linking places that have no relation and calling others into existence. A communications route – a proto-motorway, telephone and superhighway. Before its coming we might imagine a time when there were no great roads hereabouts for moving animals, goods or armies over many miles, only isolated settlements joined by little more than local tracks.

The new bearing picks up a bridleway describing the edge of Ann's Wood. The field margins are scrubby here and rock-strewn. I emerge in the fading light of a cold day across a small field on the road to somewhere called Catmere End, half-expecting, half-hoping, half-fearing that this is a place where in the right conditions you might once again see coming down the road three figures drawing their hooded cloaks about them.

♦ ♦ ♦

From the air, these fields are badged with a strange spoor, antlered with dark branches and tines. The mark of Herne. Oil on water, birds in flight, strange auguries for the Roman seer. A white hart stalks the vanished trail. The ghostly badge of a tragic king and Celtic omen. It was there at the start of our quest, the White Hart Inn in Puckeridge, next to the road hub, and we find it has never left us. Looking east towards Howe Wood, where Miller Christy found his oxlips, in the distance moves a herd of deer, and in their midst three striking white deer of these chalklands. A good omen as we near the end of our journey, this local wild herd. What can we read in their movements, in the wisps of cloud overhead, fleeing like smoke from a sacrificial pyre? Did you dream of owls in the watches of the night? Beware bandits or storms. If you dreamed of donkeys then the fates will look kindly on you, you will make steady progress and it will be a good day to tangle with white harts and red herrings. The route is over-loaded now with clues, contradictions, correlations and cockamamie.

The landscape of the chalk downs here is one of soft hills folding into one another as we drop into shallow valleys and ravines only to climb out again towards our destination. Shaped by wind, the land billowing, alive, the contours seeming to shift from visit to visit and the field boundaries unreadable on the ground. The sky is an encyclopedia of cloud forms projecting an ever-moving front of sunlight across the fields, scanning the land for traces. Several times today I will stand waiting, hoping to catch a hint of the road's course in this changing shadowland.

The mind searches for patterns on the ground and on its maps. There are geological maps, soil maps, Google Earth elevations, endless Ordnance Survey maps, old estate maps, tithe maps, enclosure maps, field maps, definitive maps of footpaths and bridleways, street maps and road atlases, maps of the itineraries of medieval kings. They all promise to reveal something, these beautiful objects made to help us find things, but make us lose ourselves.

I'm fond of the *Ten Mile Road Map* published in 1932. It strips the landscape back to its pre-motorway essentials: the caramel relief of the East Anglian heights is easily read within an oblong defined by the A-roads, faintly dissected by the county boundary and a shaky colophon of B-roads. That is all. A perfect canvas to draw our secret road on and see how neatly it transects the polygon. As with all maps, the mind begins to play with such shapes, reaching for significance. Along the roads the mapmakers have scattered the letters 'A' and 'R' at junctions and, sometimes, accompanied by a black dot, along a length of road. I had to call my eighty-four-year-old father to ask if he knew what these were. They were the old AA and RAC boxes. Members had keys to them and could take shelter inside, use the maps and provisions, make free local calls on the telephones. What might we learn from these and their positioning? How closely might such boxes correlate to Roman roads? What archaeological remnants will they leave behind centuries from now?

They were harbours from the weather. Coldharbours. There is a place name calculated to make ears prick up and eyes roll among Roman road followers. The nearest Coldharbour to our road is just south of Braughing on Ermine Street. It is 'a name which in the south of England is found constantly accompanying Roman roads, the meaning of which has been a moot point,' wrote Codrington back in 1903, by which time the word had already acquired legendary status among antiquaries as a source of much heated debate.

We must blame the antiquary Richard Colt Hoare for sitting down in his Wiltshire mansion and inventing the connection. The meaning of the word has quite literally been taken to mean a harbour or shelter from the cold, a way station. It is clearly not of Latin origin nor thought to be of Old English, so we are forced to accept that such shelters survived for many centuries up to a time when they could be given the name in recognisable English. And why not? What more natural thing than to provide shelter for travellers along a road?

The language expert Richard Coates, in an ingenious article for *Nomina* in 1984, did a good job of debunking what he wonderfully called the 'caravanserai hypothesis' – referring to the roadside inns found along the Silk Road. 'Few place names can have had so much historical and archaeological weight thrust undeservedly upon them as Coldharbour,' he begins, going on to point out that there is not a single piece of archaeological evidence for a wayside shelter or inn at one of the over two hundred places – mostly in the south and south-east – called Coldharbour.

Coates assumed that, having nothing to do with Romans or their roads, the word is in fact a derogatory name like the better-known Cold Comfort that we find as a place name. His article was taken to draw a line under the centuries-old debate, although in a brief appendix to his paper he added a new provocation, pointing out that in the *Ravenna Cosmography* there is a place near Pisa known as 'Tabernis frigidis', which ought to mean at the 'cold booths or shelters'. That, as Coates tells us, is exactly analogous to Coldharbour.

In an analysis by the statistician Keith Briggs, many place names that had been commonly associated with Roman roads were shown to be equally linked with any random point on the map of England. And yet Coldharbour withstood his methods. In fact, it proved to be one of the few place names or sites that had a real, undeniable correlation with Roman roads. Only Roman villas were more closely linked. Nobody knows why.

The landscape is full of revealing names, densely packed with history, not just for roads but for brick kilns, fairy rings, magic places, treasure, dovecotes, memories of what once stood there and how people lived their lives. Some might even lead us back to Roman times or to that boundary between the Romans and Early Middle Ages. Margary saw the potential of scouring early maps for field names and local place names when trying to find new roads or prove a course.

Richard Bagshawe advises that the first phase in researching a supposed Roman road, or searching for lost ones, is to examine the place-name evidence for hints of occupation. The most common word bequeathed to the Anglo-Saxons by the Romans was *castrum*, a military camp, which survives in the various *-chesters*, notably Colchester, in the *cester* of Cirencester, the *caster* of Lancaster, in names like Leicester – the Roman site of the Ligore tribe – less obviously, in the two Norfolk *caisters*, and in our destination at Great Chesterford. Odder place names have been associated with Roman roads, some of them with more doubtful or tentative associations such as 'folly' that you find in Folly Farms and Folly Lanes, but nobody knows why. As Bagshawe concedes, they make no sense but 'occur with uncomfortable frequency along Roman roads'.

Words that carry the road above the level of the surrounding land might hint at the existence of an *agger*: ridges, causeways and dykes. Stones also turn out to be clues. We meet them in place names, such as Stane Street, literally the stone road, akin to the Stanegate in the north, which runs roughly parallel to Hadrian's Wall, but not street this time, rather the Old Norse *gata* for road. Or the nearby village of Stansted Mountfichet, where the first part means the stony place.

In the 1960s, Margaret Gelling, the most influential place-name expert of them all, noticed that of the twenty-eight English place names formed from the Old English word *wīchām*, all but four were near to a Roman road. The second part of the word is from Old English *hām*, which meant a homestead or village (thought to be one of the very earliest English place name elements). The first part of the name comes from the Latin *vicus* and Gelling argued that names derived from *wīchām* were given by the early Anglo-Saxon settlers to anywhere that had been a Romano-British *vicus*, that is the 'smallest unit of self-government in the Roman provinces'. Importantly, she thought it was assigned by settlers who understood what it meant because they had lived so close to the time of the Romans, had perhaps lived through the dying days of the occupation, possibly as Saxon mercenaries in Britain from the fourth century. Later she would revise her view. Wichams were not villages, but small towns and had nothing to do with early mercenaries, and were applied to Roman towns that were still lived in sometime after the Romans had left. The traditional notion of *vici* was that of small towns attached to a fort, or to a civilian settlement with a military origin where the fort had disappeared, but the town had flourished. The *vicus* would be attached to a larger town, a *civitas* centre that functioned as the administrative hub for a particular 'tribe'.

It is not just place names: medieval battle sites, castles, homestead moats, early churches, Anglo-Saxon cemeteries, religious houses – all have been associated with Roman roads. This should be no cause for surprise. People came along the roads for centuries to build things, to trade, to fight, to worship. The case for some is more compelling than for others. The writer and Romanist Mike Bishop has argued that the military history of Britain was often conducted along those same roads: 'There is an undeniable broad correlation between battle sites in Britain – especially England – and the Roman road network,' he writes and he goes on to narrate the battlefield history of the Middle Ages and Early Modern England from the Battle of Natanleaga in 506, via the campaigns of 1066, to the final undoing of the Jacobeans in the 1740s when roads built by the Romans were still influencing the movement of troops and where blood would be shed. For historians, not only do the roads provide a strategic and tactical background to military history, they also enable them to guess at the location of lost battle sites on the assumption that these would probably have been reached along a Roman road.

The place names most closely associated with Roman roads contain the Old English *straet*, a word for a paved or metalled road, taken from the Latin *strata*. Observing that the only such roads in Britain in the first millennium were Roman ones, linguists have translated the word to mean a Roman road. Hence we have Earninga Straet, the 'Roman road of Earn's People', and Waeclinga Straet, the 'Roman road of Wacol's People', names that have come down to us as Ermine Street and Watling Street. We don't know if the Romans named any of their roads in Britain, but if we have to guess what the later Romano-Britons called the roads, we probably should plump for the Latin *strata* rather than the *via* commonly found in Italy. We met a 'street' already in Streetly, the old name for Littlebury Green and here is another in our path: the tiny village of Strethall.

Strethall would have proven a good harbour from the cold, a sanctuary from the storm for travellers. Early settlers on the land there, grazing their sheep four hundred feet above sea level, sheltered from the cold winds on the southern boundary of Strethall Wood at the edge of the boulder clay next to the chalk escarpment. *The sheltered corner on the Roman road*, is how one local historian elegantly translated the Old English elements *straet* and *healh*, more literally rendered as the 'Roman road nook of land'.

King Aethelred guards this nook, this harbour. Carved out of neighbouring estates over a thousand years ago as a 'gift' to the abbot of Ely, in Cambridgeshire, in exchange for *nine pounds of the purest gold*, little Strethall has remained largely unchanged since. This is lucky because Aethelred's curse on anyone who would undo the gift is quite spectacular. Among other torments, they risk being 'punished in the melancholy fires of foolishness' and 'joined with Judas, the betrayer of Christ'. And so, while in the words of one historian, Strethall has been *confiscated, rented, bequeathed, bestowed, usurped, and given in dower* over the centuries, it survives intact as one of the smallest parishes in the country. Just 629 acres of clay farmland and chalk downland, ten houses, ten fields and an ancient church. Perhaps intact too as a remnant of Roman countryside that has survived the road that ran through the heart of it.

Its shape suggests that it was part of a Roman estate, a *territorium* encircling Great Chesterford. There is some evidence of metalworking, but Roman fieldworkers left few records beyond the pattern of fields, the spolia of brick and tile in the church walls, and the ubiquitous, tell-tale pottery alongside the road. Huddled south of the farmland, the modern village sits squeezed into the south-western corner of the parish.

The Romano-British forebears, working fields gathered into segments of a pie, were not so different from those who came after them and shaped a medieval field system that would still be in place as recently as the nineteenth century: fields divided

into furlongs, in turn divided into narrow strips of land. Here are ten fields beautifully filleted into 227 parcels: a pattern engraved on the first large-scale Ordnance Survey map and still visible today from the air in the ghosts of field baulks and lynchets that terrace the steep fields tumbling into the Cam valley.

It would not be too surprising to meet Mabel the widow on a headland, or Hugh Buc, or Elias the son of William, or any one of the other labourers who in 1222 worked the manor soil in payment for their own half virgate of land; exchanging toil and money for older dues: for *whitepund* (a payment of ale), winesilver (of wine) or even scharpenny (of dung).

The tiny church of St Mary the Virgin, with its Anglo-Saxon origins, contains Roman brick and tile in its walls, thought to have been plundered from the site of a nearby Romano-British farmstead. Its location away from the houses, but very near to the road – like the churches at Braughing, Brent Pelham and Meesden – might be another historical clue along with the mid-Saxon pottery found there. Both attest to the notion that some rural settlements were established from scratch alongside Roman roads in the middle Anglo-Saxon period, before moving away from them in later years, perhaps as the roads lost their importance in the lives of the villagers.

♦ ♦ ♦

The eye is enticed by a path, and the mind's eye also.
The imagination cannot help but pursue a line in the
land – onwards in space, but also backwards in time to
the histories of a route and its previous followers.

Robert Macfarlane, *The Old Ways* (2012)

♦ ♦ ♦

The soil darkens with the silt of centuries washed down off the slopes to enrich the valleys and bury the roads. An old track makes an arc here. In 1949, the archaeologist M.R. Hull notified the Ordnance Survey that this was the line of the road, but when a field investigator walked south this way the following spring they found nothing. Another correspondent disagreed with Hull; Major John Brinson placed the line of RR21b along the eastern edge of the field.

Brinson was right. The road shadows the parish boundary, keeping to its direct line. Here the sweeping track meets that boundary running north-south and we are finally on the section of the modern Icknield Way trail – a tree-lined terrace way between two fields. The poet Edward Thomas might have been describing it when he wrote the lines, 'and the path that looks / As if it led on to some legendary / Or fancied place where men have wished to go'.

Thomas might have walked it when he went in search of the Icknield Way, that great, long-distance, prehistoric ridgeway littered with stone axes and burial mounds. *Icknield Way*. Those two words support a great weight of history, of millennia of travel and more recently of travel writing. Anyone who doubts that roads are romantic need only read the opening chapter of Thomas's book on the Icknield Way, in which he invokes the ways of literature, of Bunyan and Malory. It is a lyrical, digressive book and a good starting point for anyone wanting to write about walking and looking.

'I could not find a beginning or an end of the Icknield Way,' he writes. 'It is thus a symbol of mortal things with their beginnings and ends always in immortal darkness.'

After fifty pages of detailed history, myth, charters, deeds and much speculation and supposition, Thomas concludes, pragmatically for a poet, that 'The Icknield Way is sufficiently explained as the chief surviving road connecting East Anglia and the whole eastern half of the regions north of the Thames, with the west and the western half of the south of England.' No one knows its true course. The best that can be said is that it was a routeway from Thetford, in Norfolk, to Wanborough, in Wiltshire. The consensus is that it is an 'ancient complex of branching pathways,' writes landscape historian Richard Muir.

> In attempting to visualise the great highways, we should not picture a single deeply worn and bustling routeway, but rather wide corridors or zones of movement containing many little trackways which follow roughly parallel courses, branching, widening, merging and narrowing to pick their individual ways through the local terrain within the broad highway zones.

The sweep of the path, the crescent of the Icknield Way, helps organise the fields here, the strips following its shape, so naturally and pleasingly; reluctantly I remember Thomas's complaint against straight roads: he is upset by the modern roads of the motorist – this before the First World War – and in condemning them ends up condemning Roman roads as well: 'If we make roads outright and rapidly for a definite purpose, they may perish as rapidly ... and their ancient predecessors live on to smile at their ambition.' Our road did not perish rapidly, dismissed ignominiously, punished for its arrogance. The evidence proves otherwise, but perhaps here for a short stretch, its ancient predecessor is smiling. Here is where our road and the Icknield Way intertwine and become one.

As I approach it for the first time, I expect to find a clear and ancient trail to follow and find little to guide me until I reach the hawthorned terrace way to a fancied place. Not the road, I think, but a stepped field boundary formed by soil banking up against it over the centuries? James Albone, in his thoughtful thesis, has written of another similar landscape where the 'presence of ridge and furrow earthworks overlying the Roman road ... provides a strong indication that it must have fallen out of use as a continuous long-distance routeway by, or at least during, the medieval period'. And studying the old and not so old maps, we might suppose the same happened here.

My attention is caught by signs of excavation in the field bank to my left. Badgers have been raising mighty earthworks, building their own tumuli from great spoils of chalk scored with powerful claw marks. I glance at the spill, hoping to find something antique thrown out of the earth, and marvel at the sheer quantity of material heaped by the creatures. The name of Tasciovanus, the chieftain who once ruled here, means 'badger killer', perhaps with good reason.

For the first time since I stepped out of Drage's Mead in Braughing, the outside world intrudes. The M11 is below and ahead, a great bow of noise and impatience. I cross the footbridge. If the road is below, where it should be, it is deep beneath the modern debris of motorway architecture.

While Thomas didn't come this way, in more recent times his great disciple Robert Macfarlane did. He stood on the bridge where I am standing. In one of his many beautiful meditations on paths he wrote simply, 'Following them, we are reading one of the earliest stories, told not in print but in footprint.' He invoked the writer and artist John Emslie who walked the Icknield Way in the late nineteenth century and claimed to have met people who said it went all around the world, to the fiery mountains, from sea to sea. 'If you keep along it and travel on you will come back to the place you started from', which is true in a multitude of ways.

I rested on the motorway bridge where Macfarlane had rested and watched the rush of cars as he had, contemplating the meeting of the Icknield Way and the M11. It is a meeting with a Roman road too, as archaeologists discovered in 1977, racing to keep ahead of the opening of the motorway. Down there, marooned by the asphalt and its vortex of traffic, in a tear-shaped plot of land they found our road.

♦ ♦ ♦

> The ancient world ... was henceforth separated from their own by an unbridgeable historical caesura. It was this historical shock ... that lies at the basis of the modern search for ancient fragments, and endows the very term fragment with an emotional tone connoting loss, injury and deprivation ... It was Petrarch who first extended the use of the word fragmentum to encompass with deep pathos all that was left over from the fall of Rome.
>
> Glen W. Most, 'On Fragments' (2009)

♦ ♦ ♦

In 1774, the antiquary Edward King watched the legions pass through Great Chesterford's south gate and described in detail the marching order. They came north along our road, led by the future emperor Vespasian:

> Those auxiliaries which were lightly armed, and the archers, marched first; that they might prevent any sudden insults from the enemy; and might search the woods that looked suspicious, and were capable of

> ambuscades. – Next to these followed that part of the Romans, which was most completely armed; both horse and foot; (usually called the heavy armed.)

Next came the surveyors who would lay out the camp and after them the men who made the roads they marched on, 'such as were to make the roads even, and straight; and if it were anywhere rough, and hard to be passed over, to plain it; and to cut down the woods that hindered their march; that the army might not be in distress, or tired with their marching'.

Then came the siege engines, followed by the senior officers and their guards with lance and bucklers. Next the eagle bearers, the ensigns and the trumpeters, all followed by the main body of the army, six men in each rank, wearing breastplates and helmets, two swords, a spear and a long buckler. They didn't carry just weapons; here too were the tools needed to build their camps: a saw, a basket, two axes, a thong of leather and a hook. It was a formidable burden. As much as fifty kilograms a man by modern estimates, but since the army reforms of the second century BCE general Gaius Marius, Roman military training had equipped them well for the ordeal. They were Marius' mules, expected to cover nearly twenty miles every five hours on a forced march, although they were a fair bit slower with a large baggage train. This was the purpose of Roman roads. To hurry the legions to battle or camp. 'Speed in war is more important than courage' was the famous maxim of the Roman military theorist Vegetius.

Before King came to see the Roman ruins at Chesterford, his imagination had been fed by the first-century historian

Josephus's description of Vespasian and the Roman army marching on Galilee in the first Jewish War – some twenty years after Vespasian led the II Augusta Legion in the invasion of Britain, and three years before he would wrestle with his rivals for the purple in the civil wars of 69 CE.

'Nothing can be more interesting to us, than to attend to his minute description of the order of marching,' wrote King, explaining how Josephus conjured the ghostly army in his mind's eye:

> It really carries us back, in imagination, to the very scenes that presented themselves, when either Suetonius Paulinus or Agricola, or even Vespasian himself, and Titus, marched, in this Island, from any one of those very Castra we are describing, or from any one of their inferior camps, and stations, to another ... Thus, by this intelligent Author, we are brought, almost to stand in imagination, on the original walls of Chesterford.

He was lucky to see those walls still, let alone the legion afoot. Throughout the 1700s they had been under attack. William Stukeley, half a century before King, had lamented that Chesterford's walls were being rapidly dismantled: 'In one part they have been long digging this wall up for materials in building and mending the roads.' A year later he wrote to Roger Gale, recalling, 'I saw the wall to the foundation; they are pulling it up with much labour to mend their highways, though materials might be had at easier charge as near, for which I heartily anathematised them.' A few years later, the engraver Joseph Strutt would write disconsolately that the walls had been 'stubbed down'. An ignominious word, *stubbed*, for these once mighty defences raised with such labour.

So King knows he is preserving their memory when he describes what is left in his vast and charming *Munimenta Antiqua*, in the chapter 'Observations on the Works of the Roman in this Island – And Particularly on those of a military kind'. He writes:

> At Chesterford, in Essex, are the traces of another great Roman Castrum; now almost levelled with the ground. On digging, however, into the bank, or apparent vallum, still existing, there appear in numbers of places, the manifest foundations of the original great wall. It surrounded the whole of this great Castrum, which was, like that at Richborough, nearly in the figure of a square; but had the corners rounded off, more than those at Caster.

King describes the walls in loving detail. They were made of flint and brick 'very pale red; but the other of a deep red colour, with an inward substance of a deep blueish colour; plainly bearing the marks, to this hour, of the streakiness, and rude working up of the clay'. It produced 'a very beautiful effect to the eye'.

I warm to Edward King, for the evidence he has saved for us, his attention to detail, his appreciation that the texture and colour of an old brick might not only be of interest and of evidential value, but also beautiful. For his great learning too, his obsession, his eccentric range of interests, but most of all his ability to pull all this together and imagine the past back to life.

King drew a diagram of the walls and on the side nearest the River Cam he placed a gate, calling it the *Decuman* gate. He was writing at a time when antiquaries didn't distinguish between civil and military remains in Britain; everything was martial, so he treats what we now know were Great Chesterford's town walls as if they surrounded a military camp.

'In this wall, the place of the great Decuman gate may plainly be traced,' he says, telling us that there were four main gates: the *Decuman, postern, praetorian* and *second principal.*

> The Decuman gate; or largest gate of all; which took its very name, from being wide enough to permit ten men at least to march through it abreast; and which always conveyed such an idea of magnificent dimensions; that the very word decumanus was classically used by the Romans, to signify anything that was both huge, and fair; – beautiful, and of vast size.

At Great Chesterford, King decided that the southern gate must have been this most magnificent of gates because there it was best defended by the river.

As he grew older, King held ever stranger views and as the end of the eighteenth century approached he became more convinced of the Second Coming, looking for signs in scripture and finding passages that prophesied the course of the French Revolution. He grew obsessed with secret ways and hidden passages, writing about hiding pits and imagining the existence of false entrances into castles built to confuse the invader. He was perfectly equipped to find our secret way running through his great *Decuman* gate and find it he did.

He added it to his drawing: 'For there appears to have been a broad raised paved way, constructed of flints and mortar, passing directly through the gate; and carried out quite across the ditch surrounding the castrum, and even beyond it.' Though he didn't know where it went and gave it no name, it is the earliest description we have of RR21b and the only road on King's plan. He adds ominously that there used to be the foundations of another way passing through the western gate but the locals 'were removing and carrying away the stones of

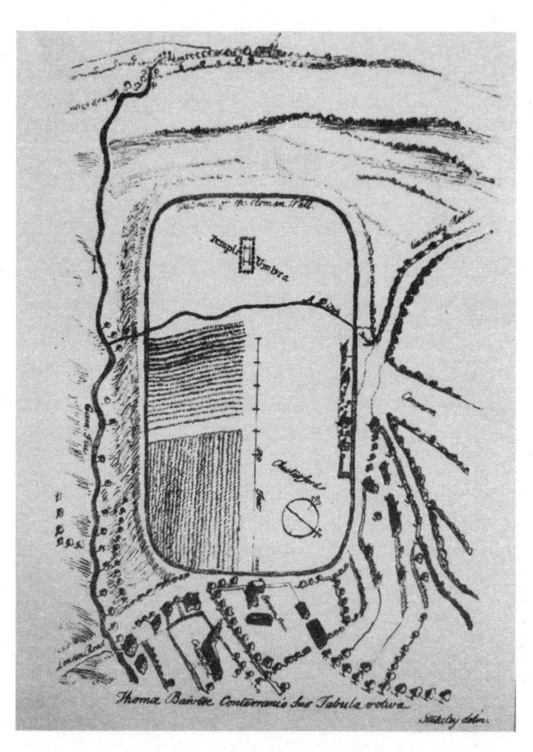

the pavement as fast as they could, when I saw it in the year 1774'. Our road would no doubt meet a similar fate. It too would finally be torn up and scavenged, leaving only a ghost road seen for the first time from the air in the early 1970s and still clearly visible today on Google Earth. Beginning at the edge of the River Cam and crossing a field called Borough Ditch Shot – an incongruous smudge, 140 metres long.

♦ ♦ ♦

Stop to taste the pendulous elderberries as you follow the footpath down from the motorway bridge round a sheltered trail. Was this holloway route the way the road took into the Roman town or an older way, a newer way even, or both? A way that pre-dates and outlasts the Roman way. We know it was in use when the road and walls were being stripped, because in about 1711, a miller – a 'fortunate miller' – discovered a hoard of Roman coins there, along with several urns, a bronze head, burned bones and, beneath a thick bronze bowl, a bar of gold, shaped like a horse's bit and said to be worth as much as £600.

Two hundred years after Edward King's visit they found the road again. If 1976 had been so hot that it revealed the connecting stretch of road near Bozen Green at the beginning of our journey, the following year saw such heavy rainfall that the Cam flooded, breaking its banks and uncovering a river crossing: a series of wooden stakes, with limestone, flints, tiles and mortar under the water in a riverbed that was solid with debris. The remains of a paved ford or bridge. The grid reference is on our line.

The late 1970s saw the gradual opening of the M11, and before its cheap, cost-saving concrete surface could be poured, archaeologists decided to investigate further the aerial ghost road, joining both Edward King's south gate and the recently uncovered river crossing. A little way to the south-west in a meadow unploughed for over a century – now the middle of an island formed by the M11 slip road at Junction 9 – they dug a trench. The *agger* they found was seven metres wide and fifty-five centimetres thick, the original surface of flint and clay worn hollow by centuries of traffic despite repairs that had been made with larger flints and gravel. Within the surface were the sherds of jars, porridgy blue-grey and dark brown, thought to have been thrown into the gravel pits quarried to make the road.

I could finally join the dots with confidence. The dot where I thought the line changed direction and pointed this way, nearly three miles behind me in the dip between Bixett and Ann's Wood; the dot through a cropmark west of Howe Wood; the dots of the excavation in the meadow, in the riverbed and at the cropmark within the lost walls of Great Chesterford's Roman town, where some 250 years ago, Edward King saw the road still passing through a gate. A single straight line for us to march along in the footsteps of King's revenants, past junction 9 of the M11, dodging the traffic, past a Roman glass and pottery warehouse, the hints of a Roman temple and a burial ground, where urns and bones abide in the ground south of the river, over the ford or bridge to walls of flint ragstone where King and Stukeley stood.

The walling of a town in Roman Britain was a major undertaking. Most towns with walls saw their defences evolve over two or three centuries. Typically, they began with an earthwork in the second century. In the third century came a stone wall, which might be upgraded with towers in the fourth. Great Chesterford, however, was one of only a handful of towns that appears to have had its huge stone wall built out of the blue in the middle of the fourth century. Why did it suddenly need such elaborate and costly defences? As with so much of the archaeological evidence, the temptation is to link it to known historical events. The year 367 CE saw the start of the Barbarian Conspiracy, when Britannia came under attack from sea and land by the Saxons, Picts and Scots – acting in concert. For two years, the raiders spread mayhem and bloodshed as far south as London and the Romano-British army mutinied, with desertions becoming rife. Eventually, Theodosius, the father of the future emperor Theodosius I, arrived in Britain with an expeditionary force and after securing London proceeded to regain control of the country – a feat for which he won the title Count of Britain. Historians have suggested that Great Chesterford was walled both against future attack and so that it could act as a military supply base for the campaign to retake Britain. The town may also have been part of the hinterland of Saxon shore defences, a base from where reinforcements could hurry into East Anglia if sea-borne raiders broke through the line of coastal forts.

We have computer-generated maps of the town now, precise, but lacking the charm of the rough sketches that the antiquaries made. The course of the wall has been charted with the grainy precision of geophysics. The earth's magnetic resistance probed in the hope of encountering artificial things that interfere with it. The readouts look like brass rubbings of the buried town. The dark line of the wall nearest to the river is unmistakable. The road is there too with its ditches. It begins at the river, eleven metres wide, and runs through the wall, narrowing as it passes a large courtyard building to meet other roads in the large marketplace or *forum* of the second-largest Roman town in Essex after Colchester. Here are disturbances in the soil made by long-forgotten shrines, temples and a blacksmith's. Here in Roman times the gods would have been there to welcome you: Venus, Mercury and, most potent of all, Jupiter. The king of the gods looking down from the heavens. We know because a blacksmith's trough was found in 1803, probably near the mill where the eighteenth-century miller hoarded his treasure. This crude trough, hacked from a larger stone, has been called the most important find in the whole of the town. Now in the British Museum, it is all that remains of the octagonal base of a towering Jupiter column that raised the god high over Great Chesterford. The blacksmith needed just half of the base to hold his water, so only some of its niches survive. There would originally have been seven; one for each day of the week. One niche contains a figure that was once Venus holding her mirror, to represent Friday. Wednesday is Mercury with his caduceus, and for Tuesday, part of the god Mars with his long spear – both barely recognisable, even to experts. It might be another Jupiter in the Thursday hollow. Hacked and weathered, worn and shaped by time, the stone has slowly come to emulate the rough stones and chalk and clay lands, the valleys and landforms over which the road has come. A fine destination.

Except the road is too old. That pottery found in its surface, not Roman but native, the porridgy and blue-grey remnants of

large storage jars, patterned with vertical furrows. Dark-brown and flint-tempered ware too, thrown on a wheel in the first century CE. Which leaves us with a first-century road surface heading for a fourth-century gateway leading to a second-century marketplace. This was the destination in space, but not in time. Where was the road headed when it was first driven through the countryside? Why was it built? If they chose Great Chesterford to play a crucial role in the military adventures of the closing years of the occupation, might it not have been vital in earlier times too, perhaps even at the time of the most celebrated challenge to the Romans in the entire history of Roman Britain?

◆ ◆ ◆

An archaeological layer of terrible violence, a band of ashes seven metres underground, the blackened remains of wattle and daub, Roman armour and human skulls; this is what Queen Boudicca and her uprising in 60–61 CE has bequeathed us. If the archaeological boundary between Iron Age and post-conquest Roman Britain is vague, not so that between pre- and post-Boudicca. Consider the head of a Roman emperor. Found by a schoolboy playing in the River Alde in Suffolk in 1907, it had been hacked and torn from a life-size bronze statue by the vengeful army of Britons as they rampaged through Britannia's first Roman colony at Colchester. Or so the story goes. Today, from its display case in the British Museum, vacant black eye sockets stare at you from under a thick Roman fringe parted over the right eye. Based on the hunches of historians, it was said to be the head of Claudius wrested from a toppled statue, probably at the temple to the emperor, who had become a god. Was it later flung in the river by someone wishing to get rid of their booty in the aftermath of the rebellion? Or placed there ritualistically, a sacrifice to much older deities. It is now thought to be the head of Claudius's infamous successor Nero, emperor when south-eastern Britain rose up in fury against the invaders. The British Museum's description of the head claims it was removed 'by a heavy blow to the back of the *skull*'. My italics. A slip perhaps, a transference, because bronze heads do not normally have skulls, but someone attacking it might imagine that they do. The description captures the bloodlust in the minds of those who smashed the head from the statue and conjures 'Celtic' head-hunters on the rampage. A recent forensic analysis of the sculpture also reads like a post-mortem report. Here was a violent *decapitation*, a *series of chopping punctures*, a *ripping* and *distorting* of the head: 'Nine or 10 separate blows evident above the left clavicle and around the neck appear to have been created by a single iron axe, mattock or small entrenching tool ... One, possibly two, hefty blows to the back of the head, ostensibly with a blunt object.' These were delivered by a second *assailant*.

Here is the anger and rage of an oppressed people against Rome. There is nothing really to link the head to Colchester. If it is Nero, it's possible that the statue was vandalised during the *damnatio memoriae* of the reviled emperor after his suicide, when his image was deliberately destroyed across the empire. Having quashed the Claudius hypothesis, the authors of the post-mortem have enough imagination and good sense to cling to traditional and neatly satisfying guesswork, writing that the most likely scenario is that this provincial bronze statue of Rome's fifth emperor was 'toppled and decapitated during the Boudiccan Revolt of 60/61. The final deposition of

the head in a watery context at the boundary between the Iceni and Trinovantes tribes was probably a religious or ritualised act as an offering to native deities following the destruction of a major Roman urban, religious or military centre.'

There is an even better memorial to the horror visited upon Colchester: a tombstone from the city. Nearly two metres high, it is a statue of a Roman soldier standing in an arched stone niche on a block carved with the letters that tell us, among other things, that this was Marcus Favonius Facilis, a centurion of the XX Valeria Victrix Legion. Marcus has an uncannily similar face to the bronze head from the river. Perhaps it's the same staring eye sockets from beyond the grave. Marcus grasps the pommel of a sword in his left hand and leans on a centurion's stick in his right. Here is no slashing or hacking or violent blow. The fate of the monument carries a more subtle echo across the centuries. Dating from before the revolt and found in 1868 near to a lead cylinder containing burned bones, this two-thousand-year-old stone looks fresh from the stonemason's yard. It has been protected and preserved from time and weather, because it was knocked onto its face. By the passing rebels? For me – improbably, remarkably – the stone's pristine condition freezes in time a momentary, transient, intangible, human act of intense emotion: the hurling down of the hated Roman all those centuries ago.

We know the Boudiccan revolt through such moments, captured in stone, in bronze, in ash, but also thanks to the mythmaking of two Roman authors. Tacitus and Cassius Dio both relished this story of a warrior queen – as they knew their Roman readers would too. The idea of a woman leading an army was exotic and alien and Boudicca had her perfect foil in the despised memory of the emperor Nero, who was said to be less virile than the barbarian queen. As others have pointed out, we have no separate evidence for her existence. Everything we know of one of the great characters and set-pieces of British history was gifted us by an admiring and sensationalising enemy.

It is less than twenty years after the Roman invasion that the figure of this outraged woman strides into the history of Roman Britain. We picture her shaking a spear from the back of a British war chariot, tall, with a piercing glance, her long auburn hair flowing out behind as she incites a vast and ferocious army of Britons to a war of terror that would nearly put an early end to Roman rule in Britain.

According to the Roman historians, the first signs of trouble were dire portents in the blackness of night, when wailing could be heard coming from the theatre, and barbarian voices shouted and laughed in the senate house, but no one was there, at least no one living. On the banks of the Thames, houses were seen under water, presaging the fall of the city. Blood pooled in the estuary and corpses floated out to sea. 'For no apparent reason,' wrote Tacitus, 'the statue of Victory at Camulodunum fell, with its back turned as if in retreat from the enemy. Women, converted into maniacs by excitement, cried that destruction was at hand.'

Boudicca was the widow of Prasutagus of the Iceni in East Anglia, a client king of Rome, who had recently died, leaving half of his wealth to Nero as death duty, or rather as protection money to the gangster emperor. His ruse failed. Perhaps the province's Roman procurator and his officials scorned a female ruler or just decided it was the right moment to annex the Iceni lands. The invaders pillaged the royal household and when Boudicca protested, she was beaten and her daughters raped. It was the catalyst for revolt and the tribe rose up against their oppressors.

'You have discovered the difference between freedom in humble circumstances and slavery amid riches,' shouted Boudicca to the rebels in a speech put into her mouth by the Roman authors. Her people marched south in their thousands to join with their allies the Trinovantes.

The impulse for rebellion was more complex than the rage of a vengeful queen. Here too was the bottled-up resentment of a people oppressed, their lands seized. Colchester had been turned over to retired soldiers, who proceeded to seize more land at will. The overwhelming burden of taxes, and the payment to Rome of huge loans (that had suddenly been called in) also helped create the conditions for the war. As did tribal enmities, particularly between the Trinovantes and their rivals to the west, the Catuvellauni, who, despite their initial resistance, may have been thriving under their new masters. We have to imagine less a spontaneous uprising and more a carefully planned operation. Surely it was no accident that at the moment the tribes fell on Colchester, the Roman governor was hundreds of miles away with two of the province's four legions, fighting a campaign in Anglesey against the druids. Some have suggested that the slaughter of the druids may even have played its part in inciting the rebellion.

As the Britons rampaged through the streets, the townspeople took shelter in the temple. In Robert Graves' *Claudius the*

God, the emperor resists deification and is appalled to hear that a temple has been built in his name in Britain, yet is eventually persuaded to accept the honour. More likely it had been built after his death six years before (in 54 CE) at the expense of the local British population – hence the loans. The temple proved a poor refuge for the colonials, and the small band of soldiers who had been sent to rescue them. They held out for two days, but once the Britons had finished plundering and despoiling the town (hacking the heads off statues and throwing down tombstones), the temple was put to the torch and all inside were massacred unprotected by a reluctant, impotent god.

Ironically, the military invasion roads of Watling Street and Ermine Street speeded the fury of the Iceni and their allies as they killed and burned their way to the trading post of Londinium. Much of the savagery appears to have been focused on places where foreigners were thriving, not just those working for the state, but merchants and craftsmen from the continent. London 'thronged with merchants' and was 'a famous centre of commerce', Tacitus tells us.

On their way to London, Boudicca's army encountered and destroyed a battle group of the IX Hispana Legion that had rushed from their fort at Longthorpe, in Cambridgeshire, to head off the Britons. The battle is traditionally said to have been in a marshy field, Sharpfight Meadow, next to the River Stour, in Suffolk. The legate of the Ninth only just escaped the field with his cavalry. In London, the procurator, who was largely responsible for the incendiary treatment of the Iceni, fled Britain for Gaul, never to return. By now the governor Suetonius Paulinus had raced back from Wales with a small contingent of troops, probably with his staff officer Julius Agricola, the future governor of Britain and the father-in-law of the historian Tacitus, our main source. Suetonius beat the rebels to London, but on hearing what had happened to the Ninth and in the face of overwhelming odds – writing a hundred years later, Cassius Dio put the number of rebels at 230,000 – Paulinus decided to sacrifice the future capital and, ignoring the pleas of the Londoners, retreated north to link up with the legions marching from Wales. He took with him only those who could keep up; those too weak, too young or too elderly were left to a dreadful fate. Boudicca razed London to the ground.

With no one to stand in their way, the Britons headed north towards St Albans in Hertfordshire, in search of booty, say the Roman authors, but perhaps also to destroy the old capital of their Catuvellauni enemies. There they hanged, burned and crucified their unlucky victims. Dio recounts even worse war crimes. Seventy thousand fell at the hands of the rebels.

Meanwhile, Paulinus had met with the XIV Gemina Legion, elements of XX Valeria Victrix and auxiliary cohorts returning from the war on the druids. Somewhere north of Hertfordshire, the governor chose a hillside flanked by woodland, probably near Watling Street. It is one of those unknown battle sites scattered throughout English history that provide a lifetime of distraction for historians and enthusiasts. The huge but ill-disciplined British force that had previously only faced a battle group took the field against a much larger army of hardened Roman legionaries, who had fallen back to a position of the governor's choice and were ready and waiting.

What happened that day has been called the Battle of Watling Street. The writer John Higgs suggested that it was the largest number of British deaths in a single day until the First World War and probably the largest single gathering in prehistoric Britain. The victors tell us that after the Britons fell back against their own vast wagon train under an initial javelin attack, eighty thousand of Boudicca's soldiers met their end (more than twice the number said to have been killed at Brunanburh in 937 and nearly three times as many as slain at Towton in 1461 during the Wars of the Roses, often cited as the bloodiest battle in British history). Tacitus wrote that only four hundred Roman soldiers died.

It was one of the worst uprisings in Roman imperial history. Nero nearly withdrew the legions from Britain, but the ensuing chaos and reprisals hurt the Britons immeasurably more. They had neglected the harvest, expecting to plunder Roman supplies, and now faced famine. As for Boudicca, she poisoned herself, like all good epic heroines. For that, she lives on in myth and legend, the site of her reportedly rich burial still hotly contested by towns and villages wishing to claim this strange and savage national hero for their own.

◆ ◆ ◆

While investigating traces of Great Chesterford's Roman town in 1940, Major John Brinson found a piece of the aftermath of Boudicca's revolt: a V-shaped ditch, four metres deep with a squared-off shovel slot at the bottom, an ankle breaker. To the archaeological eye, it looked like a military ditch, a *fossa fastigata*, the last remnant of the outer perimeter of a permanent Roman fort, not walled, but enclosed by a single ditch and earthbank once topped with a wooden staked palisade.

It was certainly in the right place for a fort: occupying a strategically important position on the River Cam and the Icknield Way, guarding the approaches to London from Icenian territory. 'The more the topography of the district is studied the clearer the military importance of the site becomes, and the greater the likelihood therefore of its having been a military station in the middle of the 1st century A.D.,' wrote the eminent archaeologist Cyril Fox, even before evidence of a fort had been found.

Further investigations over the years uncovered other short sections of the ditch and a plan projecting its outline soon found its way onto maps. The fort was early and short-lived. It could have been built in the years immediately after the invasion, but the best clue is the absence of any Claudian pottery in the ditches. It all dates from the mid-50s to about 70 CE, during the reigns of Nero and the first of the Flavians, Vespasian – to the time of the Boudiccan revolt and its repercussions.

At a little under thirteen and a half hectares, it would have been a large fort, the second largest in Essex after Colchester. Not big enough for a legion, but certainly for a vexillation or battle group of one.

Who was it built for? We need Tacitus again. He wrote that Suetonius embarked on a campaign of vengeance. Those who had supported the uprising were 'harried with fire and sword'. An intelligent and sympathetic provincial procurator, who – out of compassion or because he worried there would be no one left to pay taxes – eventually had the governor replaced so that he could begin the process of rebuilding and pacifying the province, as well as ensuring nothing like the revolt could happen again. After the defeat of Boudicca, 'the whole army was united and kept under canvas to finish the war,' wrote Tacitus. 'The emperor reinforced it with 2,000 legionnaires, eight auxiliary cohorts and 1,000 cavalry from Germany. On their arrival, the IX Hispana was brought up to strength and the auxiliaries were placed in new winter quarters.'

The word used for winter quarters was *hibernacula*, and suggests a single fort. Since the late 1970s, a consensus has formed around the idea that this single fort was built at Great Chesterford. It's the right size, from the right period and in the right location. Yet the evidence is slight. Its outline is based on small stretches of ditch, less than half of the eastern perimeter of the fort, and less than a quarter of the northern ditch, but with a distinctive corner section, rounded like a playing card. Nothing of the southern or western ditches has been found.

The roads help. In the summer of 1961, Dr J.K. St Joseph flew over the field called Borough Ditch Shot one morning and took one of the oblique photographs he was best known for. Described by his biographer as a geologist, archaeologist and aerial photographer, St Joseph stands second only to O.G.S. Crawford in the pantheon of aerial archaeologists and in some respects surpassed his friend and mentor. The air unit at Cambridge that he founded and headed from the 1940s until the 1980s discovered over 40 Roman garrison forts and over 185 temporary camps. It was claimed that in just a few hours' flying time in 1945, 'St Joseph discovered more Roman military sites in the North than had come to be known in the previous two hundred years.' In 35 days in the hot summer of 1949 alone, he clocked up an astonishing 154 hours in the air.

The photograph St Joseph took of Borough Ditch Shot clearly shows the cropmarks of three roads meeting in the field, within the circuit of the later town walls. They meet exactly where the elusive south ditch of the fort was projected. The road crossing the River Cam from the south-west is RR21b. So let us sketch in the fort's southern gate at the meeting of the roads as we stand in the obscuring stubble, golden and vast, twenty-five acres of it, fringed by dark-green hedges. Once more squinting into the sun at something that is and isn't there.

Archaeologists contend that the ditches they have traced were deliberately backfilled before 70 CE. The fort was built for a purpose and then vacated, while a settlement that would become a town grew outside its south gate.

The fort was abandoned, but the road remained.

◆ ◆ ◆

Roman Britain was built on a great military transport network, fashioned road by road as necessity demanded, for armies, their supply trains, their scouts and their couriers to move along quickly in all weathers at all times of the year. RR21b was one short line on this complex graph, built from a major junction to supply a new fort after the Boudiccan revolt, to speed troops on their command and control missions.

For four hundred years, Britain was occupied by the troops of the empire. Throughout much of the occupation, the

Romans stationed some 12 per cent of their army in its tiny northernmost province. The story of Roman Britain that we have encountered would suggest that even after much of the country had been pacified, large numbers of troops needed to move rapidly along the roads throughout all the centuries of occupation: to react to uprisings, raids, invasions, mutinies and usurpations. The army would always have needed to act as a police force along the roads, protecting against brigandage, escorting lead and silver from the mines, collecting taxes and guarding convoys of coin to pay the legions or grain to feed them. The military necessity for the roads never went away. They were first and foremost the army's transport conduits, but they came to be other things too and, in time, secondary roads were built with more than one purpose in mind.

In places they were also temporary frontiers and boundaries following lines surveyed to define territories – of client kingdoms, of land distributed to Roman troops – or to limit the influence of British tribes. They were for transporting ores from the mines, crops from the farms, stone from the quarries and goods to market. They were also expressions of power, of the incredible feats of mathematics and engineering that mastered the landscape, a shock and awe tactic on the one hand and the means for the Romanisation of a territory, at least of the elites, and for satisfying their new Roman tastes – for pottery, say.

Fragments of jars and dishes help us to date the fort, the roads that led to it and the settlements alongside it, but they play an even more important part in the later history and survival of our road long after the fort had gone. The first clues for this lie in embarrassing abundance across acres of ploughland, just south of where we started the journey. We must return to the beginning to get to the end.

The fields at Bromley Hall farm in Much Hadham, a few miles south of Braughing, spawn sherds of pottery, a crop of rims, bases and handles, fragments that reassemble into the daily necessities of Roman cooking and dining. Within the shadow of ancient Caley Wood, the land is sprawling and lonely and broken. When a section of it was field-walked by the Braughing archaeology group in the 2000s, they found an extraordinary fourteen and a half potsherds per square metre – that was just the average; some sections contained much higher densities – but fourteen and a half means there were somewhere in the region of thirty-six million pieces of salt and pepper grey ware and upmarket orange burnished ware for the dinner table. No one has yet found the boundary of the area, not a point where the average diminishes.

This was where Romano-British potters crafted bowls and flagons for nearly four hundred years. The first kiln was found by accident in the 1960s. When the second was unearthed, it contained nearly half a tonne of pottery. These Hadham ware products, as they came to be known, had been shaped and fired from the local clay as early as the late Iron Age, around the time of the invasion, although the potters would not be at their busiest for another three hundred years.

Picture this landscape through the seasons long ago. In autumn the worker digging clay. In winter laying it out, weathering it and tempering it so that when spring came they could start the wheels turning and throw the flagons and dishes and the ever-popular large globular bowls, burnished by hand to make the clay shine. In late spring, early summer, some built the kilns, while others gathered fuel or readied the pots for firing: the rough reduced wares or grey wares would be fired in sealed kilns, 'reduced' because the oxygen was kept out of the process; the fancy orange burnished ware would be oxidised in kilns with a chimney hole, the temperature and oxygen expertly managed and monitored.

Where were these pots going?

Beneath the eighteenth-century Bishop's House, just beyond where the Great Chesterford town walls once ran, archaeologists have unearthed and bagged another multitude of sherds. Here, they were not scattered across fields but usefully stratified, and so datable. They have been stored carefully in little bags, hundreds of them in boxes in the archives of Saffron Walden Museum. Slide open the grey archaeology racks along their tracks to reveal long, light-grey shelves from floor to ceiling, laden with the treasures from digs: sheep bones – 'mandibles and maxilla' – horse bones, antiquarian finds, stones, shells, flints, daub, slag, mortar and box after box from various sites marked simply 'Sherds' or 'Roman pottery' or 'Misc. Roman Pot'.

Box 236 of site GC24 is a strong-cornered cardboard box of amphorae, Samian and fat, clear plastic bags of 'Illustrated Roman pot'. These are the characteristic pieces. Those that can be identified as coming from a particular type of vessel. Their shape and fabric known and perhaps more besides: their date and origin and distribution.

Fractured triangles of rims and bases in burnished blacks and oranges, some belonging with each other, so painstakingly glued into larger fragments. Of the thirty bags that contain samples of pot illustrating the finds by type, twenty-five are from Hadham. In fact, Hadham ware makes up over 50 per cent of the finds by weight.

Archaeologists have plotted the growing popularity of Hadham ware in Great Chesterford. It is found in ever-increasing numbers from the Flavian period, shortly after the road is built, until the bitter end, the fine orange ware booming when the supply of Samian dried up with the troubles on the continent.

We read that 'one of the outstanding features of pottery assemblages from Great Chesterford is the quantity of material from the Hadham kilns, which increases throughout the Roman period ... It appears to have completely dominated the market for "black wares" in the third and fourth centuries in Great Chesterford to a degree not seen elsewhere in Essex.' Not just the black wares but the grey wares and red wares also. The Hadham industry had gained a 'virtual stranglehold' over pottery supply to Great Chesterford by the fourth century. Not only there. It is found widely throughout the local area and as far away as the continent. There is so much Hadham ware in the archaeological record that the handful of kilns found here can only be a tiny part of the story waiting to be discovered. Archaeologists think there must have been a hundred or more kiln sites over a much greater area than merely the Bromley Hall fields.

Also telling is the lack of other types of pottery that are common elsewhere. That makes it 'probable that Roman Great Chesterford acted as a regional market centre for the redistribution of Hadham wares,' say the archaeologists. Did our road outlive the fort it was built for and the decline of

Braughing because it came to be a vector of trade for the Hadham pottery industry? That doesn't meant that its primary role stopped being a military one, and we might pause to ask who was buying all that pottery within those impressive defensive town walls. Throughout the history of Roman Britain, the largest buyer was always the army.

The trade finally stopped in the early fifth century. The evidence suggests that by 430 CE, Great Chesterford no longer received new supplies of pottery from any source, and by 450 CE, if still occupied by anyone, it had become aceramic. The pottery stops. Sherdless strata for the archaeologists.

These pots are the one thing I can say with any certainty moved along the road ahead of me, nearly two thousand years ahead of me. We can even put a face to their potters. Or at least to their face pots. Faces turned out of moulds to smile faintly from the bellies of pots. Noses pinched out of clay, eyebrows and thick lips protruding. A local face, or a god? A personification of beauty perhaps, or health? Used for decoration, at the table and sometimes for the ashes of a beloved. Another face from the grave. Someone who travelled our road. Heading northwards before the weather turned, in a cart laden with the kindness of Mother Earth.

♦ ♦ ♦

> What happens here? What is at work in the work? Van Gogh's painting is the revelation of what equipment, the pair of farmer shoes, is in truth. This entity steps out here into the unconcealment of its being. This unconcealment is what the Greeks called *alêtheia*.
>
> Martin Heidegger, *The Origin of the Work of Art* (1950)

♦ ♦ ♦

Flick through any number of archaeological reports on Roman Britain and you will find the pleasing outlines of dishes and flagons, tableware, cook ware and storage jars. Faint outlines of detective work and improbable attention to detail with tiny curved sections of the bases or rims picked out in thick black lines that tell which bit has actually been found. The rest has been deduced and imagined back into existence. From a black-slipped lip picked out of the till, an expert can reconstruct a whole beaker and its rouletted design as it once was on a potter's wheel in Gaul, on a Romano-British farmhouse table in Essex.

Not just pottery: reports and museum displays reconstruct entire artefacts from the smallest fragments. At Chelmsford Museum, an elaborately decorated Iron Age mirror is 80 per cent drawing, the handle and a small segment are all that really survive. At Saffron Walden Museum, a large detailed view of an entire British chariot pulled by two horses and driven by a Celtic warrior has sprouted from three tiny pieces of metal – a lynch pin from a wheel hub, a harness fitting, a strap fitting. And so a Boudiccan fort from a short section of V-shaped ditch and a rampaging army from a fallen tombstone and a battered bronze head.

Here I have tried to make something whole again from its few surviving parts, to mend and rebuild with the fragments I have collected. To lay them end on end along that line on a map we began with. A road built from letters and photos and stories is not as useful for travelling along as it once was, but not bad for imaginative journeys, for travelling into the past; much better for the dead to travel, for mendicant friars and legionaries to walk on.

I wanted to unconceal the road too. Not the road as it was in 70 CE or at any point in the past, but how it is now, impossibly thick with layers of time. Not to time travel back to Roman Britain, but to experience the folding of time, the immanence of things separated by the years but occupying the same physical space – events, themes, objects, lives far apart in time yet related to each other in ways that alter them and what they mean to us now.

Commentators have recently debated whether or not UNESCO was right not to replace the Bamiyan Buddhas with replicas because their destruction forms part of their history. Do we want the Buddhas as they were when they were carved into the cliffs in central Afghanistan in the sixth century – or as they were when they were destroyed by the Taliban in 2001, or as they were at some other point in their story, all points in their story? Impossibly, I want it all. I am more inter-

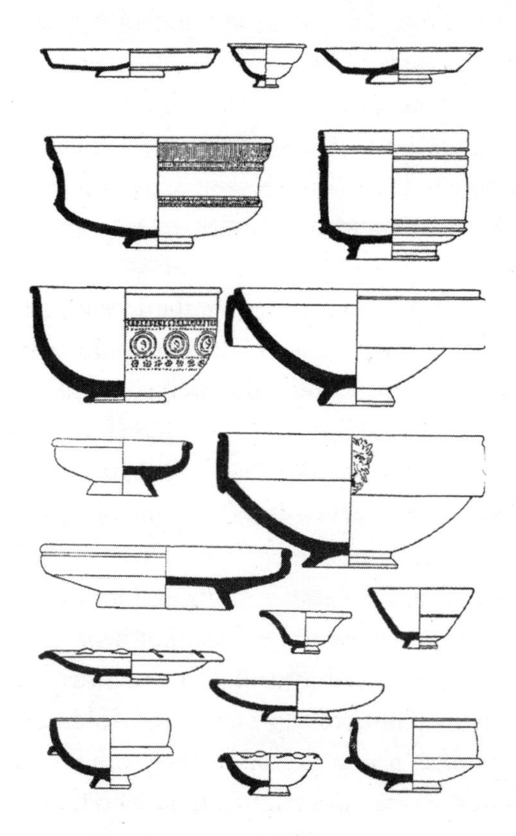

ested in the history that accrues. I want the palimpsest, in which we hope to recover as much of the original text as we can, but I want the writing on top as well, the finished painting and the shadowy figure lost beneath layers of paint revealed only under ultraviolet light. This is to pick examples where it is possible to separate the events; a better analogy might be our memories of moments in our lives that are repeatedly re-remembered into inseparable layers.

To unconceal is also to lay bare the experience of searching for a road, including the daft seductive ideas, the errors of logic and the flights of fancy, the resonances fuelled by popular culture as much as by history books. The journey along our road is replete with the vanished, the misinterpreted, the never-there-in-the-first-place (except in the imagination) propagated by amateurs and the greatest experts of their day. They are fragments too and we cannot mend the road without them.

Roman roads might be unique in the archaeological record. I cannot think of a comparable artefact: something built in antiquity to a standard not surpassed for nearly two millennia, which is still used today for its original purpose, if only in part, that still dictates where we travel and determines which places prosper, and survives as other things too that we find useful: a footpath, a boundary, the subject of a photographic work of art. It is as if an amphora were still being used to store and transport olive oil. What thing so ancient continues not only to be repaired and reused, but even when lost or hidden, to still influence the behaviour of moderns? In one sense the road is a finite resource that can be used up as it succumbs to the wear and tear of those who travel along it, or yields to neglect or destruction. In another sense it will last for ever. Its surveyed line can never be used up. It would never go away, even if the last fragment of stone were removed. Its entire length, its roadness might exist for ever as a concept, an alignment, a route. In this way it is like a story. An epic poem, say. Our road is both the text and the scroll itself. We must treasure it and keep on reading it anew.

♦ ♦ ♦

ACKNOWLEDGEMENTS

This book couldn't have been written without the generosity and expertise of Mark Landon. He endured many pints in the Golden Fleece, Braughing, to tell me everything he knows about that village in the Iron Age and Roman period. He shared his research about the road, Eric Stacey's diary – which is in his care – and some terrible jokes. Isobel Thompson encouraged my interest in the road when she was at the Hertfordshire Historic Environment unit some years ago and as publication of this book rapidly approached, she was still happily sharing the latest research on south-east Britain in the first century CE. At Hertfordshire, Rebekah Hart helped me track down the last few hard-copy records relevant to the road as well as teaching me how to use LiDAR more effectively. At Essex County Council, Maria Medlycott gave freely of her time to talk to me about Great Chesterford and discussed the course of the road north of the River Stort and finds within its corridor. Carolyn Wingfield at Saffron Walden Museum was especially kind and helpful and continued to send ideas and useful references following my visit to the storeroom there. At Chelmsford Museum, Mark Curteis patiently answered all my questions about the coins found en route. Thanks are also due to Janet Tocqueville at Hertford Museum for answering my enquiries about finds and dig archives in their possession and for arranging for me to see the Newell sketches among other things. My research took me back to the Hertfordshire Archives where I am always met with kindness and helpful advice from all the staff, but especially from Nick Connell.

Further afield, Mike Haken and Dave Armstrong at the Roman Roads Research Association extended the hand of friendship and were generous with their time and responses to my questions. Mike welcomed me into his home, fed me from his much-loved vegetable garden and set me on the right path. A chance encounter with a group of metal detectorists while walking the road one weekend led me to Zoe Williams and Klaine Fegan, who didn't hesitate to invite me to their home and share their stories about metal-detecting 'T-shirt field' and beyond. My long conversation with Stewart Ainsworth was invaluable; the section on J.R.L. and the work of the Ordnance Survey field investigators would have been impossible to write without his help. Jacqueline Cooper and Simon Coxall were very generous with material and ideas about Beard's Lane and Rumberry Hill. Andy Peachey at Archaeological Solutions told me everything I wanted to know about Hadham ware. Further details on my debts to these kind people and others are in the notes.

Over the years, I walked sections of the road with friends. Matthew Free, who long ago studied archaeology at university, walked the whole road with me and this book has benefited greatly from his thoughts and observations. The filmmaker Nick Edwards, who contacted me about my last book, turned out to know the road and we walked Beard's Lane together. He introduced me to David Ahn and put all sorts of ideas into my head that have found their way into these pages. My friend Dominick Tyler walked much of the road with me over the years and, among other things, his photographer's eye did lots of the looking for me.

Thanks also to Steven and Linda Bratt for their encouragement and advice; to Chris and Hannah Hines for their support. Thanks also to Terry Kenny who is kindness itself and helped me rejuvenate my writing shed during the pandemic when everyone here got sick of me monopolising the kitchen table. I also want to remember the late Bob Mills, who originally built what he called my 'crappy old shed', and his partner July Ramsey, who probably told him he had to build the shed for me. She quietly championed and encouraged my endeavours for years and was the loudest fan of my last book – her humour and kindness are missed by many.

Arabella Pike made this book possible. My gratitude to her is magnified by the fact that she was nursing this book and its author to a finished draft during a period when she was fighting one of the most arduous and important legal battles a publisher has had to endure for a long time. Also at William Collins, thanks to the ever-patient Iain Hunt and to Sam Harding, and to Martin Brown, Richard Rosenfeld and Ben Murphy. To the genius Joe McLaren for another beautiful cover. David Godwin is the most discerning and supportive of agents. A heartfelt thanks to all.

Finally, I must thank Max, Daisy and Caspar who not only fill me with pride, joy and inspiration every day, but contributed to this book in many practical ways. And to Rebecca.

This book is appropriately dedicated to her as she is the great walker in the family; she taught me the patience to walk when sprinting was no longer getting me very far. I take my bearings from her and every time I have lost my way over the last thirty odd years, she has brought me back to the road. She is my long-distance alignment, my compass and my companion on the great journey.

SELECT BIBLIOGRAPHY

Here is a selection of books and articles on Roman roads in Britain and the history and archaeology of Roman Britain that I have found useful. Asterisked titles deal specifically with RR21b. Works on more specific topics can be found in the notes.

♦ ♦ ♦

Adams, Colin, 'Transport', in *The Cambridge Companion to the Roman Economy*, ed. Walter Scheidel (Cambridge: CUP, 2012), pp. 218–40

Albone, James, *Roman Roads in the Changing Landscape of Eastern England c.AD 410–1850*, University of East Anglia, DPhil. Thesis, 2016, available at https://ueaeprints.uea.ac.uk/id/eprint/63543/

*Babington, Thomas, *Ancient Cambridgeshire: Or an attempt to trace roman and other ancient roads that passed through the county of Cambridge* [etc.], revised edn (Cambridge: Deighton, 1883)

Bagshawe, Richard, *Roman Roads* (Princes Risborough: Shire Publications, 1979)

*Barr, Bernard and Geoffrey R. Gillam, 'Excavation and Fieldwork on the Roman Roads at Braughing, Hertfordshire', *East Herts Arch. Soc. Trans.* 14/2 (1958–61), pp. 108–16

Bédoyère, Guy de la, *Roman Britain: A New History* (London: Thames & Hudson, 2010)

Berry, Bernard, *A Lost Roman Road: A Reconnaissance in the West Country* (London: George Allen & Unwin, 1963)

Bishop, Mike, *The Secret History of the Roman Roads of Britain* (Barnsley: Pen and Sword, 2014)

*Brinson, J.G.S., 'Chesterford, Great', in *Victoria History of the County of Essex*, Vol. 3 (London: Institute of Historical Research, 1963), pp. 72–88

*Burnham, Barry C. and J. Wacher, *The 'Small Towns' of Roman Britain* (London: Batsford, 1990)

Carlà-Uhink, Filippo, 'The Impact of Roman Roads on Landscape and Space: The Case of Republican Italy', *The Impact of the Roman Empire on Landscape* (Leiden: Brill, 2019), pp. 69–91

Casson, Lionel, *Travel in the Ancient World* (Baltimore and London: Johns Hopkins University Press, 1994; first pub. 1974)

Chevallier, Raymond, *Roman Roads*, trans. N.H. Field (London: Batsford, 1976)

*Christy, Miller, 'On Roman Roads in Essex', *Transactions of the Essex Archaeological Society*, 15 (1921), pp. 190–229

*Codrington, Thomas, *Roman Roads in Britain* (London: S.P.C.K., 1903), pp. 130–6

*Cussans, John Edwin, 'Edwinstree Hundred', in *History of Hertfordshire*, Parts III and IV (London: John Camden Hotten; Hertford: Stephen Austin, 1872)

Davies, Hugh, *Roads in Roman Britain* (Stroud: Tempus, 2002)

Entwistle, Robert, *Britannia Surveyed: New Light on Early Roman Britain through the Work of Military Surveyors* (Pewsey: Armatura Press, 2019)

Fields, Nic, *Boudicca's Rebellion AD 60–61: The Britons Rise Up Against Rome*, illus. by Peter Dennis (Oxford: Osprey, 2011)

*Fox, Cyril, *Archaeology of the Cambridge Region* (Cambridge: University of Cambridge, 1922)

Highways, Byways, and Road Systems in the Pre-modern World, eds Susan E. Alcock et al. (John Wiley, 2012)

Hindle, Brian Paul, *Roads, Tracks and Their Interpretation* (London: Batsford, 1993)

Hoffmann, Birgitta, *The Roman Invasion of Britain: Archaeology versus History* (Pen and Sword Archaeology, 2013)

*Holmes, John, 'Excavation and Fieldwork at Roman Braughing', *East Herts Arch. Soc. Trans.* 13 (1952), pp. 93–172

Johnston, David E., *An Illustrated History of Roman Roads in Britain* (Bourne End: Spurbooks, 1979)

*Landon, Mark, *The Great Chesterford Roman Road: Investigations 2000–2013* (Braughing: Braughing Archaeology Group, May 2014). Unpublished

Literary Sources for Roman Britain, eds J.C. Mann and R.G. Penman (London: LACTOR, 1985)

Livingston, Helen, *In the Footsteps of Caesar: Walking Roman Roads in Britain* (Shepperton: Ian Allen/BCA, 1995)

*Margary, Ivan D., *Roman Roads in Britain*, third edn (London: John Baker, 1973)

Mattingly, David, *An Imperial Possession: Britain in the Roman Empire* (London: Penguin, 2007)

*Medlycott, Maria, *The Roman Town of Great Chesterford*, East Anglian Archaeology Reports No. 137 (Chelmsford: Essex County Council, 2011)

*Munby, Lionel M., *The Hertfordshire Landscape* (London: Hodder & Stoughton, 1977)

New Visions of the Roman Countryside 1: The Rural Settlement of Roman Britain, eds Alexander Smith et al., Britannia Monograph Series No. 29 (London: Society for Promotion of Roman Studies, 2016)

New Visions of the Roman Countryside 2: The Rural Economy of Roman Britain, eds Martyn Allen et al., Britannia Monograph Series No. 30 (London: Society for Promotion of Roman Studies, 2017)

New Visions of the Roman Countryside 3: Life and Death in the Countryside of Roman Britain, ed. Alexander Smith, Britannia Monograph Series No. 32 (London: Society for Promotion of Roman Studies, 2018)

*Niblett, Rosalind, *Roman Hertfordshire* (Wimborne: Dovecote Press, 1995)

The Oxford Handbook of Roman Britain, eds Martin Millett, Louise Revell and Alison Moore (Oxford: OUP, 2014)

*Partridge, Clive, 'Braughing' in *Small Towns of Roman Britain*, eds Warwick Rodwell and Trevor Rowley, *British Archaeological Reports*, No. 15 (1975)

Partridge, Clive, 'In the Territory of the Catuvellauni: Braughing before and during the Roman Occupation', *EHAS Newsletter* (September 2010)

*Potter, T.W. and S.D. Trow, 'Puckeridge-Braughing, Hertfordshire: The Ermine Street Excavations 1971–2', *Hertfordshire Archaeology*, 10 (1988)

Poulter, J. 'The Date of the Stanegate, and a Hypothesis about the Manner and Timing of the Construction of Roman Roads in Britain', *Archaeologia Aeliana*, Series 5, Vol. 26 (1998), pp. 49–56

*Rackham, Oliver, *A History of the Countryside* (London: Dent, 1986)

Rivet, A.L.F. and Colin Smith, *The Place-names of Roman Britain* (London: Batsford and BCA, 1981; first pub. 1979)

Rodwell, Warwick, 'The Roman Fort at Great Chesterford, Essex', *Britannia*, Vol. 3 (1972), pp. 290–3

Roman Britain [map], fourth edn (Southampton: Ordnance Survey, 1978)

Roman Roads: New Evidence – New Perspectives, ed. Anne Kolb (Berlin; Boston: De Gruyter, 2019)

Roman Roads Research Association Newsletters Nos. 1–23

Rowe, Anne, and Tom Williamson, *Hertfordshire: A Landscape History* (Hatfield: University of Hertfordshire Press, 2013)

Salway, Peter, *Roman Britain* (Oxford: Clarendon, 1981)

Scheidel, Walter, *The Shape of the Roman World, Version 1.0* (Stanford University, April 2013), https://orbis.stanford.edu/assets/Scheidel_59.pdf retrieved 11/3/2020

Sedgley, J.P., 'The Roman Milestones of Britain: Their Petrography and Probable Origin', *BAR* 18 (Oxford: BAR, 1975)

Small Towns of Roman Britain, eds Warwick Rodwell and Trevor Rowley, British Archaeological Reports, No. 15 (1975)

Smith, Nicky, *Pre-industrial Roads, Trackways and Canals: Introductions to Heritage Assets*, eds Joe Flatman and Pete Herring (Swindon: Historic England, 2018) retrieved from HistoricEngland.org.uk/listing/selection-criteria/scheduling-selection/ihas-archaeology/ 14/10/19

Smith, Urban, 'Roman and Pre-Roman Roads in Hertfordshire', *East Herts Arch. Soc. Trans.* 5 (1912), pp. 117–30

Taylor, Christopher, *Roads and Tracks of Britain* (London: Orion, 1994; first pub. 1979)

*Thompson, Isobel, *Braughing: Extensive Urban Survey Project Assessment Report*, 2002. Retrieved from http://ads.ahds.ac.uk/catalogue/projArch/EUS/herts_eus_2005/downloads.cfm 23/09/2010

*Thompson, Isobel, 'Roman Roads', in *An Historical Atlas of Hertfordshire* (Hatfield: University of Hertfordshire Press, 2011), pp. 36–7

Thompson, Isobel, 'When Was the Roman Conquest in Hertfordshire?', in *Archaeology in Hertfordshire: Recent Research. A Festschrift for Tony Rook*, ed. Kris Lockyear (Hatfield: University of Hertfordshire Press, 2015), pp. 117–34

Von Hagen, Victor W., *The Roads that Led to Rome* (London: Weidenfeld and Nicolson, 1967)

Williamson, Tom, 'The Roman Countryside: Settlement and Agriculture in N.W. Essex', *Britannia*, Vol. 15 (1984), pp. 225–30

Williamson, Tom, 'The Development of Settlement in North West Essex: The Results of Ancient Field Survey', *Essex Archaeology and History*, Vol. 17 (1986), pp. 120–32

Williamson, Tom, *The Origins of Hertfordshire*, revised edn (Hatfield: Hertfordshire Publications, 2010)

NOTES

These notes are organised under the incipit of each section of the book and identified by a key word or phrase from the text. They are mostly short introductions to the main sources along with warnings, elaborations, qualifications, citations, last-minute additions, hedging of bets, asides and, most importantly of all, expressions of gratitude and acknowledgements of debts incurred.

I identify texts by author and date if the text is in the bibliography or after it has already been mentioned in the notes. I have been highly selective with references; when the text makes it clear where something has come from or where you can find out more, I am unlikely to give any further signposts here.

A general note on telling the story of Roman Britain. Much of the conventional story of Roman Britain is tenuous and disputed. We would do well to remember what Hoffmann (2013) has to say about what we know about the invasion from the surviving sources and the archaeology: 'The amount of material recovered, which is usually considered to be between one per cent and 0.1 per cent of what was originally there, makes it unlikely to ever get to the bottom of what really happened at any given time in Roman Britain [p. 11] ... With the exception of Julius Caesar's Commentaries, we have no records of Romano-British events from the perspective of an eyewitness [p. 15] ... If this journalistic standard of reliability is applied, then the only facts that can be trusted are that there was a successful invasion of Britain, that Aulus Plautius was in charge, that Vespasian had a lesser command and that Claudius came for a short period [p. 70].'

In a similar vein Lacey Wallace applies this caution specifically to the roads when discussing problems with the historiography of Roman Britain: 'The effort to "match up" the events in the surviving accounts – for example, to link the construction of roads to the movements of troops described – led to a situation where archaeologists decided what they were going to find before they dug it up.' 'Early Roman Horizon' in *The Oxford Handbook of Roman Britain*, eds Martin Millett, Louise Revell and Alison Moore (Oxford: OUP, 2014).

Throughout this book I endeavour to give the most up-to-date research and thinking on the history of Roman Britain and its roads. More traditional accounts are likely to interpret the archaeology in the light of the few, often unreliable texts left to us by classical authors. As we can see from the above quotations, many historians and archaeologists are a lot more cautious these days. However, my intent is to tell the story of Roman roads and I don't want to strangle that story at birth with endless qualifications and caveats. While at times I discuss the historiography, especially around the end of Roman Britain, this can quickly turn into endless handwringing and excursions into the weeds. Though important and fascinating to experts, many nuances of interpretation often don't change the bigger picture and with this in mind I haven't shied away from leaning on traditional narratives or having it both ways.

♦ ♦ ♦

PREFACE 1–5

Roman Roads Research Association – see https://www.romanroads.org and the acknowledgements. They produce a quarterly newsletter and, more recently, *Itinera*, the first academic journal dedicated to the study of Roman roads.

map being redrawn weekly – for example, see the recent work of David Ratledge in the Roman Roads Research Association Newsletter and on their The Roads of Roman Britain website https://roadsofromanbritain.org/index.html. Also the recent work of Chris Smart and colleagues at Exeter University in identifying the Roman roads in Cornwall.

Hollow Places – an unusual history of land and legend (London: William Collins, 2019) where our road first caught my imagination. It appears on the second page of the prelude. I am describing an ancient yew, where nineteenth-century labourers thought they'd found a dragon's lair. 'There she grew in this remote spot near the Hertfordshire–Essex border, within five or six feet of where a Roman road lay beneath the soil of the field.'

great ways or iconic roads – some of these are suggested by Margary (1973).

Lincoln – for the names of places, I usually give the modern place name, although we should always bear in mind that the modern settlement and the Roman settlement were not necessarily in the same place. Where I give the Romano-British name it is relevant to the context and always accompanied by the modern name.

Braughing – incidentally, Braughing is pronounced Braffing or Broffing.

province of Britannia – I use Britain and Britannia interchangeably. The latter was the name of the Roman province in the early years of the occupation before Roman Britain was divided into two provinces, *Britannia Superior* and *Inferior*, and later still into four and possibly five. For the sake of simplicity, I refer to the province of Britannia throughout.

After London – Jefferies, Richard, *After London Or, Wild England* (London: Cassell, 1885), cf. the opening par of 'Part I, The Relapse into Barbarism', 'Chapter 1 The Great Forest': 'The old men say their fathers told them that soon after the fields were left to themselves a change began to be visible. It became green everywhere in the first spring, after London ended, so that all the country looked alike ...'

◆ ◆ ◆

THE GRASS SPREAD INWARDS FROM THE MARGINS 9–13

Willowherb, groundsel and bindweed ... bluebells ... Dog's mercury – some are taken from Leonard Wooley's description in *Digging Up the Past* (Harmondsworth: Penguin, 1937) of what happens to a Roman camp after it is abandoned. The others are from personal communication with Trevor James, the author of *Flora of Hertfordshire* (Welwyn Garden City: Hertfordshire Natural History Society, 2009) and from Brian Sawford's *Wild Flower Habitats of Hertfordshire* (Ware: Castlemead, 1990).

Ten thousand miles of them – an often repeated estimate. See Smith (2018).

coming of the railways ... first motorways – see Hindle (1993).

hoggin – a great word, culled from Landon (2014) and defined by the *OED* as 'Finely sifted or screened gravel; (now chiefly) a material consisting of a mixture of sand, gravel, and clay.'

blackthorn hedge – see Rackham (1986). Also see below in section beginning 'Beyond the mill'.

Only flights of rooks – Richard Jefferies writes about the collective memory of rooks: 'They have their laws, from which there is no deviation: they are handed down from generation to generation ...' He imagines their flightpaths remembering lost woods and ancient clearings. 'Rooks Returning to Roost' in *Walks in the Wheat-fields*, English Journeys No. 9 (London: Penguin, 2009) pp. 1–13, first published in *Wild Life in a Southern County* (1879).

ginks – Cussans (1872): 'The road itself has been disused and "stocked up" for many years, but its course may be readily traced through the wood, by the peculiar water-worn pebbles, locally known as "ginks", which lie scattered about throughout its length. These stones, with which the road is paved, or rather macadamized, are nowhere else to be found in the neighbourhood, and were probably brought here from the bed of the Quin.'

smoring – to smore means to suffocate or to smother – a wonderful word.

wanton outrage – taken from *Old England: A Pictorial Museum*, ed. Charles Knight (London: Bracken Books, 1987; first published London: James Sangster, 1847). I use it so as to put this quote in the notes: 'Somehow it has happened that during these last two centuries there has been a greater destruction of ancient things, and a more wanton desecration of sacred things, perpetrated by people in authority, sleek, self-satisfied functionaries, practical men, as they termed themselves, who despised all poetical associations and thought the beautiful incompatible with the useful – there has been more wanton outrage committed upon the memorials of the past, than all the invaders and pillagers of our land had committed for ten centuries before. The destruction has been stopped, simply because the standard of taste and of feeling has been raised amongst a few.' We find the same sentiment echoed over a century later in a review of a book about Roman roads in the South East Midlands by the group calling themselves the Viatores: 'In reading this it becomes painfully clear how rapidly ancient remains, even tracks, are disappearing. The Viatores are explorers, but they are also fighting a rearguard action, for the visible evidence of much of the information they are salvaging is too often being swept away by motorways, housing developments and factories.' See *Journal of Roman Studies*, Vol. 55, No. 1/2, Parts 1 and 2 (1965), pp. 298–9.

humanity's struggle against distance – the phrase is famously Fernand Braudel's; see Scheidel (2013), citing Braudel's *La Méditerranée et la monde méditerranéen à l'époque de Philippe II* (1966).

mist – the first-century BC geographer Strabo wrote of Britain: 'The weather tends to rain rather than snow. Mist is very common, so that for whole days at a stretch the sun is seen only for three or four hours around midday.' Strabo, *Geography*, Book 2. The translation is from *Literary Sources for Roman Britain* (1985).

at the world's end – the Roman poet Virgil's description of Britain in his Eclogues 1:66 in Cecil Day Lewis's translation: 'Meliboeus: But the rest of us must go from here and be dispersed – / To Scythia, bone-dry Africa, the chalky spate of the Oxus, / Even to Britain – that place cut off at the very world's end.' Virgil, *The Eclogues. The Georgics*, trans. C. Day Lewis (Oxford: OUP, 1983).

birrus – a long wool garment with a hood. See Casson (1974), where you will find a selection of capes a Roman traveller might have taken with them on a journey.

drayman in his Leyland – driving to Rayments Brewery in Furneux Pelham in the twentieth century.

one of Sir John's men leads the mortuary cow – in the fourteenth century. 'Next I bequeath one red cow to Sir Alan the vicar of the same township to go before my body on the day of my burial.' From the testament of Sir John Chaumberleyn of Pelham Arsa in 1340 – see No. 1,161 in *Ninth Report of the Royal Commission on Historical Manuscripts* (London: Eyre and Spottiswoode, 1884). Now in the London Metropolitan Archives MS 2512 1161.

dolabra – an entrenching tool, pick axe or mattock. 'The *dolabra* was one of the standard pieces of Roman military kit. It combined a cutting blade with a spike. Each soldier was issued with one, along with a basket (for carrying soil), rope, saw, bill-hook, chain, pickaxe and turf cutter. The *dolabra* was used as an entrenching tool to building overnight marching camps and other fortifications. It was carried on a soldier's belt and would have had a bronze sheath to protect the soldier from its sharp cutting edge.' – Display label at Vindolanda Roman fort.

Mr Sworder – Mr Sworder's bit part in the history of the road is recorded in a letter written by the Revd Woolmore Wigram in about 1870. 'Concerning the ... Roman roads at and near Furneux Pelham', Hertfordshire Archives D/ECu 9 310.

dark-toned anomalies – an interesting phrase encountered in archaeological reports and historic environment records.

fourteen parishes ... one watershed – these are Standon, Braughing, Hormead, Furneux Pelham, Brent Pelham and Meesden in Hertfordshire; Langley, Clavering, Elmdon, Arkesden, Littlebury and Strethall in Essex; Ickleton in Cambridgeshire; and Great Chesterford, back in Essex again. The hundreds are Braughing, Edwinstree, Clavering, Uttlesford and Whittlesford. The rivers: Rib, Quin, Ash, Stort and Cam, as well as tributaries such as the Wicken Water (which appears to have been filled in where the road crosses it). The watershed is between the Thames and the Ouse.

No Trace ... Faint Trace ... Remarks on Ordnance Survey file on RR21b now held at Historic England Archive.

◆ ◆ ◆

In the beginning was the road – cited by Charles Homer Haskins in his 'The Spread of Ideas in the Middle Ages', *Speculum*, Vol. 1, No. 1 (January, 1926).

◆ ◆ ◆

THE ROADS BEGIN AT A BEACHHEAD 13–17

The roads begin at a beachhead – On the development of the early road system, I have followed the traditional sequence of events in first-century Britannia and imagined, as others have before me, how the barebones of the network might have developed in the early years of the invasion. See the general note on telling the story of Roman Britain above.

For the development of the roads in the first century, see Bishop (2014), especially p. 41f. and figure 12. Also Entwistle (2019) is a fascinating analysis of particular routes. I consider the development of the road system immediately following the invasion, before the Romans arrived and in the subsequent years of the occupation later on in the journey.

four legions – Mattingly (2007). See also Hoffmann (2013) for a more cautionary analysis.

'unprecedented width' – this is suggested by the always entertaining Von Hagen (1967). As an aside, it recalls the discovery of mammoth bones near the Thames which were originally thought to be the skeletons of Claudius's elephants (at least that's what the classicists thought; the theologians thought they were elephants who weren't lucky enough to get on the Ark and had drowned in the Flood) – a classic case of archaeology being made to fit the historical sources.

symbol and a concrete expression – Anne Kolb, 'Roman Road Building: An Introduction to Its Significance, the Sources and the State of Research', in *Roman Roads* (2019): 'For Rome, the roads were not merely a symbol of power, but also served as a concrete instrument of rule.'

Fosse Way – or Foss Way. In a well-known and influential 1924 paper, R.G. Collingwood argued that the Fosse Way differed from other parts of the road network and represented the first frontier in Roman Britain. This has been written about extensively and is no longer thought to be the case. 'The Fosse', *Journal of Roman Studies*, Vol. 14 (1924), pp. 252–6.

Mendips – see Hoffmann (2013).

IX Hispana – I have opted for a hybrid naming of the legions: legion rather than *legio* but with no attempt to translate the *cognomen* or nickname.

250,000 dead – 'somewhere between 100,000 and 250,000 Britons are likely to have perished in the conquest period 43–83'. See Mattingly (2007).

Solent along Stane Street – or possibly he marched the other way, especially, as some conjecture, if the main invasion force or a secondary force landed on the Solent. See Entwistle (2019) for a detailed discussion of what the road itself can tell us about this.

driven directly over the low hills towards East Anglia – 'a direct road was driven over the hills from Braughing to Great Chesterford, thus shortening the journey from London into East Anglia, the country of the Iceni'. 'An Outline Survey of Saffron

Walden and its Region, Section VI, The Roman Period, ed. G Morris', in *The Avenue* (December 1916).

♦ ♦ ♦

IN A FIELD SOMEWHERE YOU'VE NEVER HEARD OF 17–25

goblin ridge – the literal rendering of the place name Puckeridge. Roman Braughing straddles both its modern namesake and Puckeridge, which is part of Standon, Hertfordshire.

eight dials – from *Herts and Bucks*, ed. L. Russell Muirhead (Harmondsworth: Penguin, 1949), where the road hub is described as a five dials, but now we know there were more roads. Some say seven. Mark Landon counts eight.

unbroken channel of communication – the phrase is Cyril Fox's in *Archaeology of the Cambridge Region* (Cambridge: University of Cambridge, 1922).

River Guadalquivir ... Arles ... Campania – all associated with Braughing by archaeological finds. More later on.

six most important towns – Mattingly (2007), Figure 10.

Eric's diary – this was bequeathed to Mark Landon and is used with his permission.

lynchets – old strips of a terraced field.

John Holmes, will find – see Holmes (1952).

One of the earliest accounts of a cropmark – the early examples of cropmarks are all taken from Martyn Barber's excellent *A History of Aerial Photography and Archaeology: Mata Hari's Glass Eye and Other Stories* (Swindon: English Heritage, 2011). Long ago, when I was first pulling together notes on RR21b, Martyn very kindly sent me the relevant chapters in draft.

sown with wheat – Barr and Gillam (1958–61).

ghostly monks – Doris Jones-Baker, *Old Hertfordshire Calendar* (London: Phillimore, 1974): 'Five spectral monks "walk" at Horse Cross, Braughing, one night in every five years ... The ghostly walk is said to be the monks' penance for eating trout caught without leave in the River Rib ... it was considered an omen of good fortune to see the Braughing spectres, and their appearance was carefully watched for.' Those in search of good fortune should note that the next appearance is scheduled for May 2026; see you there.

♦ ♦ ♦

I STAND ONE SPRING DAY AT A BERMUDA TRIANGLE OF ROADS 26–29

Bermuda triangle – not just Roman roads go missing here: an uncanny number of lost roads hem this field as well as the Roman ones that cross it. On its left flank is the old course of the B1368 coach road to Cambridge, which now comes to a dead end. On its right a lost lane has long since vanished.

Eric sank a trial trench – Barr and Gillam (1958–61).

apparent diversion – Margary (1973).

Four Great Ways – see Roger Gale, 'An Essay Towards the Recovery of the Courses of the Four Great Roman Ways' in *The Itinerary of John Leland the Antiquary, Vol. 6*, Published from the original ms. in the Bodleian Library by Thomas Hearne M.A., 2nd edn (Oxford: 1744) pp. 10–14. See also Francis Palgrave, 'Part I and Part II: Proofs and Illustrations', *The Rise and Progress of the English Commonwealth: Anglo-Saxon Period* (London: John Murray, 1832).

drew the archaeologists – Barr and Gillam (1958–61).

brooch – Barr and Gillam (1958–61). The brooch was M.R. Hull's Langton Down C type. See C.F.C. Hawkes and M. Reginald Hull (1947). *Camulodunum. First Reports on the Excavations at Colchester, 1930–1939*, Reports of the Research Committee of the Society of Antiquaries, XIV (Oxford: OUP, 1947). Also Guy de la Bédoyère, *The Finds of Roman Britain* (London: Batsford, 1989).

slabs of venison ... vineyard – see 'Standon', in *A History of the County of Hertford: Volume 3*, ed. William Page (London, 1912), pp. 347–66., British History Online http://www.british-history.ac.uk/vch/herts/vol3/pp347-366

Herbert Tompkins – Herbert W. Tompkins, *Highways and Byways in Hertfordshire* (London: Macmillan, 1902), p. 277, where Tompkins also rhapsodises about Dick Turpin, imagining him riding Black Bess through Puckeridge. See the later epigraph taken from Tompkins.

♦ ♦ ♦

BURIED TWICE AMONG US 30–32

Buried twice among us – see epigraph to section.

Thomas Codrington – Codrington (1903). There is an earlier pencil line marking the road, scored on the early 1-inch OS map by Woolmore Wigram, but it has not survived. For his description of marking the road see 'Concerning the ... Roman roads at and near Furneux Pelham', Hertfordshire Archives D/ECu 9 310.

Ordnance Survey maps – current OS maps at different scales can't agree on where it should be marked.

fixed materialisation – the phrase is Isak Dinesen's (the pen name of Karen Blixen neé Dinesen) at the beginning of her short story 'Sorrow Acre', first published in 1942. The road she is writing about so beautifully is not straight like ours, but that is of little consequence. 'The thin gray line of a road, winding across the plain and up and down hills, was the fixed materialization of human longing, and of the human notion that it is better to be in one place than in another.'

♦ ♦ ♦

NODULES OF FLINT LITTER THE FIELD EDGES 32–37

The archaeology of Roman Braughing-Puckeridge in the next two sections is based largely on conversations with Mark Landon and on the following sources: Barr and Gillam (1958–61); W.B. Gerish, 'The Roman Station at Braughing' in EHAST I, II (1900) pp. 178–9; Holmes (1952); Niblett (1995); Partridge (1975); Partridge (2010); Clive Partridge, *Skeleton Green: A Late Iron*

Age and Romano-British Site, British Monograph Series No. 2 (London: Society for the Promotion of Roman Studies, 1981); Potter and Trow (1988); Rowe and Williamson (2013); Thompson (2002); Thompson (2015).

intermediate loss – taken from the section's epigraph. Filling the intermediate loss between the road hub and the plateau north of the Braughing valley is no simple task. I have lost many hours of my life assessing the most likely route before deciding that readers of this book could be spared most of the niceties; the more interesting and conclusive ones are here and in the following section. Mark Landon has made the most detailed study: Landon (2014).

first test a true Roman road – see Bagshawe (1979).

real indication – as we shall see, earlier antiquaries thought that Braughing had been a Roman settlement but their conjectures were built on sand.

'A field called Wickhams' – see below for more on Wickhams.

'Tom Tiddler's ground' – defined by *Brewer's* as 'A place where it is easy to pick up a fortune ... The name comes from the old children's game in which a base keeper, who is called Tom Tiddler, tries to keep the other children from crossing the boundary into his base. As he does so, they sing: *Here we are on Tom Tiddler's ground / Picking up gold and silver.*'

wrote one antiquary – Cussans cited by Gerish (1900).

many kilos of moulds – much of this section is based on conversations with Mark Landon. See also his *The Ford Bridge Coin Mould Assemblage* online at https://www.ehas.org.uk/html/bag.html and his *Making a Mint: Comparative Studies in Late Iron Age Coin Mould* (Oxford: Archaeopress, 2016).

where people came to meet at the end of summer – communicated by Isobel Thompson at the Archaeology in Hertfordshire: Recent Research Conference, 22 October 2022.

nearby earthworks – the Gatesbury enclosure. It is Potter and Trow (1988) who suggest that this might be the site of Cassivellaunus's stronghold. The following quotations and translation of Caesar's description are taken from there. Hoffmann (2013) argues that he had more than one powerbase. James Kemble, *Prehistoric and Roman Essex* (Stroud: History, 2009), suggests that allies would not venture so far into Catuvellauni territory as Wheathampstead, although he is promoting another candidate for the site of the *oppidum*. Recent investigations have questioned whether Gatesbury is indeed an Iron Age earthwork – see Hertfordshire Historic Environment Record 110 on https://www.heritagegateway.org.uk/Gateway/

After Caesar's departure – we know that there were merchants from the continent in Britain even before Caesar arrived. He describes interviewing them when planning his first visit. 'He gathered intelligence by inviting the traders dealing in Britain to his tent to advise him.' Hoffmann (2013). For a detailed account and discussion of Caesar's expeditions see Hoffmann (2013), pp. 24–40. Moffat (2017) tells the story particularly well.

♦ ♦ ♦

THE WALLS OF ST MARY'S, BRAUGHING 38–44

For the sources used in this section see the introductory note to the previous one.

others have suggested that our road – Thompson (2002).

not unknown for buildings to use roads as their foundations – Bagshawe (1979). See below under 'The Parish of Brent Pelham'.

They found lots of Tudor brick – Landon (2014).

Mount Falernus – forty miles north of Naples is today known as Monte Massico – the source of the grapes used to make Falernian wine, much fêted by poets in antiquity.

'You have built a strategic road' – S.S. Frere, 'The Origins of Small Towns' in Rodwell and Rowley (1975).

only about a quarter of Romano-British forts – Mattingly (2007).

none in Hertfordshire – 'no certain examples,' write Rowe and Williamson (2013).

'no more than a small ...' – Thompson (2002).

porters and pack animals – Casson (1974).

double-winged villa, was possibly a mansio – see Partridge (1975).

♦ ♦ ♦

IF ONLY THE ROMANS HAD LEFT A MAP BEHIND 44–53

If only the Romans had left a map behind – they did, it's called the Peutinger Table, but almost all the British section is missing, so the *Antonine Itinerary* and the *Ravenna Cosmography* are our best sources for place names.

Antonine Itinerary – see A.L.F. Rivet and Kenneth Jackson, 'The British Section of the Antonine Itinerary', *Britannia*, Vol. 1 (1970), pp. 34–82, and Rivet and Smith (1979), and https://roadsofromanbritain.org/antonine.html

Recent interpretations – Mattingly (2007).

99 of the 153 – Margary (1973). Mattingly says there are about 110 accepted locations.

Antiquaries intent on fitting names – Rosemary Sweet, *Antiquaries: The Discovery of the Past in Eighteenth-century Britain* (London: Hambledon and London, 2004). Braughing was 'anciently the most considerable place …' – Nathaniel Salmon, *The History of Hertfordshire* (London, 1728).

British Museum – see https://www.britishmuseum.org/collection

Leman – Charles Bertram and Thomas Leman, *The Description of Britain, translated from Richard of Cirencester etc.* (London: White and Taylor, 1809).

Bertram – on Bertram I have relied mostly upon Sweet (2004) and Stuart Piggott, *William Stukeley: An Eighteenth-century Antiquary*, revised edn (London: Thames and Hudson, 1985).

'nuisance whose influence' – see *A History of the Ordnance Survey*, ed. W.A. Seymour (Folkestone: Dawson, 1980).

Ravenna Cosmography – see Rivet and Smith (1979), and Natalia Lozovsky, 'Ravenna Cosmographer' (Anonymous Ravennas), in *Oxford Classical Dictionary Online* (2018).

Crawford and Richmond – Crawford and Richmond, 'The British Section of the Ravenna Cosmography', *Archaeologia*, XCIII (1949), pp. 1–50.

♦ ♦ ♦

Blind Road – for many years this was the working title of the book.

♦ ♦ ♦

PENNED NOW BY THICK HEDGEROWS 53–57

private carriage – from the Braughing enclosure award, 1820, Hertfordshire Archives DP/23/26/1.

Roman engineers tolerated steeper slopes – see Davies (2002) for a detailed discussion on gradients.

'hard and metalled with flint' – Holmes (1952).

sandals – the material on Roman footwear is taken from the Vindolanda museum's display labels and guidebook, and Carol van Driel-Murray, 'Vindolanda and the Dating of Roman Footwear', *Britannia*, Vol. 32 (2001), pp. 185–97.

At Heraclea – Rebecca West, *Black Lamb and Grey Falcon: A Journey through Yugoslavia* (Edinburgh: Canongate, 2006; first pub. 1941).

Thomasing – Doris Jones-Baker, *Old Hertfordshire Calendar* (London: Phillimore, 1974).

experimental short story – Rebecca West, 'Indissoluble Matrimony' in *Blast*, No. 1 (June 1914), pp. 98–117.

'Great roads were made' – H.G. Wells, *A Short History of the World*, revised edn (Harmondsworth: Penguin, 1945).

♦ ♦ ♦

I AM TRACING A TERRACED BRIDLEWAY 57–60

For more on Ivan Margary's life see the obituary below and also 'Ivan D Margary FSA, His Legacy to Roman History' at https://www.felbridge.org.uk/index.php/publications/ivan-d-margary-fsa-his-legacy-roman-history/, as well as the 2021 lecture by Dr David Rudling 'I.D. Margary (1896–1976): An Officer, Gentleman, Scholar and Philanthropist by Dr David Rudling' on YouTube https://www.youtube.com/watch?v=DLc8lQvVcvM

higher ground beyond – Margary (1973).

obituary in The Times – 27 February 1976.

numbering system – Margary (1973) explains his rationale. See also https://roadsofromanbritain.org/margarynumbers.html

RR21b – Margary's 21b runs for 19½ miles from Braughing to Great Chesterford and then on to Worsted Lodge. The section beyond Great Chesterford is not in any sense the same road.

♦ ♦ ♦

THE LINE HAS EVOLVED 61–63

Ordnance Survey file for RR21b – Linear and Roman Road Files Historic England ORD 01/04 RR21b.

Charles Phillips – see C.W. Phillips, *Archaeology in the Ordnance Survey* (London: Council for British Archaeology, 1980) and C.W. Phillips, *My Life in Archaeology* (Gloucester: Allan Sutton, 1987). Also 'Charles Phillips' in the *Dictionary of National Biography* online.

Glyn Daniel – quoted by Yolande Hodson in the Charles Close Society's *Sheetlines* No. 34 (September 1992).

Deep ploughing etc – see Phillips (1980).

♦ ♦ ♦

THE FIELD INVESTIGATOR TOOK THE TRACK UP PENTLOW HILL 65–67

J.R.L. – is John Linge who after working with the OS moved to Scotland where he worked on the Antonine Wall. See John Linge, 'The Cinderella Service: The Ordnance Survey and the Mapping of the Antonine Wall', *Proceedings of the Society of Antiquaries of Scotland*, 134 (2004), pp. 161–71.

Some years ago I was given an address and telephone for John Linge, but by the time I got round to trying to make contact he was no longer there and I have failed to track him down, although quite early on I decided it was better for us to know him only through the eighteen comments he makes on the map – I warmed to him through them and enjoyed walking the road in his company. Stewart Ainsworth (see next note) knew him and I believe the type of investigator described in this chapter is a fair description of J.R.L.: a conscientious one, possessing a genuine affinity with the past under our feet. See also John Linge, 'Blood and Glory: A Field Arch. Section Revisited' in *We Were Always Chasing Time …*' ed. Frodsham et al., *Northern Archaeology*, Vol. 17/18 (1999), pp. 31–3.

I imagine – very much with the help of Stewart Ainsworth. This chapter is indebted to him and is largely based on a lengthy telephone interview about his time at the OS. I am grateful to Wayne Cocroft for putting me in touch with Stewart and to Stewart Bryant at Herts County Council for suggesting I reach out to Wayne. On the Ordnance Survey Archaeology Division, see also M. Bowden and D.A. Mackay, 'Archaeology and the Ordnance Survey Revisited', in *We Were Always Chasing Time …*' ed. Frodsham et al. *Northern Archaeology*, Vol. 17/18 (1999), pp. 1–13. They note some interesting (and heartening) examples of how field investigators were prone to mission creep, recording invisible things, keeping files of find spots and eventually going rogue, contriving 'wide sweeps and circular routes to increase the possibility of finding new sites' (especially once it became clear that the Division was going to be shut down).

Archaeology Division Instructions – cited in Bowden and Mackay (1999).

invisibles – archaeological features not obvious to the naked eye.

♦ ♦ ♦

INTIMATE ALMOST SECRETIVE 73–76

Intimate almost secretive – Rowe and Williamson (2013).

Ordnance Survey archaeology field guide – *Field Archaeology: Some Notes for Beginners* issued by the Ordnance Survey, fourth edn, OS Prof. Papers New Series. No. 13 (London: HMSO, 1963). The first edition was written by O.G.S. Crawford in 1921. The fourth was updated by C.W. Phillips and A.L.F. Rivet.

♦ ♦ ♦

THE TWIN PROPS OF A MOSQUITO MK 34 76–79

On 540 Squadron and aerial photography in general see Barber (2011); Kitty Hauser, *Shadow Sites: Photography, Archaeology, and the British Landscape, 1927–1955* (Oxford: OUP, 2007); Roy Conyers Nesbit, *Eyes of the RAF: A History of Photo-reconnaissance* (Stroud: Sutton, 2003); National Collection of Aerial Photography website http://ncap.org.uk/; 'Photographic Reconnaissance in World War II, Seminar Monday 10 July 1991 at the Royal Air Force Museum' in *Proceedings of the Royal Air Force Historical Society*, No. 10 (1991).

ninth of July, 1946 – see TNA AIR 27/2500/17 ORB – Operations Record Book for 540 Squadron flying out of RAF Benson in 1946.

John Piper – Hauser (2007).

Frames 5240–5241 – RAF/106G/UK/1635.

♦ ♦ ♦

WHILE MILITARY RECONNAISSANCE 79–81

For this section on O.G.S. Crawford I am particularly indebted to Kitty Hauser's work: Kitty Hauser, *Bloody Old Britain: O.G.S. Crawford and the Archaeology of Modern Life* (London: Granta, 2008); Hauser (2007); also see Barber (2011); O.G.S. Crawford, 'Air Survey and Archaeology', Ordnance Survey Professional Papers New Series, No. 7 (London: HMSO, 1924); *A History of the Ordnance Survey*, ed. W.A. Seymour (Folkestone: Dawson, 1980).

'bony skeletons of an old horse' … 'a furrow, grown over with weeds' … 'emphasized one thing' … cat on a carpet … H.G. Wells – all are found in Hauser (2008).

'shadow sites' – the title of Kitty Hauser's book (and also an interesting video artwork by Jananne Al-Ani). The term refers to archaeological features that are revealed from above when the sun is low in the sky.

'No single scholar' – W.F. Grimes, ed., *Aspects of Archaeology in Britain and Beyond: Essays Presented to O.G.S. Crawford* (1951), cited in the *Dictionary of National Biography* entry for Crawford.

♦ ♦ ♦

IT IS WITH A GOD'S EYE VIEW 82

82 Squadron … two frames – 9 January 1947. RAF/CPE/UK/1917 RS 4082-83. Provided by Historic England.

♦ ♦ ♦

BACK ON THE GROUND NOW ON A GRASSY TRACK 85–93

On milestones in general and for those mentioned here see Carol Haines, *Marking the Miles: A History of English Milestones* (n.p. Carol Haines, 2000). Many of the examples in this chapter can be found there and in the Roman Inscriptions of Britain database https://romaninscriptionsofbritain.org/. Bishop (2014) is also good on milestones. Chevallier (1976) has lots of examples of milestones on the continent.

Virgil's tough wayfaring tree – Virgil's Eclogues I in the Cecil Day Lewis translation.

stamp collecting – I've borrowed J.R.L.'s dismissive phrase made in a slightly different context in Linge (2004). I have nothing against stamp collecting.

very taken with a large lump of stone – Salmon (1728).

Victoria County History –'Little Hormead', *Victoria History of the County of Hertford*, Vol. 4, ed. W. Page (London: Constable, 1914; repr. London: Dawsons, 1971).

sheer scale of quarrying – I cannot recall or discover where I read this.

Found in the bed of a Lancashire stream – all British Roman milestones mentioned in this chapter can be found on the Roman Inscriptions of Britain website https://romaninscriptionsofbritain.org/. This one is RIB 2272.

ten thousand milestones – Bishop (2014).

a series of sixteen beautiful milestones – see Haines (2000) for a detailed account.

recently recognised – Charlotte Higgins writes about this fascinating discovery in her *Under Another Sky: Journeys in Roman Britain* (London: Vintage, 2014).

In a letter to his friend Gallus – Pliny, *Letters*, 2.17, cited by Davies (2002).

♦ ♦ ♦

FAR FROM ROME NOW 94–96

I squat in the dark coppice – Colin Hambrook who at the time was Hertfordshire's countryside access officer, but was an Egyptologist by training, first showed me the road in Hormead Park Wood.

took his interest in the ancient world – Christopher Woodward, *In Ruins* (London: Chatto, 2001).

a local vicar bosing – Woolmore Wigram, 'Concerning the … Roman roads at and near Furneux Pelham', Hertfordshire Archives D/ECu 9 310.

It's been said that physicians – my wife is a doctor, so the analogy instantly occurred to me, but Kitty Hauser makes the same point: see Hauser (2008).

♦ ♦ ♦

IF YOU CANNOT FOLLOW THE ROAD BY ITS MUSIC 97–100

James Sowerby – *English Botany*, Vol. 8 (London, 1799).

local naturalist – Brian Sawford. See Sawford (1990).

Miller Christy – Miller Christy, '*Primula Elatior* in Britain: Its Distribution, Peculiarities, Hybrids and Allies' in *Botanical Journal of the Linnean Society*, Vol. 33, No. 229 (1897), pp. 172–201; Miller Christy, '*Primula Elatior Jacquin*: Its Distribution in Britain' in *Journal of Ecology*, Vol. 10, No. 2 (November 1922), pp. 200–10; Miller Christy, '*Primula Elatior Jacquin*: Its Distribution in Britain: Supplementary Note' in *Journal of Ecology*, Vol. 12, No. 2 (July 1924), pp. 314–16; see also C.D. Preston, 'The Distribution of the Oxlip Primula elatior (L.) Hill in Cambridgeshire', in *Nature in Cambridgeshire*, No. 25 (1993), pp. 29–60.

♦ ♦ ♦

ROMAN ROADS WERE BEAUTIFUL 101–107

Plutarch – from Plutarch's *Life of Gracchus* 7.1, trans. B. Perrin, cited by Carlà-Uhink (2019).

Publius Statius – in *Silvae* 4.3; see Bishop (2014).

crushed stone, pebbles and gravel – see Davies (2002).

described as typical – Niblett (1995).

'most striking feature' – Margary (1973).

local archaeologist – this is, of course, Mark Landon again.

Thomas Walford – this account is given in Christy (1921).

♦ ♦ ♦

BEYOND THE WOOD, STONES GUIDE ME ALONG THEIR HANSEL AND GRETEL TRAIL 108–110

'He speaks to the portion' – Wigram (*c.*1870), Hertfordshire Archives D/ECu 9 310.

aerial photograph taken in the 1960s – provided by Historic England MAL / 69031 075 and 076, 5 April 1969.

Margary mentions in passing – Margary (1973).

Oliver Rackham wrote – Rackham (1986).

♦ ♦ ♦

BRACKETED BY CRATERED FIELDS 113–119

a note scribbled in 1935 – see George Henry Cameron, *History of Furneux Pelham* (1935), unpublished. See Hertfordshire Archives D/P 78/29/2 p. 123. Also *Furneux Pelham Parish Magazine* 1937–9 (In private hands).

Roman historian Strabo – *Literary Sources for Roman Britain* (1985).

'dull enough in the eyes' – Tompkins (1902).

Cameron had read – in Alfred Watkins, *The Old Straight Track: Its mounds, beacons, moats, sites, and mark stones [etc.]* (London: Methuen & Co, 1925).

Lawrence Augustine Waddell – *The Phoenician Origin of Britons, Scots & Anglo-Saxons* (London: Williams & Norgate, 1924).

Archaeological Institute Journal – *Archaeological Journal*, Vol. X (1853), Various Numbers. The report of the Danesbury Hoard is in No. 39 (September 1853).

◆ ◆ ◆

IF WE CAN RESOLVE PLAUTIUS'S DILEMMA 120–125

Others are sceptical – Davies (2002).

In his Agricola – Tacitus 31.2, translated by M. Hutton, revised by R.M. Ogilvie.

in Holland in 2019 – Roman Roads Research Association Newsletter No. 10 (Summer 2019).

military roads – conversation with Stewart Ainsworth.

'If we did not have the written record' – Thompson (2015).

clients of Rome – it has recently been argued that large parts of the south-east were client kingdoms before the Claudian invasion and offered no resistance, constituting a buffer zone for the Roman forces, hence the absence of Roman forts in Hertfordshire. Communicated by Isobel Thompson at the Archaeology in Hertfordshire: Recent Research Conference, 22 October 2022.

roundhouse not the villa – see Mattingly (2007).

decision to go to the cost ... unparalleled – see Kolb (2019).

♦ ♦ ♦

THE ROAD PERSISTS 126–128

quennets – see Philip Terry, *Quennets* (Manchester: Carcanet, 2016). Terry gives David Bellos' explanation of the structure of a quennet: 'Three two lines stanzas, line 1 of each consisting of three phrases and line 2 of one phrase, each phrase formed by a noun-adjective pair'. Followed by: 'Seven lines of at least two and not more than seven syllables.' Followed by: 'One two-line stanza conforming to the same constraint as at the start.' 'Rhymes, assonances, and repetitions between phrases and the "middle lines" (what Queneau called the "refrain") are not regulated but positively encouraged.'

The LiDAR way – general sources. With thanks to Rebekah Hart for helping me use the LiDAR data at the Department of the Environment. See RRRA website for links to LiDAR sources. Historic England has an excellent page with links to in-depth reports on LiDAR at https://historicengland.org.uk/research/methods/airborne-remote-sensing/lidar/

♦ ♦ ♦

THE PARISH OF BRENT PELHAM IS FAR REMOVED 130–131

Tithe commissioner – TNA IR18 /3255 Tithe File Furneux Pelham.

Writing of those who used old roads – Bagshawe (1979), p. 22.

The last miller – see Arthur Smith, *Windmills in Hertfordshire* (Stevenage: Stevenage Museum, *c.*1986).

♦ ♦ ♦

BEYOND THE MILL WE NO LONGER NEED POETIC LICENCE 131–137

On the history of roads in general see Taylor (1994) and Hindle (1993).

Miller Christy – 'On Roman Roads in Essex' (1921).

John Oliver – see *Four County Maps of Hertfordshire* (Stevenage: Hertfordshire Library Service and Local History Council, 1985).

brought before the quarter sessions – Herts quarter sessions are calendared and extracted in Hertford County Records compiled by W.J. Hardy (Hertford, 1905).

Tudor Highways Act 1555 – see Taylor (1994).

surveyors' books – Brent Pelham Surveyors Book HALS D/P 77 21/1-2.

better known tablets – see the text of the Vindolanda tablets at Roman Inscriptions of Britain https://romaninscriptionsofbritain.org/

John Norden imagined – *Speculi Britaniae pars: A Description of Hartfordshire, Reprinted with the Addition of a Portrait of J. Norden and a Biography by W.B. Gerish* (Ware: G. Price & Son, 1903; first pub. [London] 1598).

Nathaniel Salmon poked fun – Salmon (1728).

♦ ♦ ♦

Herbert Tompkins – he is writing about the stories of Dick Turpin. See above.

♦ ♦ ♦

LET US GO SIMPLING 137–147

A great introduction to some of the issues here around the clearance of woodland in Britain is Christopher Taylor's revised edition with commentary of W.G. Hoskins, *The Making of the English Landscape* (London: Hodder, 1988), in which you get both the older and newer take on the history of the landscape.

'rich kind of verge' – Rackham (1986).

Joseph Conrad's Heart of Darkness – I am not the first to invoke Conrad in this context. I think it was W.G. Hoskins, or perhaps Christopher Taylor correcting Hoskins.

'At Black Hall the modern road' – Christy (1921).

The Hertfordshire Landscape – Munby (1977).

But for others – I'm thinking of Richard Muir, who in his *Shell Guide to Reading the English Landscape* (London: Michael Joseph, 1981), writes: 'It is hard to believe that as colonists, in what was for many an unfamiliar land, they would deliberately avoid the best routeways in a realm which they sought to penetrate and settle in.'

Adventus *debate* – this never stands still. I have leaned on *AD 410: The History and Archaeology of Late and Post-Roman Britain*, ed. F.K. Haarer (London: Society for the Promotion of Roman Studies, 2014). Also G. Halsall, *Worlds of Arthur: Facts and Fictions of the Dark Ages* (Oxford: OUP, 2013), and Simon Esmonde Cleary, 'The Ending(s) of Roman Britain' in *The Oxford Handbook of Anglo-Saxon Archaeology*, eds David Hinton et al. (Oxford: OUP, 2011), pp. 13–29. The *Nature* paper on aDNA is 'The Anglo-Saxon Migration and the Formation of the Early English Gene Pool', *Nature*, 610 (2022), pp. 112–19.

repairs were made to Akeman Street – Thomas Williams, *Lost Realms* (London: William Collins, 2022).

ancient DNA – another key finding of this study is that as time went by the percentage of continental north European DNA (the term preferred to Anglo-Saxon) in the British population declines significantly (hence the importance of studying aDNA as opposed to that of the modern population to get a true picture of what was happening in the fifth and sixth centuries). Bad news for the far-right extremists who have hijacked the term Anglo-Saxon and imagine a pure bloodline.

brilliant study of Roman Roads – Albone (2016).

'dark and miserable place' – Revd Upton's survey in *Religion in Hertfordshire 1847–1851*, ed. Judith Burg (Hertford: Hertfordshire Record Publications, 1995), brought to my attention by Linda and Steve Bratt.

♦ ♦ ♦

Quiller-Couch – cited by Bishop (2014).

♦ ♦ ♦

ONE DAY IN THE SPRING OF 1950 147–149

'There appears to be a section' – the 495 record cards associated with RR21b were not added to the OS linear file, but were distributed to county Historic Environment units. The Hertfordshire ones have gone missing, but Essex supplied a digital copy to me some years ago as part of Essex Record Card 3890.

fourth river crossed by the road – this assumes that the river crosses the Quin as it does in some versions – though not Mark Landon's – of the route out of Braughing.

160 English chalk streams – I learned about the chalk streams at the John Catt Symposium on Hertfordshire Geology and Landscape at the University of Hertfordshire in July 2019. The well-known singer Feargal Sharkey is a great champion of the chalk streams and campaigns to preserve them from pollution and over-extraction.

Auden knew it – 'In Praise of Limestone'.

They were woe waters – see 'Woe Water' in the *Spectator* (5 March 1910).

♦ ♦ ♦

I DID DISCOVER THAT THE STRATA 149–150

At the 2019 excavation – see Roman Roads Research Association Newsletter No. 11 (Autumn 2019). On width in general see Davies (2002) and Bishop (2014).

♦ ♦ ♦

THE RIVER HAS WANDERED 151–153

On Roman bridges the usual sources are indispensable: Davies (2002), Bishop (2014) and Margary (1973). On Trajan's bridge over the Danube see Von Hagen (1967).

over 560 crossing places – see Tyler Franconi and Chris Green, 'Movement' in *English Landscapes and Identities: Investigating Landscape Change from 1500 BC to AD 1086* (Oxford: OUP, 2021). Davies (2002) calculated that only 5 per cent of an estimated two thousand bridges had left a trace – a number based on how many were used on the eighteenth-century military roads in Scotland and then scaled to take into account Scotland's higher than average rainfall.

Ordnance Survey period map of Roman Britain – started by O.G.S. Crawford in the 1920s, now up to its fifth edition, but the fourth edition published in 1978 is still considered the best.

in full flood – Davies (2002) argued that Romans used fords as little as possible since the point of a well-engineered, all-weather road is that it should be usable even when the river was in full spate. Bagshawe (1979) thought differently: 'Bridges were vulnerable and only seem to have been provided where there was no practical alternative.'

♦ ♦ ♦

THE FIRST FIELD IN THE COUNTY OF ESSEX 154–157

functional continuity – see Albone (2016).

settlers chose to go other ways – Munby (1977).

Bokerley Dyke … all the major Rome routes were deliberately blocked – see Anthony Durham, 'The Afterlife of Roman Roads', Roman Roads Research Association Newsletter, No. 16 (2020), pp. 31–9: 'Almost all of Britain's major Roman roads were blocked with dykes at some point during the Early Medieval Period as explained by Jim Storr (2018). Dykes served to stop military incursions (by cavalry or formed up infantry) or bands of thieves retreating with loot.'

♦ ♦ ♦

IN THE RIVER VALLEYS 161–162

It has been argued that when roads stopped being used – see Albone (2016) and Peter Warner, *Greens, Commons and Clayland Colonization* (Leicester: Leicester University Press, 1987).

trees might have stood along the road – to learn about the most extraordinary tree that stood alongside RR21b you will need to read my last book *Hollow Places*, or at least the first part, 'Tree'.

♦ ♦ ♦

TERMINUS WAS BOTH A BOUNDARY STONE 163–167

On boundaries and their history see Angus Winchester, *Discovering Parish Boundaries*, second edn (Princes Risborough: Shire Publications, 2000). Also Elisabeth Zadora-Rio, 'Parish Boundaries and the Illusion of Territorial Continuity in Landscape Archaeology: The Evidence from Touraine', in Tomás Ó Carragáin et al., *Making Christian Landscapes in Atlantic Europe. Conversion and Consolidation in the Early Middle Ages* (Cork: Cork University Press, 2016), pp. 345–65.

Some have seen this … 'centuriation' – Brinson (1963) noticed this. See also John Peterson's papers at https://eastanglia.academia.edu/

'Thonne of hindehlypan' – see David Iredale and John Barrett, *Discovering Local History* (Princes Risborough: Shire Publications, 2003).

Where a Roman road … ignores – see Albone (2016) on Desmond Bonney's work.

♦ ♦ ♦

LET'S TAKE A WALK IN ROMAN BRITAIN 169–172

Thanks are due to Jacqueline Cooper who corresponded with me about Beard's Lane and shared some very useful extracts from her *History Walks in Clavering* (2003). She also sent me Stuart Moore's historical map of the lane and surrounding fields from his thesis on pastoral economy in the area.

I encounter David Ahn – thanks to Nick Edwards, who introduced me to David. It was Nick who first put it into my head that David was like a wonderful old wizard in the woods.

Mr Pink-Whistle ... Cadellin – with the exception of Mr Pink-Whistle who was half-brownie, the others are literary wizards, the creations of Tolkien, Susan Cooper and Alan Garner respectively.

♦ ♦ ♦

IF DAVID AHN WERE GUARDING SOMETHING 172–174

On tumuli and particularly Roman ones see Nicola Whyte, 'The After-life of Barrows: Prehistoric Monuments in the Norfolk Landscape', *Landscape History*, 25:1 (2003), pp. 5–16; *Prehistoric Barrows and Burial Mounds: Introductions to Heritage Assets* (Swindon: Historic England, 2018); Hella Eckardt et al., 'Roman Barrows and Their Landscape Context: A GIS Case Study at Bartlow, Cambridgeshire', *Britannia*, Vol. 40 (2009), pp. iv, 65–98; Laura Crowley, 'Creating a Community: The Symbolic Role of Tumuli in the Villa Landscape of the

Civitas Tungrorum', *Proceedings of the Eighteenth Annual Theoretical Roman Archaeology Conference, Amsterdam 2008* (Oxford: Oxbow Books, 2009), pp. 113–26; G.C. Dunning and R.F. Jessup, 'Roman Barrows', *Antiquity*, Vol. X (1936), pp. 37–53; L.V. Grinsell, *The Ancient Burial Mounds of England*, second edn (London: Methuen, 1953); J.M.C. Toynbee, *Death and Burial in the Roman World* (Baltimore: Johns Hopkins University Press, 1971).

Since 1816 the Ordnance Survey's standing orders – see John Brian Harley, *The Old Series Ordnance Survey Maps of England and Wales, Scale 1 Inch to 1 Mile: A Reproduction of the 110 Sheets of the Survey in Early State*, in 10 volumes, Vol. 1.

Guy Maynard ... used brown envelope – this was spotted by Carolyn Wingfield at Saffron Walden Museum. The quote is not Maynard, but from his travelling companion Miller Christy.

Find Audley End House – much of the material that follows is from my *Archdeacon's Doodles*, privately published (2008). See also Hon. Richard Cornwallis Neville, 'Notes on Roman Essex (Read at the Meeting at Waltham Abbey, 1857)', *Transactions of the Essex Archaeological Society*, Vol. I (Colchester, 1858), pp. 191–200.

♦ ♦ ♦

BELL BARROWS AND DISC BARROWS 179–184

My greatest debt here is to the landscape archaeologist Simon Coxall, who pointed me towards the Tungrian theory and to the work of Andrew Reynolds and Nicola Whyte on barrows. He generously shared all his research on Rumberry and the field known as 'Qualmstoweslappe'. Thanks to Maria Medlycott for pointing him in my direction. See also the bibliography to the previous section.

Collins field archaeology – Eric S. Wood, *Collins Field Guide to Archaeology in Britain*, fourth edn (London: Collins, 1975).

At nearby Bartlow Hills – see Essex HER 4751.

King John himself – see Grinsell (1953).

One compelling theory … Tungrians – Simon Coxall's, see above. Also Crowley (2009). The individual Tungrian tombs are from the Roman Inscriptions of Britain database online https://romaninscriptionsofbritain.org/

Brougham in Cumbria – see Mattingly (2007).

♦ ♦ ♦

RUMBERRY IS SOLITARY 185–187

John Aubrey – cited by Grinsell (1953).

a monument's viewshed – see Eckardt (2009).

'This material had been stacked … marshland' – Rosalind Niblett, *The Excavation of a Ceremonial Site at Folly Lane, Verulamium,*

Britannia Monograph Series No. 14 (London: Society for the Promotion of Roman Studies, 1999).

♦ ♦ ♦

BARROWS ARE THE WORK OF THE DEVIL 188–189

In general see Andrew Reynolds, 'Crime and Punishment' in *The Oxford Handbook of Anglo-Saxon Archaeology*, eds David Hinton et al. (Oxford: OUP, 2011), and Andrew Reynolds, *Anglo-Saxon Deviant Burial Customs* (Oxford: OUP, 2009) and Whyte (2003).

a nest for dragons – see Whyte (2003).

until someone noticed – this is Simon Coxall.

♦ ♦ ♦

THEY FEASTED HERE ONCE 191

savouring wine from southern Italy – see Essex HER SMR 46359.

♦ ♦ ♦

WITH ITS FOLDS AND LITTLE RAVINES 192–194

There is evidence for freshwater fish ponds – Alison Locker, '*In Piscibus Diversis*; the Bone Evidence for Fish Consumption in Roman Britain', *Britannia*, Vol. 38 (2007), pp. 141–80.

Urban Smith – Smith (1912).

♦ ♦ ♦

LET'S PLOT THE UPS AND DOWNS 196–197

'Woods are not on land that was good for growing trees' – Rackham (1986).

Anglo-Saxon law code – see Albone (2016).

♦ ♦ ♦

LISTEN 198–207

I am indebted to Zoe and Klaine for their help with this chapter. Various people helped me compile a list of finds along the road, including Maria Medlycott, Rebekah Hart and Carolyn Wingfield; other finds mentioned in this chapter were found using the Portable Antiquities Scheme and the Hertfordshire and Essex HER. Mark Curteis at Chelmsford Museum gave me a masterclass in Roman coins, answered all my follow-up questions and guided my reading. I took him a list of finds and he had something fascinating to say about all of them and was able to quickly cut through to the most interesting ones and what they could tell us about the past. Much of the information here is taken from my conversation with Mark. See also Mark's *Harlow Roman Temple and Other Essex Temples: A Numismatic Study*, Essex Society for Archaeology and History, Vol. 6 (2015), pp. 164–88; and P.J. Casey, *Roman Coinage in Britain*, third edn (Oxford: Shire Publications, 2009). I also used Philippa Walton and Sam Moorhead, 'Coinage and the Economy', in *The Oxford Handbook of Roman Britain*, eds Martin Millett, Louise Revell and Alison Moore (Oxford: OUP, 2014).

Thanks also to Tom Brindle at Cotswold Archaeology, the numismatist on the New Visions of the Roman Countryside project, for kindly responding to my questions.

Peter Frankopan – Silk Roads (London: Bloomsbury, 2015).

Clipping has been seen – see Andrew Burnett, 'Clipped Siliquae and the End of Roman Britain', *Britannia*, Vol. 15 (1984), pp. 163–8.

♦ ♦ ♦

THEY ARE BROWNS AND REDS 208–213

This chapter is based entirely on two early papers by the eminent landscape archaeologist Tom Williamson: 'The Roman Countryside: Settlement and Agriculture in N.W. Essex', *Britannia*, Vol. 15 (1984), pp. 225–30, and 'The Development of Settlement in North West Essex: The Results of Ancient Field Survey', in *Essex Archaeology and History*, Vol. 17 (1986), pp. 120–32.

grey durable pot – this is so-called South East Midlands shell-tempered ware – see potsherds.org and P.J. Drury and Warwick Rodwell, 'Settlement in the Later Iron Age and Roman Periods', in *Archaeology in Essex to AD 1500*, ed. D.G. Buckley, Research Report No. 34 (Council for British Archaeology, 1980).

'a kindness of Mother Earth' – cited by Guy de la Bédoyère, *Pottery in Roman Britain* (Princes Risborough: Shire Publications, 2004).

outnumbered at least twenty-five to one – Mattingly (2007).

THE FIELD-WALKING GRIDS 214–215

Richard McGuire, *Here* (Hamish Hamilton, 2014).

much-celebrated account – this was given in *An Adventure*, published pseudonymously in 1911; it has spawned many responses and commentaries. I mostly used Terry Castle's study 'Contagious Folly: "An Adventure" and Its Skeptics', *Critical Inquiry*, Vol. 17, No. 4 (Summer, 1991), pp. 741–72.

◆ ◆ ◆

THE EASTERN EXTREMITIES 216–218

Mary Seymour – spotted in the excellent *Littlebury: A Parish History*, eds Lizzie Saunder and Gillian Williamson (Littlebury: Parish of Littlebury Millennium Society, 2005).

G.K. Chesterton's – His 1913 poem begins: Before the Roman came to Rye or out to Severn strode / The rolling English drunkard made the rolling English road. / A reeling road, a rolling road, that rambles round the shire, / And after him the parson ran, the sexton and the squire; / A merry road, a mazy road, and such as we did tread / The night we went to Birmingham by way of Beachy Head.

Joe Moran – see his *On Roads: A Hidden History* (London: Profile, 2009).

◆ ◆ ◆

LET US CONTEMPLATE 219–222

On the surveying of Roman roads I have leaned heavily on Bishop (2014), Davies (2002) and most recently and profitably on Entwistle (2019).

1066 and All That – *A Memorable History of England*, is the classic tongue-in-cheek retelling of our island story by Sellar and Yeatman. First published in 1930.

surveyed line – see Entwistle (2019).

Belloc – in *The Road* (Manchester: British Reinforced Concrete Engineering Co., 1923).

♦ ♦ ♦

YOU MIGHT BE FORGIVEN 227–228

The altars mentioned in this section can all be found on the Roman Inscriptions of Britain database, see above.

pyschogeography ... 'genius loci' – this is the folklore blogger Icy Sedgwick in her 2019 piece 'Psychogeography and Folklore: Walking the City's Legends'. You can read it here: https://www.icysedgwick.com/psychogeography/

♦ ♦ ♦

FROM THE AIR, THESE FIELDS ARE BADGED 231–235

The opening is inspired by the patterns on the ground in aerial photographs and a chance spotting of white deer one day.

Did you dream of owls ... donkeys – Roman portents for travellers given by Casson (1974).

Coldharbour – see Richard Coates, 'Coldharbour for the Last Time?', *Nomina*, 8 (1984), pp. 73–8. Bagshawe (1979) suggests they might be tents and so might leave no archaeological trace.

Briggs – 'The Distribution of Distance of Certain Place-name Types to Roman Roads', *Nomina*, 32 (2009), pp. 43–57.

wīchām – Margaret Gelling, 'English Place-Names Derived from the Compound *wīchām*', *Medieval Archaeology*, Vol. XI (1967), pp. 87–104; and Margaret Gelling, 'Latin Loan-words in Old English Place-names', *Anglo-Saxon England*, Vol. 6 (1977), pp. 1–13. It was the county archaeologist Stewart Bryant who pointed out that wīchām is unique among place names associated with Roman sites because it's thought to identify the nature of the site as it was given by people who remembered what a *vicus* was.

♦ ♦ ♦

STRETHALL WOULD HAVE PROVEN A GOOD HARBOUR 237

This chapter is largely based on D.A. Melford, *A History of the Manor and Parish of Strethall* (1998).

♦ ♦ ♦

THE SOIL DARKENS WITH THE SILT OF CENTURIES 240–244

Edward Thomas – the lines are from *The Path* (1915). See also his book *The Icknield Way* (London: Constable & Co., 1916).

Robert Macfarlane – The Old Ways: A Journey on Foot (London: Viking, 2012).

♦ ♦ ♦

Glen W. Most, 'On Fragments' (2009) – cited and constructed by Charles Nicholl on Petrarch in *LRB*, 7 February 2019.

♦ ♦ ♦

IN 1774 244–249

All sections on Great Chesterford rely heavily on Medlycott (2011).

Edward King – Munimenta Antiqua, Vol. 1 (London: Nicol, 1799). See also *Field Report No. 2 Roman Road from Braughing*, Great Chesterford Archaeology Group (1978), which drew my attention to Edward King's drawing.

♦ ♦ ♦

STOP TO TASTE THE PENDULOUS ELDERBERRIES 251

The walling of a town in Roman Britain … Barbarian Conspiracy – see Mattingly (2007).

♦ ♦ ♦

AN ARCHAEOLOGICAL LAYER OF TERRIBLE VIOLENCE 254–262

On Boudicca see Fields (2011), Mattingly (2007) and Hoffmann (2013).

Consider the head of a Roman emperor – see Miles Russell and Harry Manley, 'A Case of Mistaken Identity? Laser-scanning the Bronze "Claudius" from near Saxmundham', *Journal of Roman Archaeology*, Vol. 26 (2013), pp. 393–408.

John Higgs – *Watling Street: Travels through Britain and Its Ever-present Past* (London: Weidenfeld and Nicolson, 2017).

♦ ♦ ♦

WHILE INVESTIGATING TRACES 262–264

This chapter is built on Brinson (1963), Medlycott (2011) and Rodwell (1972). Isobel Thompson has recently suggested that there was no fort at Great Chesterford, at the same time conceding that while the evidence is very slight, the strategic case is strong and a Boudiccan fort is conceivable.

Cyril Fox – but it is not uncommon to find people inventing forts on the basis of where you would expect to find them.

J.K. St Joseph – see Hauser (2007).

♦ ♦ ♦

ROMAN BRITAIN WAS BUILT ON A GREAT MILITARY 265–267

12 per cent of their army – this figure comes from Bethany Hughes' TV series *The Roman Invasion of Britain.*

The fields at Bromley Hall farm – see Mark Landon, *Bromley Hall and Caley Wood Fieldwork*, Braughing Archaeology Group (2009).

Hadham ware – thanks to Carolyn Wingfield, who showed me the archive of Hadham ware from Bishop's House. Also Andy Peachey at Archaeological Solutions was incredibly generous with his time and expertise on Hadham ware. See also T.S. Martin on pottery in Medlycott (2011); A. Garwood et al., 'Late Roman Buildings at Bishop's House, Great Chesterford: Excavations 1999', *Essex Archaeology and History*, 35 (2004), pp. 1–25; and Robin P. Symonds and Sue Wade, *Roman Pottery from Excavations in Colchester 1971–86*, Colchester Archaeology Report No. 10 (1999).

MAPS AND ILLUSTRATIONS

Maps (drawn by Martin Brown)

Illustrations

page 256 – Head of Nero found in the River Alde in 1907. Author's photograph

page 270 – Hadham ware face pot. Fourth-century CE. Chelmsford Museum. Author's photograph

page 273 – Samian ware outlines. Anonymous drawing from *A Guide to the Antiquities of Roman Britain* (London: British Museum, 1922)

HarperCollins has used all efforts to credit the authors of the works used herein, and if any work has been wrongly credited, please contact us and we will provide the correct credit in future editions.

INDEX

Page entries in *italics* indicate images.